LETTERS OF
FORD MADOX FORD

LETTERS
OF
FORD
MADOX
FORD

EDITED BY RICHARD M. LUDWIG

PRINCETON, NEW JERSEY
PRINCETON UNIVERSITY PRESS
MCMLXV

For Ned

PREFACE

FORD MADOX FORD was born in Merton, Surrey in 1873 and died in Deauville, Normandy in 1939. During the course of his life he published seventy-eight books. This impressive achievement is detailed in brief at the front of this volume so as to offer the reader of these letters a guide to the titles mentioned in passing and a survey of the genres Ford worked in. He is known to the world as the author of *The Good Soldier* and the tetralogy out of World War I, *Parade's End*. Though he wrote twenty-seven novels in addition to these five, fiction was only one of his interests. Ford was among the distinguished group of young poets in London before World War I—Ezra Pound, H. D., Richard Aldington, T. S. Eliot, and others; and he knew the critics F. S. Flint and T. E. Hulme at the time when the theory of Imagism was first being talked about. He was a brilliant editor of two magazines, *The English Review* and *The Transatlantic Review*; had he known as much about business management as he did about manuscripts, he might have had a quite different career, particularly in the 1920's. We could also argue that Ford's four autobiographical volumes—*Ancient Lights, Thus to Revisit, Return to Yesterday,* and *It Was the Nightingale*—and his fascinating novel *No Enemy*, which is only disguised autobiography, show us still another and equally vital side of his talent and make us wish he had finished the three-volume *History of Our Own Times* on which he labored so long during the 1930's. Some of his observations and comment crept into the four hundred articles he contributed to periodicals and into his critical studies of Dante Gabriel Rossetti, Henry James, Joseph Conrad, and the English novel. He reserved his more caustic social criticism for *New York Is Not America,* for *Great Trade Route,* and especially for that lovely paean to the South of France, *Provence*. But will any one of these genres, or indeed all of them, show us the real Ford?

We will never know this man by facts alone. In the dedicatory letter to *Ancient Lights and Certain New Reflections* (1911)— addressed to his young daughters, Christina and Katharine, and beginning "My Dear Kids"—Ford talks briefly about "impressions" and "facts." It is a memorable, even necessary, distinction he makes, one which any reader of Ford will have to bear in mind continually if he is not to become confused and exasperated with Ford's tricky memory, his carelessness with details, his occasional outright fantasies. "This book," he tells his daughters, "is full of inaccuracies as to facts, but its accuracy as to impressions is absolute. . . . My business in life, in short, is to attempt to discover, and to try to let you see, where we stand. I don't really deal in facts, I have for facts a most profound contempt. I try to give you what I see to be the spirit of an age, of a town, of a movement."

It is too much to hope that these letters will recreate the spirit of their author as exuberantly as Ford recreates the spirit of an age in his autobiographical writing. But they are offered with the knowledge that they can hold a mirror to Ford in their own peculiar way. We have heard so much gossip about this man, read so many conflicting stories, heard in interview so many contradictory reports that it is refreshing to hear Ford tell his version of certain events in his life. These letters are only a skeletal biography. They begin in 1894 with the young Ford living in Kent, recently married and only casually interested in writing, and run sporadically through the next forty-five years of his life to the last letters he wrote from America, in May, 1939. The lacunae are numerous and patent, but what facts are here established are important and will assist a future biographer. But again, facts alone will not bring back Ford in all his panache—at one moment the editorial genius, at another the dogged infantryman, later the small producer living off his own land, later still the professional man of letters, author of one of the great novels of this century, trying to make a living with his pen. The spirit of the man is of more importance, at least to his admirers, and that spirit—his endless generosity, his deep respect for literature, his professional standards, above all his perseverance—is fully evident in these pages.

Collections of letters are by their nature collaborations, and I wish to acknowledge here much kind assistance given me over the past several years. Without the generous advice and hospitality of Ford's literary executor, Janice Biala, this collection could never have been completed, nor indeed begun. She brought the Ford papers out of France at a time when the country was falling to the Germans and has preserved them ever since. Ford's daughters, Katharine Lamb and Julia Loewe, have been equally generous with hospitality and with advice about the papers they own. Edward Crankshaw gave me much needed help in meeting Ford's friends in London and has allowed me to excerpt one of his own letters to Sir Stanley Unwin. Frank MacShane has for many years shared with me his research on Ford; likewise David Dow Harvey, whose bibliography of Ford is a splendid achievement. Edward Naumburg's collection in New York City is so vital to any work on Ford and his faith in this project has been so great that his part in this edition is acknowledged on a separate page.

Thanks for assistance are also due to: Frederick L. Arnold, Carlos Baker, William T. Bandy, Paul Alexander Bartlett, Francis L. Berkeley, Anthony Bertram, Mrs. William A. Bradley, the late Gerald Bullett, Alexander P. Clark, Earle E. Coleman, the late A. E. Coppard, Leon Edel, Robert Fagles, John V. A. Fine, Donald Gallup, David Garnett, the late Douglas Goldring, Malin Goldring, John D. Gordan, Caroline Gordon, Graham Greene, Rupert Hart-Davis, Mary M. Hirth, Samuel L. Hynes, Frederick R. Karl, Harold Loeb, Faith Mackenzie, Robert B. Martin, Lucy Masterman, Margaret Nash, Glendon T. Odell, Jr., Reginald Pound, Princess de Rachewiltz, Gordon N. Ray, Sir Herbert Read, D. W. Robertson, Robert Rogers, Bertram Rota, the late R. A. Scott-James, Albert Sonnenfeld, Sir Frank Soskice, Edward D. Sullivan, Frank Swinnerton, Allen Tate, Gerard Tetley, Willard Thorp, James Thorpe, Rayner Unwin, Sir Stanley Unwin, Alexander D. Wainwright, Monroe Wheeler, Harris W. Wilson, John Cook Wyllie, Marjorie Wynne, and Kenneth Young.

Acknowledgment in the printing of certain letters is due to:

E. P. Dutton and Company, Inc., for permission to reprint letters quoted by Douglas Goldring in *Trained for Genius*: *The Life and Writings of Ford Madox Ford* (New York, 1949).

Faber and Faber, Ltd., for permission to reprint two letters to Sir Herbert Read first reproduced in his *Annals of Innocence and*

Experience (London, 1940) and later in his *The Contrary Experience* (London, 1963).

Henry E. Huntington Library, for permission to print letters to James B. Pinker.

Alfred A. Knopf, Inc., for permission to reprint a letter to Gertrude Stein reproduced in *Flowers of Friendship*: *Letters Written to Gertrude Stein*, edited by Donald Gallup (New York, 1953).

The Lockwood Library of the State University of New York at Buffalo, for permission to print letters to Iris Barry and James Joyce.

The New York *Herald Tribune,* for permission to reprint letters to the Editor reproduced on February 20, 1927, and March 14, 1937.

Princeton University Library, for permission to print letters to Joseph Conrad, James B. Pinker, Allen Tate, and Alec Waugh.

Saturday Review, for permission to reprint letters to the Editor reproduced in the issues of October 22, 1938, and June 3, 1939.

Charles Scribner's Sons, for permission to reprint two letters to John Galsworthy reproduced in H. V. Marrot, *The Life and Letters of John Galsworthy* (New York, 1936). Copyright 1936 Charles Scribner's Sons; renewal copyright © 1964 A. J. P. Sellar.

The South Atlantic Quarterly, for permission to reprint letters to R. A. Scott-James reproduced in the Spring, 1958 issue.

Time, Inc. for permission to reproduce the frontispiece photograph of Ford Madox Ford.

University of Chicago Library, for permission to print a letter to Harriet Monroe.

University of Illinois Library and Gordon N. Ray, for permission to print letters to H. G. Wells and his wife.

University of Pennsylvania Library, for permission to print letters to Theodore Dreiser.

University of Texas Library, for permission to print letters to F. S. Flint, Harold Monro, and Hugh Walpole.

Yale University Library and Donald Gallup, for permission to print letters to George T. Keating, Sinclair Lewis, and Gertrude Stein.

Finally, I wish to record my appreciation to Princeton University for the assistance it has given me in completing this edition: a Bicentennial Preceptorship and grants from the University

Research Fund; to Mary Bertagni for preparation of the type-
script; and to Eve Hanle for invaluable editorial advice.

A brief note on emendations will facilitate the reading of these
letters. Throughout the collection I have silently corrected Ford's
typographical errors and occasionally supplied marks of punctua-
tion. Other misspellings and miswritings, particularly of proper
names and titles, have been left uncorrected, followed by [*sic*].
Where it was necessary to insert omitted words in order to make
sentence sense, I have used brackets. Likewise, approximate dates
of letters undated in the originals have been bracketed. Illegible
words and questionable readings have been so marked, with
brackets. In some instances I have condensed the place at which
the letter was written, from four or five lines to one or two. The
date, the salutation, and the valediction remain as Ford wrote
them, but throughout the volume I have omitted his signature.

Deletions created a peculiar problem. In his fiction as well as
as his letters, Ford habitually used points of ellipsis to indicate
an unfinished thought or the tapering off of an idea. He variously
used from three to eight such marks, according to his mood.
I have consistently regularized them to the standard three, but
some other means of indicating my own deletions has had, therefore, to be devised. The symbol [. . . . .] indicates my omission
of several words, a sentence, or a whole paragraph.

Letters taken from carbon copies in the Ford archive are marked
with an asterisk after the name of the recipient.

A LIST OF FORD'S BOOKS

(*Chronologically arranged, first publication only,
with a brief designation*)

1891. *The Brown Owl,* London, T. Fisher Unwin. Children's fairy tale.

1892. *The Feather,* London, T. Fisher Unwin. Children's fairy tale.

1892. *The Shifting of the Fire,* London, T. Fisher Unwin. Novel.

1893. *The Questions at the Well,* London, Digby, Long & Co. Poems. Published under the pseudonym Fenil Haig.

1894. *The Queen Who Flew,* London, Bliss, Sands & Foster. Children's fairy tale.

1896. *Ford Madox Brown,* London, Longmans, Green & Co. Biography.

1900. *Poems for Pictures,* London, John MacQueen.

1900. *The Cinque Ports,* Edinburgh and London, William Blackwood and Sons. Descriptive history of Kent and Sussex port towns.

1901. *The Inheritors* (with Joseph Conrad), New York, McClure, Phillips & Co. Novel.

1902. *Rossetti,* London, Duckworth & Co. Critical biography.

1903. *Romance* (with Joseph Conrad), London, Smith, Elder & Co. Novel.

1904. *The Face of the Night,* London, John MacQueen. Poems.

1905. *The Soul of London,* London, Alston Rivers. Essays.

1905. *The Benefactor,* London, Brown, Langham & Co. Novel.

1905. *Hans Holbein,* London, Duckworth & Co.; New York, E. P. Dutton & Co. Critical monograph.

1906. *The Fifth Queen,* London, Alston Rivers. Novel. The first volume in the Katharine Howard trilogy.

1906. *The Heart of the Country,* London, Alston Rivers. Essays.

1906. *Christina's Fairy Book,* London, Alston Rivers. Children's fairy tale.

1907. *Privy Seal,* London, Alston Rivers. Novel. The second volume in the Katharine Howard trilogy.

1907. *From Inland and Other Poems,* London, Alston Rivers.

1907. *An English Girl,* London, Methuen & Co. Novel.

1907. *The Pre-Raphaelite Brotherhood,* London, Duckworth & Co.; New York, E. P. Dutton & Co. Critical monograph.

1907. *The Spirit of the People,* London, Alston Rivers. Essays.

[1907. *England and the English,* New York, McClure, Phillips & Co. Essays. A one-volume edition of *The Soul of London, The Heart of the Country,* and *The Spirit of the People,* but published about five months before the last volume of the trilogy appeared in England.]

1908. *The Fifth Queen Crowned*, London, Eveleigh Nash. Novel. The third novel of the Katharine Howard trilogy.

1908. *Mr. Apollo*, London, Methuen & Co. Novel.

1909. *The 'Half Moon'*, London, Eveleigh Nash. Novel.

1910. *A Call*, London, Chatto & Windus. Novel.

1910. *Songs from London*, London, Elkin Mathews. Poems.

1910. *The Portrait*, London, Methuen & Co. Novel.

1911. *The Simple Life Limited*, London, John Lane. Novel. Published under the pseudonym Daniel Chaucer.

1911. *Ancient Lights and Certain New Reflections*, London, Chapman and Hall. Reminiscences. Published by Harper & Brothers in New York, 1911, as *Memories and Impressions*.

1911. *Ladies Whose Bright Eyes*, London, Constable & Co. Novel.

1911. *The Critical Attitude*, London, Duckworth & Co. Essays.

1912. *High Germany*, London, Duckworth & Co. Poems.

1912. *The Panel*, London, Constable & Co. Novel.

1912. *The New Humpty-Dumpty*, London, John Lane. Novel. Published under the pseudonym Daniel Chaucer.

[1913]. *This Monstrous Regiment of Women*, no publisher, no date. Suffragette pamphlet.

1913. *Mr. Fleight*, London, Howard Latimer, Ltd. Novel.

1913. *The Desirable Alien* (with Violet Hunt), London, Chatto & Windus. Historical essays.

1913. *The Young Lovell*, London, Chatto & Windus. Novel.

1913. *Ring for Nancy*, Indianapolis, The Bobbs-Merrill Company. Novel. Revised version of *The Panel*, 1912; published only in America.

1913. *Collected Poems*, London, Max Goschen, Ltd.

1914. *Henry James*, London, Martin Secker. Critical monograph.

[1915]. *Antwerp*, London, The Poetry Bookshop, no date. Long poem.

1915. *The Good Soldier*, London, John Lane. Novel.

1915. *When Blood Is Their Argument: An Analysis of Prussian Culture*, New York and London, Hodder and Stoughton. Essays. War propaganda.

1915. *Between St. Denis and St. George: A Sketch of Three Civilisations*, New York and London, Hodder and Stoughton. Essays. War propaganda.

1915. *Zeppelin Nights* (with Violet Hunt), London, John Lane. Historical sketches.

1918. *On Heaven and Poems Written on Active Service*, London, John Lane.

1921. *A House*, London, The Poetry Bookshop. Long poem.

1921. *Thus to Revisit*, London, Chapman & Hall. Reminiscences.

1923. *The Marsden Case*, London, Duckworth & Co. Novel. The first book to appear with Ford Madox Ford as the author's name.

1923. *Women & Men*, Paris, Three Mountains Press. Essays.

1923. *Mister Bosphorus and the Muses*, London, Duckworth & Co. Long poem.

1924. *Some Do Not*, London, Duckworth & Co. Novel. The first volume of the Tietjens tetralogy.

1924. *The Nature of a Crime* (with Joseph Conrad), London, Duckworth & Co. Novel. Previously published in *The English Review*, in 1909, under the pseudonym Baron Ignatz von Aschendrof, and in *The Transatlantic Review*, in January and February, 1924. Published as a book two months after Conrad's death.

1924. *Joseph Conrad: A Personal Remembrance*, London, Duckworth & Co. Biography and criticism.

1925. *No More Parades*, London, Duckworth. Novel. The second volume of the Tietjens tetralogy.

1926. *A Mirror to France*, London, Duckworth. Essays.

1926. *A Man Could Stand Up*, London, Duckworth. Novel. The third volume of the Tietjens tetralogy.

1927. *New Poems*, New York, William Edwin Rudge.

1927. *New York Is Not America*, London, Duckworth. Essays.

1927. *New York Essays*, New York, William Edwin Rudge.

1928. *The Last Post*, New York, The Literary Guild of America. Novel. The last volume of the Tietjens tetralogy. Published almost simultaneously in London by Duckworth.

1928. *A Little Less Than Gods*, London, Duckworth. Novel.

1929. *The English Novel: From the Earliest Days to the Death of Joseph Conrad*, Philadelphia, J. B. Lippincott Company. History and criticism.

1929. *No Enemy*, New York, The Macaulay Company. Autobiography disguised as fiction.

1931. *Return to Yesterday*, London, Victor Gollancz, Ltd. Reminiscences.

1931. *When the Wicked Man*, New York, Horace Liveright, Inc. Novel.

1933. *The Rash Act*, New York, Ray Long & Richard R. Smith, Inc. Novel.

1933. *It Was the Nightingale*, Philadelphia, J. B. Lippincott Company. Reminiscences.

1934. *Henry for Hugh*, Philadelphia, J. B. Lippincott Company. Novel. A sequel to *The Rash Act*.

1935. *Provence*, Philadelphia, J. B. Lippincott Company. History and travel reminiscence.

1936. *Vive Le Roy*, Philadelphia, J. B. Lippincott Company. Novel.

1936. *Collected Poems*, New York, Oxford University Press.

1937. *Great Trade Route*, New York, Oxford University Press. History and travel reminiscence. With *Provence*, planned as part of a trilogy which was never completed.

1937. *Portraits from Life*, Boston, Houghton Mifflin Company. Critical essays. Published by George Allen & Unwin in London, 1938 as *Mightier Than the Sword: Memories and Criticisms*.

1938. *The March of Literature from Confucius' Day to Our Own*, New York, The Dial Press. Criticism.

CONTENTS

1894 · 1918

KENT, LONDON, THE WAR

$\mathcal{I}$N 1869, Ford's father, Franz Xaver Hüffer, left his Roman Catholic family in Münster to settle in England. He had earned his doctorate at Göttingen and had published at the age of twenty-four a critical edition of the works of Guillem de Cabestanh. Nine years later he finished his more ambitious work, THE TROUBADOURS: A HISTORY OF PROVENÇAL LIFE AND LITERATURE IN THE MIDDLE AGES. By that time he was a naturalized British subject and was known as Francis Hueffer, music critic for THE TIMES of London, author of RICHARD WAGNER AND THE MUSIC OF THE FUTURE, and husband of Catherine Brown, the youngest daughter of Ford Madox Brown, mentor to the Pre-Raphaelite Brotherhood and prominent English painter.

These bare facts are more vital to Ford's biography than they may at first glance seem to be. Had Dr. Hueffer not died suddenly at the age of forty-three, his eldest son, christened Ford Hermann Hueffer, might well have followed him into journalism, historical scholarship, and language study. Ford was only fifteen when his father succumbed to a heart attack. He had already absorbed Dr. Hueffer's passion for Provence, and in later years he was to write glowingly of his father's versatility and his cultivated taste. Ford might well have attended a good public school, followed by Oxford or Cambridge, and thus might have had a greater independence in choosing a profession. After his father's death in 1889, however, he and his brother Oliver were forced to leave Praetoria House, a boarding school in Folkestone, and join their mother at No. 1 St. Edmund's Terrace, Regent's Park, the house which Ford Madox Brown had taken only the year before and which, with typical generosity, he offered to share with his daughter and grandsons. Ford lived here for about three years and, for at least one of them, attended University College School on Gower Street. Since his sister Juliet was living at No. 3 St. Edmund's Terrace with the William Michael Rossetti family (Catherine Hueffer and Lucy Rossetti were half-sisters), it was inevitable that Ford should find his home life more instructive and certainly more exciting than a London day school.

Of all the formative influences which Ford recalls from these precarious years, Madox Brown was clearly the strongest. As benevolent grandfather and passionate liberal, he gave Ford all the encouragement he needed to pursue his own interests, though it was clear he preferred a literary career for his grandson over the Civil Service or the Army which at the time seemed attractive to the young Ford. The Rossettis were equally encouraging. Dante Gabriel was dead, but "Aunt" Christina was always for Ford "the most satisfactory of all the poets of the nineteenth century," and she continued to write verses during the years Ford lived in London. "Uncle" William, the Secretary of the Inland Revenue, offered practical assistance as well as affection and advice. But for the rest of "the bitter, enormous, greybeard assembly of the Victorian Great"—with the exception of Swinburne—Ford had little sympathy and less patience. "To me," he wrote in 1911, "life was simply not worth living because of the existence of Carlyle, of Mr. Ruskin, of Mr. Holman Hunt, of Mr. Browning, or of the gentlemen who built the Crystal Palace. These people were perpetually held up to me as standing upon unattainable heights, and at the same time I was perpetually being told that if I could not attain to these heights I might just as well not cumber the earth. What then was left for me? Nothing. Simply nothing." Ford longed to escape this hothouse atmosphere, to find his own way.

Grandfather Brown helped in many ways, particularly with Ford's first publication. Dr. Richard Garnett of the British Museum was a close friend of Brown and the Rossettis. His son, Edward, only five years older than Ford, was literary adviser to T. Fisher Unwin, the publisher. Ford claims his grandfather forced the manuscript of THE BROWN OWL on Edward Garnett, much to Ford's embarrassment, promising two illustrations for the book. In 1891, Unwin published the delightful fairy story. The critical notices encouraged Ford, and in 1892 he published THE FEATHER and his first novel, THE SHIFTING OF THE FIRE. Two years later Ford married Elsie Martindale, daughter of a prominent London chemist, and the young couple took a house at Bonnington, near Hythe and Romney Marsh. Both Ford and his wife knew this part of Kent from earlier days. They had first met at Praetoria House in Folkestone; the Martindales had a cottage at Winchelsea; and the Hueffers used to make summer visits to Hythe. From 1894 to the spring of 1904, Ford and Elsie Hueffer lived in the country on a slim budget and family charity. A more ambitious young writer might have chosen London.

After Madox Brown's death, Longmans Green and Company wished to commission a biography. William Morris refused; surprisingly, so did William Michael Rossetti, but he suggested his nephew for the assignment and Ford accepted. Throughout the writing of the book, Rossetti supplied information and materials, and Edward Garnett acted as adviser and agent. FORD MADOX BROWN: A RECORD OF HIS LIFE AND WORK, handsomely published in 1896, brought Ford compliments from THE TIMES ("in every way an admirable biography"), THE SPECTATOR, and THE ARTIST, among other journals. During the next four years, however, he produced little he wished published, chiefly because of ill health. He and Elsie moved from Bonnington to the Pent Farm near Postling, from there to Limpsfield, Surrey, and then to a small cottage called Stocks Hill at Aldington.

LETTERS OF
FORD MADOX FORD

To Edward Garnett

Bloomfield [Villa]
Bonnington, Hythe, Kent
[1894?]

Dear Garnett,

Thanks for your letter—I am glad the style meets with your approval.—As regards the chapters, I will do as you direct in a few days time—letters and anecdotes keep turning up & I shouldn't want to leave anything out.

About Uncle Bill[1]—I believe you misunderstand the situation. —There is *nothing whatever* of the nature of a quarrel between us —He is most cordial and kind—I don't mention this to hide a family scandal or that sort of thing—but merely as a fact. What I meant to imply in my last is that he is really in an almost hysterical condition owing to his sister's state.[2]—Personally I should like to leave him alone for a little—certainly not see him—but if you think well, I will, whilst returning him some letters he has lent me (F.M.B.'s to him),[3] enclose your letter to me as if to ask his approval on points & he will see for himself how the matter is.

From my knowledge of him, I know he will do anything to help me, with the exception of detracting from the interest of D. G. R.'s correspondence that he is publishing.[4]—So that it will I fear only be skim milk—i.e. letters of secondary interest that he does not want—that I should get—Of course it is a misfortune— but so it is.—I have asked him already.—If you see no objection to the above mentioned plan of sending him your letter, don't answer this. If you do, let me have a p. c. *by return* (otherwise I shall write) saying *no* & let your letter follow in a week or two as God wills giving reasons for same.

Thanks for your trouble.

Yrs,

[1] William Michael Rossetti.   [2] Christina died in December, 1894.
[3] Ford Madox Brown.
[4] *Dante Gabriel Rossetti: His Family-Letters, with a Memoir* (London, 1895). Ford reviewed it in *Longman's* in March, 1896.

I reopen to make myself clear on this point. You heard, of course, about W. M. R. & the copyright of F. M. B.'s letters.—That was merely an exhibition of W. M. R.'s red-tapeism & came from his desire to guide my feet aright. There was of course a long standing feud between my mother and Mrs. W. M. R. (but for God's sake whisper not a word of that to *anyone*)—but W. M. R. never joined it & has always been a *brick*—bound round with official red tape.

To Edward Garnett

[Bonnington, Kent]
Dear Edward—   [1895?]

Enclosed are the 1st two chapters—I have accepted your emendations with the exception of the description of the physique of M. B.—That is a subject abt. which I have a nanny goat to commence the next chapter with & it is reserved. You may tell Longmans that W. M. R. had offered to revise my chapters as they go to Press wh. is better than in the proof stage I shd. think.—I thought the frost & our 40 miles of skating wd. have been a pretext for conducing you to visit us—but the frost has broken up,—but you might try somebody's water shoes & walk the waters.

I am thinking of writing a novel all about smugglers.[1]—It seems this was the centre of one of the famous gangs of smugglers & the people can tell some famously realistic stories about those gentry.—There are one or two nonagenarians who were actually smugglers.—One of them a venerable bloke only escaped the noose by turning King's evidence.—Tho' I don't know why I shd. bother you with that.—I meant to ask about the bloody novel that Dent wouldn't have—I s'pose it is still with you?

I've done a good deal of work at the life lately—all that I *can* do here, so I rather hope to be able to touch some of Longman's gold to be able to get up to London—A lot of people have offered to let me 'interview' them & will give me anecdotes as you suggested about F. M. B. & when I get them I shall be able to go straight ahead—till then I'm rather stuck in the mud—but one gets used to that here.

[1] Ford is formulating here the plot for *Seraphina*, the novel he rewrote with Joseph Conrad and published in 1903 under the title *Romance*.

Thanks for all you've done—I don't know why you do it. If I were F. M. B., I should imagine some R. A. had been getting at you & you were mixed up in a horrible conspiracy to get my work —as it is I can only say to quote him again—'The whole thing's a mystery to me.'

Yours ever,

Compliments to Madame.—Mrs. H. has gone to bed or no doubt she wd. send you her love or something of the sort—I think I shall send you one of her effusions one of these days—She has taken to writing short stories, having exhausted the possibilities of the novel form some time ago.

To Edward Garnett

Dear Edward:

Aldington, Hythe
[December? 1898]

We are now permanently & satisfactorily settled here & shall be delighted & proud to be honoured by a visit from you whenever the same suits you. The situation is perfect, & on the whole the house is exactly what we wanted. So come along. E[lsie] commands me to command you to catch those pigeons & forward them here.

I don't personally think them worth either yr. time or trouble —but the fiat has gone forth, as far as I am concerned.

I enclose a cutting from a Speaker.

I'd take it kindly if you would send the Outlook when it contains any of my MS.—They don't send me it & we are far from bookstalls here.—There is a thing called "The Evolution of a Lyric," wh. I haven't got a copy of & wd. like to see in print— otherwise I wdn't bother you.[1] Xtina Margaret[2] flourishes on the whole. If you persuaded Connie to bring Bunny[3]—or brought him yourself—I feel convinced she wd. positively rejoice.—She has been rather upset because our rooster has once or twice flown at her & knocked her down—So he goes into the pot. Poultry at present occupy my thoughts to the exclusion of graver things.

Yrs.,

[1] It appeared in the April 22, 1899 issue.
[2] Christina Margaret Hueffer was born in July, 1897.
[3] Constance Garnett and son, David.

To John Galsworthy[1]

Aldington, Hythe, Kent
[October, 1900]

My dear Galsworthy,

Excuse my writing by machine; Christine[2] at this moment monopolizes the only pen there is in the house. I have just finished reading the *Villa Rubein*, with a great deal of pleasure and with my interest sustained to the last page—to the last word, even, and that is the great thing, it seems to me. I don't write as a critic, which I am not, but as a fellow craftsman who looks at a piece of work and wonders what he would have made of it himself. The mere writing is of course all right, lucid and excellent, very level, and felicitous in places—quite beyond the ordinary. Of course "writing" isn't very much; one has or hasn't it just as one has or hasn't a sense of smell; one can acquire it, but you have it and it's just as well not to have to worry, I mean rather for the reader than the writer. What however is essential for me is the "distinction" of the book; that is there beyond doubt and that *is* the essential, is why I can read the *Villa Rubein* when I can't read more than three or four of the other books that the weary year brings out. I say distinction, but there is not any word to express exactly what I mean; perhaps "temperament" comes nearer the mark. When one reads a book one is always wondering more or less what kind of a man the writer is—as writer be it said. In this case the writer is all right; speaks with the right sort of voice; has things to say worth listening to; has a philosophy and finds expression for it. I don't mean to say that the *Villa Rubein* is a flawless masterpiece. It isn't of course. But by reason of those qualities one is made to think that the writer stands not infinite distances away from the small band in which the elect keep apart; that, given chance, luck, exemption from death, weariness, disease, old age and power to keep his face steadfastly towards the light that he has seen, the writer ought to make his way across the rough ground where the light shines on hillocks, antheaps, mounds, and

---

[1] Ford met Galsworthy through Edward Garnett and Joseph Conrad. He admired *From the Four Winds*, Galsworthy's first book, a collection of short stories T. Fisher Unwin published in 1897 under the pseudonym John Sinjohn. Three years later, Galsworthy's second novel, *Villa Rubein*, appeared.

[2] Christina Margaret, Ford's daughter, aged three.

stretch of stubble and plough, into the very circle of the light itself.

This is monstrous, patronizing, fine writing and it seems necessary to postulate that I don't write as one warming my hands by that fire and calling out: "Keep on, young man: a little to the right . . . now, a little to the left . . . mind the broken bottles or you'll cut your toes. . . ." Rather—looking towards the fire too, but from a slightly different angle, I think I see reflected light on obstacles that perhaps you do not see, and give a friendly hail.

There isn't, in fact, any doubt that you have the *right* to write, and I who am a jealous Trade Unionist cannot pay you a greater compliment or mean it more sincerely. As a matter of fact I only accord it to about a twohandsful fingers of others, if so many. That being said, I will go on to what *I* should have desired to get into the book—over and above what it has—if it were my own work. In the first place what I am always striving to get at is:

> The ultimate reasons of the futile earth
> And crawling swarms of men . . .

I mean that I want to know the writer's attitude towards the Post, if not Super Natural. I don't think, whatever you have that takes the place of my Destiny—that whatever it is has enough of a show. Mind you, one asks for something to take the place of the Trinity and the Finger of God, one wants to feel after reading a book: this happened because it was absolutely impossible for it to have happened otherwise. One may or may not feel this about the *Villa Rubein*. I think myself that, given your characters, your events are all right. But that is not enough. One wants to feel, not that the Finger of Chance is the ultimate factor of the lives set before us, but that all the little chances and all of the few great haps of a life are only manifestations of the only thing that is worth the thinking about . . . of cause and effect. She was so and so because of her heredity; he was so and so because of the hardships of his life acting like certain acids on certain salts. Yes, yes, *I* know it because I look out for it; but what you have to do is to prove, to the man who does not look out, that they could not possibly have *done* but what they did: because, in the scheme of things as you see it and (what is more essential) as you have hypnotized them into seeing it, such and such contacts of a and b make $a^2 + 2ab +$

b^2. It is all there in the book, the Cornish-Devonshire ancestry, the contact of a hunger-weakened mind with Russian Nihilism. ... But the points are not *quite* made, the destiny of it not *quite* brought out after being put in. One has to stop and think. Now a perfect County Council puts sign-posts at its ventways because the roads are made for country-people primarily and only secondarily for tourists furnished with good, bad or indifferent maps.

Then again: there is not enough vinegar in the salad. You are too kind, too deferential to your characters; you haven't enough contempt, enough of the *saeva indignatio*. Perhaps you have not enough aloofness from them; have drawn them too much from the life. Catholicity is the first necessity of a writer on men; but there must also be room for the reaction. Turgenev had plenty, plenty, plenty of human sympathy, but all the time he was putting in his Bazarovs and his young men and old, his maids and matrons, he knew that he, as Creator, was infinitely above them, and at times that peeped out. Let it come out in your work too. You too are miles above any of the characters you create; you must be or you could not create them. Keep that always in your mind; it is one of the defects of your qualities, of your temperament. It is true there are no villains in the world; you have the sense to see that I, who am an Anarchist, a destroyer, am not, when all the shouting is over, ethically a bit worse than Mr. Cecil Rhodes who is an Empire Builder. I am not a bit better. I am just as futile, just as human, deserve spitting on just as much. Yes, spit at them sometimes, because your Christian[3] (why Xtian, which seems to me to be the *masculine* of Xtine?) your Xtian would most probably not appreciate one bit the technical merits of the *Villa Rubein*. Put more shadow into it; there *is* more shadow. One's fellow-creatures are despicable as well as pathetic; one is oneself, but that doesn't come into the story.

This is of course vastly *ex parte—ex mea parte*—and there is more to be said for your sympathy than for my disdain. I was thinking, when I was reading your *Villa Rubein*, of a girl[4] I once treated of; a girl of much the same character; very charming; a

[3] Galsworthy's heroine, Christian von Morawitz.

[4] Probably Edith Ryland, heroine of his first novel, *The Shifting of the Fire* (London, 1892).

girl I am very fond of in my way. I took hold of that young woman and ran in every bit of her charm I could think of and then smashed in all the repulsion I could think of; the boredom of her, the washed-out look of a morning, the inevitable nerves, the hysteria—and yet she was a charming girl.

Your Xtian is better done than that; she isn't one side pink muslin and the other black and purple checked cloth; it's not with her I'm quarrelling. Indeed I'm not quarrelling with any of the characters except perhaps Greta who is all charm. To me she is an undesirable; the danger with children is that they set for the reader very much the tone of the book. One is inclined to say: "Ah, this man, this writer, only sees the charm and not the hideous worry and bother of the dressing and washing, the Latin lessons and the rest. He is only a visitor in this House of Life." A child like that is a danger throughout; she takes up room; introduces dangerous touches of naïveté into scenes where the nerves are a-tremble for the saving of a situation (I am thinking of her remark about bats in the scene in Harz's unscrewed studio) and so on. I can't for a moment say that she is a superfluous character, she is, on the contrary, very necessary, for the story, for relief and so on. But I cavil at her as I did at the idyllic touches in the Cosmopolitan[5] because she takes up too much space and has worried me a little in the *progression d'effet*[6] of the end of the scenes with Treffry— very fine work that, all, by the bye.

Looking back I find I have attacked you somewhat viciously in parts of the story. I did not mean to do that, but rather to use the defects—or what seemed to me defects, as pegs to hang theoretic disquisitions upon art, as I see it in my limited field of view. As I said before, my dear fellow, you gave the right personality, your work has undeniable distinction. The *Villa Rubein* seems to me a little weak in form and in other essentials. But it shows very plainly that *you* are not weak in the essentials and, as I said before, I read the book with real pleasure who read hardly any books

[5] The story now known as "A Knight."

[6] One of Ford's favorite critical terms. In his book *Joseph Conrad*, he recalls: "In writing a novel we agreed that every word set on paper—*every* word set on paper—must carry the story forward and that, as the story progressed, the story must be carried forward faster and faster with more and more intensity. That is called *progression d'effet*, words for which there is no English equivalent."

with any pleasure, except those of three or four men whom you know very well. Because it is distinction, and again distinction and again distinction that one wants, and that you have.

Pardon this inordinate length. I have rattled on as if I were talking to a better listener than I deserve and I am a dogmatic cuss at best; also a typewriter lends itself to excesses because, not being able to amend words, one has to amplify until one flounders and flounders, over boots and over spurs.   Yours,

To John Galsworthy

Dear Galsworthy,   [March, 1901]

I am returning the *Swithin Forsyte*[1] herewith; I think it is far and away the best thing you have done; there is more "grip," more force and more reticence as well, and it makes its way along *aceto infuso* like Hannibal somewhere. The girl—both girls—are excellently done and Swithin himself is a finely ground glass. I congratulate you.

I should be inclined to shorten the death-dream towards the end, that is if you feel like doing it. It could be done, I think, without detracting from the atmosphere of Swithin's later life and would I think bring the story better into proportion. But that is a matter of a word or a phrase here and there. I am sending it back rather earlier than I should normally because we are in the middle of moving operations. I would like to re-read it; perhaps you will let me look at it in proof; it really has given me a great deal of pleasure. It has, in fact, "charm,"—all your work has had that. But in this story it comes out more because all the characters fuse (compose, perhaps) better. That comes from the treatment—from the using Swithin as a visualising medium—a glass. Excuse the machine and the incoherence; I have been packing books and writing letters to furniture removers all day and can't get any kind of a second wind.

Upon impulse I enclose "a little thing of my own," not because I want to bother you so much as because I fear my former refusal

----

[1] "The Salvation of a Forsyte," one of four stories in the volume called *A Man of Devon* (London, 1901).

to send my Katharine[2] may have appeared churlish. This is supposed to be a volume of verse.[3] Keep it for a week or so, look at
a line or two and then send it to me at the Bungalow,

WINCHELSEA, nr. RYE, SUSSEX

Or if you will bring it yourself we should be still more pleased.
[Joseph] Conrad talks of coming over as soon as we get settled;
he is going to drink somebody's waters in early morning, wander
round the church, and imagine himself doing a continental cure.
If he does it would do him good, I think, and we could all make
merry together.

Good night; I am too sleepy to see the letters any more and I
have more to write.

Yours,

To Edward Garnett

The Bungalow
Winchelsea, Nr. Rye
[1901?]

Dear Edward:

The idea keeps booming in my head: Why shouldn't there be
a popular Library of Literature on the lines of yr. Library of Art?
—conceived on the broad general idea of making manifest, to the
most unintelligent, how great writers *get their effects*. As distinct
from the general line of tub-thumping about moral purposes, the
number of feet in a verse, or the amiable & noble ideas entertained,
by said Great Writers, of elevating & of making the world a better
place.

The idea, I say, keeps booming in my head—why couldn't one
make some sort of nucleus, just some little attempt at forming a
small heap on which people could stand & get a point of view with
their heads a few inches above the moral atmosphere of these
Islands. You obviously are out of sympathy with the whole drift.
But wouldn't it be worth while just trying?

I ask you, because there *is* the P. L. of A—a sort of machinery,
& there is *yrself*, a sort of centre. It's, after all, the thing I've most

[2] His year-old daughter.

[3] Perhaps the collection published in 1904, *The Face of the Night: A Second
Series of Poems for Pictures.*

at heart in a dismal world of falling leaves—&, if it doesn't appeal to you, I shall—I feel it really!—make a desperate attempt, oh yes, a (very) forlorn hope, in other quarters.

Yrs,

To James B. Pinker

The Bungalow
Winchelsea, Sussex

Dear Mr. Pinker,

28/9/02

I happened to be at the Pent when yr. letter of the 26th arrived & Conrad asks me to answer it for my own part.[1] I can't myself feel—& I don't think Conrad feels—inclined to let Romance go at the present terms. I must point out to you that at our first interview—when I had come up with Conrad especially to enquire—you expressed yourself confident of getting £400 for the work. (Yr. exact words were: "Oh, I don't think you need have any doubt about getting that.") The sum at present offered seems to be £230. I myself would not start a work at such rates & it certainly does not seem fair play for what Conrad has done.

Yrs sincerely,

P.S. If you think that cutting down the story wd. help its chance as a serial I expect to have some leisure shortly & might see to it. The point is: supposing it cut down, say, to 70,000 words or less, what price could we expect to get for the serial—from the Cornhill or elsewhere? Perhaps you wd. let me have an answer on this point.

[1] The Conrad-Ford collaboration is a long, complex story. Edward Garnett introduced the two men in September, 1898. By late October, the Conrads had rented the Pent Farm from the Hueffers who lived in nearby Aldington and then later in Winchelsea. During the next two years, they labored over an experimental *roman à clef* called *The Inheritors*. By the time it appeared to mixed reviews in 1901, they were at work on a rewriting of Ford's draft of a novel he called *Seraphina*. The novel was finished in July, 1902, and went at once to James B. Pinker, the literary agent who was handling Conrad's affairs and, in a short time, Ford's as well. They called the new novel *Romance*.

To James B. Pinker

The Bungalow
Winchelsea, nr. Rye

Dear Mr. Pinker,

[January, 1903]

I haven't had the grace to answer yr. letter because I have been at the Pent until just this morning. I send you now those stories. The first four have appeared—the one called "A Mother" as I told you has been to the Cornhill—but is too long for them. The last long one I tried to serialize in all my usual dumping grounds—to no purpose. I should not, as a matter of fact, care for it to appear alone because it's a kind of experiment in virtuosity (not in *realism*) & at the present juncture it might get jumped on—whereas in a volume with other things as a foil it wd. probably get commended.

I imagine that I cd. place the *Mother* with Macmillan's (who'll generally give me all the space I want) or any of the other mags of that type—The trouble is that they pay so deucedly badly (Macmillan's got a story of mine just coming out).[1]

I've been slaving—for years and years—at a novel that I've just finished re-writing for the fourth or fifth time.[2] I'd offer it to you instead of these things, only at various early stages of its career I tried it on several publishers who just stopped short of taking it and to another who wanted to publish it without making an advance—wh. I refused.

I'd be content with a small sum for these stories—say £50 for the *Mother* serial and the book—because I shd. rather like to publish some fiction just now—say next spring. ([Illegible] asked me to send them something a little while ago wh. I haven't yet contrived to do, by the bye.)

Yrs. sincerely,

[1] "The Baron; (A Love Story)," *Macmillan's,* LXXXVII (February, 1903), 304-320.

[2] Possibly *The Benefactor*, which Brown, Langham & Company published in 1905.

To H. G. Wells

My dear Wells: [1903]

I have written you an immense long letter about "Mankind in the Making"—& have put it into the w[aste] p[aper] b[asket]. Chapman & Hall discharged the particular, large stone into the duckpond of my mind &, altho' I was fully determined not to read it (to muddle my poor Gray Matter)—I've read it, every word, with extreme animation: it's delightful reading; it's delight-fully interesting—& I've never been able to keep my mind down to the page of a sociological work before.—Yes, it's charming. . . .

As to whether it ought to convert one to New Republicanism: well, if one accepts your dogma that the perpetuation of the race of men is GOOD & all that militates against it EVIL,—if one grants that one must, except in certain details, go the whole way with you. (And I don't ask for a pleasanter companion.) But. . . .

Anyhow I quite seriously congratulate you on a good piece of work—& for me the aim of life, the GOOD is turning out good pieces of work. And I suppose yr. ethical purpose (as opposed to the personal, propagandist aim) was to promote thoughts in imbeciles, tels que moi.—In that you have succeeded, oh my friend.

With all sorts of good wishes,
                                                  Yrs,

By the bye: I lament to see you fall into the error of upholding "Elizabethanism."—That sort of thing is the curse of modern Eng-lish.—What we want is to use our vernacular so skillfully that words, precious or obsolete, will not stick out & impede a reader. —You practise that well enough yourself: why seek to lead astray the young? Or why fix the limit at "Elizabethanism"?—Why not uphold the "Wellwenning by the wan waters," of the late W. Morris?—Or why not pepper your page all over—as I do, for my sins—with foreign words?—I *did* think that you at least had a hearty contempt for the British classic.—Elizabethans!— Oh Lord: what single one of them, except Shakespeare, cd. express a clear thought clearly?—No, sir: their vocabulary seems better than ours because we are creatures of association—precisely because we consider a ploughed field "Nature."—We have been taught to consider Elizabethan words as "poetical"—& so we do. And we all of us have in us a little touch of the pedant: we like to twist things round to shew off: But really it's much better to write: "not pertinent" & to keep "impertinent" for its present use. If you don't you will have to use some periphrasis to express the latter sense.—If you will reconsider the matter you will see that slang is an excellent thing. (Elizabethan writing is mostly slang.) And, as soon as is practicable we sh'd get into our pages every slang word that doesn't (in our selective ears) ring too horribly. . . . We must do that or we shall die, we & our language.

Again you undervalue Latin: it's not a thing valuable as making a Don turn up his nose: but it's of inestimable use as helping to acquire foreign languages & to understand our own without the help of dictionaries.—I really think that one might as well set out to make laws without having seen a man, or sociology without the intimate historic sense, as easily as learn any of the Romance or quasi-Romance languages without a knowledge of Latin. Even Greek is useful to this end: how otherwise do I remember such a word as "cacodglate" wh. I have heard only once in my life—or shododendra or UTOPIA.

Consider, oh my friend, these points—for, very justly, you make the sense of language so important a part of yr. scheme: what we want is rather to cultivate that "sense" than to increase our vocabularies with obsolete words that are attractive merely because they're *allusive*.

To Richard Garnett[1]

Dear Dr. Garnett:

Winterbourne Stoke
Nr Salisbury
[Summer, 1904]

Thank you very much: I daresay the small volume won't set the Thames on fire. . . .[2]

I'm always digging into the times of Henry VIII F[idei] D[efensor] etc. & sh'd. be very grateful if you c'd. lend me the 1st vol of the Camb Modern History series. What I particularly

[1] Keeper of printed books in the British Museum and father of Edward Garnett.

[2] Probably *The Face of the Night* (London, 1904).

want to discover is: to what extent the theological struggles of
the Reformation were affected—in the case, say, of the upholders
of the Six articles—by the Homousian etc. struggles of Athanasius
—& to what extent the (Latin) Classics of the Renaissance reacted
upon, say, the same Six Articles.

I have read a great many texts without being able to crystallize
any views of my own—& if I c'd. run against anyone else's views
it might help me on. What I mean is: What effect did the constant
reading of, say, Plautus have upon the minds of theologians of
that amiable epoch?—Or, to what extent did Henry himself read
Tertullian? And what Classical Texts & what Texts of the Fathers
were in general circulation?—I don't put these questions to you,
of course: but c'd. you tell me where I c'd. read of such matters—
in what book that is easily come-at-able?—However: it's dis-
graceful to worry you.

I trust you're well & busy: I'd just, as it happens, been re-reading
the Twilight of the Gods[3]—with great delight, when yr. letter
came—& had just before laid down Gibbon.

Elsie sends her kind wishes & I'm

Yrs very sincerely,

To James B. Pinker

Winchelsea
Monday
Feb. 1905

Dear Mr. Pinker,

I wish Ouida, who used that title, *The Altruists*, wd. be hung
and her book burned by the public executioner. But I suppose even
a Literary Agent can't reasonably be asked to arrange that?

As it is pray tell B. L. & C.[1] that—since I've heard of Ouida's
work for the last fortnight—I've been wracking my poor brains
for a new title. I can't think of anything better than *The Benefactor*. If they could do better I wish they would, for I believe titles
are all important. Or would they prefer *A Helping Hand*?

I suppose they can let me have the 1st pp. in slip to give me
longer to think it over, not that I think I can do better. I wish
there were no such thing as titles.

Yrs,

[3] Garnett's apologues in Lucian's mode, published in 1888.

[1] Brown, Langham & Co. published *The Benefactor* in 1905.

To H. G. Wells

The Bungalow
Winchelsea, Sussex
[May, 1905]

Oh Sir!

I've read you with pleasure[1]—& I hope & believe, with profit. If the latter does not accrue it will assuredly be the fault of my muddled brain not of your clear writing.

You present, of course, an attractive picture: dyspepsia or whatever bad fairy was present at my Sunday birth makes me cavil at each item & sympathise by turns with the Botanist or the double of G[ilbert] K[eith] C[hesterton]—as opposed to the narrator; I.—But, I take it, that, whatever wings a narrator; I, may have, the reader is always against the angels. I mean that one reads to disagree.

The [illegible] impression of the book is, however, *one* of many thoughts I've thought, many I might have, many I ought to have— & God alone knows how many that are whole abysses too deep for me.

And there are many heresies I sniff! To the stake with Samurai![2] And what sort of reactionary stuff is this of sumptuary laws against women's clothing—however carefully the prohibition be snuffled and hid away.

But the book leaves an impression—not so much picturesque as of a ~~picture~~ no!—a *landscape* looked at and remembered. It suggests, when I close my eyes:

"The wending cities, rich & warm
"Smouldered & glittered in the plain."

And that's what one asks of a book—a retainable picture, or colour, or note. This will rile you—& I'm an ass to write it. Alas! One's attitude, tho' it have no business, will out—with however inarticulate an organ.

—Well: God bless you & turn you into a Samurai when you're tired of writing.—Hind visited us the other day & meditates in-

[1] *A Modern Utopia* (London, 1905).

[2] Chapter Nine is called "The Samurai." Wells describes "certain men and women of a distinctive costume and bearing" constituting an order, the *samurai*, "the 'voluntary nobility,' which is essential in the scheme of the Utopian State."

vading you, I gather. My *London*³ goes out to the papers today &
this morning I received a frantic letter from the publishers asking
me to *use my influence with my friends on the Press to get it reviewed on the day of publication.*

Figure to yourself my doing it! And I know one and one only
journalist! Kind regards from us both—   Yrs,

To H. G. Wells

Dear H. G:

The Bungalow
Winchelsea, Sussex
[October] 1905

Don't for god's sake put yourself out to write about that rot.—
And I won't write about Kipps tho it's 50 times better worth
writing about.—But it w'd look like a dare.

I expected to meet you at a silly dinner last Thursday. They
told me you were to be there or I should not have gone. And I had
intended then & there to talk about Kipps. It's to my mind a
long way the best thing you've done. It opens out my mental
image of you by several petals. From my lofty heights I say "This
young man *will* do the trick after all!"—& I say it to every one
that I meet. So that I have become—what I never expected to be—
a propagandist. This, I know, is patronizing—but I don't want
to mar my expression of what I really feel by unbridled eulogy.

Your *end* does look as if it had been a little hurried—but it seems
to me to break such new and rich good ground that I'm no end
overjoyed: you see, I want immensely to see you make a really
great success—& Kipps makes me feel certain that you will—
I mean a human-artistic success. I know you will discount this
by saying that it reads like: "This book shows promise!"—But it
means, really, a great deal more than that: it means that I'm
really no end pleased & that my hat is just *itching* to be taken off
to you.—However I said I wasn't going to write about "Kipps,"
so farewell.

If you're in town *do* lunch with me on Wed. or Thursday—
or if not, I might come to Sandgate on Saturday to lunch.

Best wishes to Mrs. Wells.
            Yrs ever,

³ *The Soul of London: A Survey of a Modern City.*

To James B. Pinker

My dear Pinker:

What I wish to do in Russia is briefly this:

To go to Petersburg with my brother-in-law, David Soskice, who is a revolutionist of some considerable position—if that's the right word: to see as much as is practicable there of the revolution which is coming on (It has really only begun)—& to write, for as early publication as the posts will allow, a series of articles, forming a book of say 75,000 words—a book rather of impression than of statistics, of course.[1]

I think I may claim to be able, in all human probability, to see the revolution from within, for I have, for a number of years, been connected with most of the Russians who are now prominent in the revolutionary movement. Father Gapon,[2] who organized the great movement which led to the January massacres, was actually hidden in my mother's house for a considerable time, &, since he is at present organizing the general strikes in Russia, he would be able to give me a great deal of help. From Petersburg I should arrange to go to Moscow, where I have friends, to Odessa where I also have friends, & to Poland—where I have a number of introductions to help me—that is, if either or all of these places were in a state of real disturbance.

I don't know what I can say any more except that, with a willingness to see, and opportunities to see, a great deal, I ought to be able to write a fairly good book on the subject. I should, I suppose, run a good deal of risk—but I don't fancy that I should shirk that, as far as I know myself.

Yrs, sincerely,

To James B. Pinker

My dear Pinker:

May ruin and desolation wait upon the day when you inspired me to come to this land! It is hot, dusty, dull, and uninspiring,

---

[1] There is no record of Ford's having made this trip.

[2] Georgi Apollonovich Gapon, Russian priest, murdered by the socialist revolutionaries in April, 1906.

and the expenses are *appalling*! *No* one is anywhere—on the contrary, everyone is always 5,000 miles away: I can't imagine what I came for. May the Lord pardon you.

But I suppose, being here, I had better stay till some people return to the various towns—&, in the meantime, I am working on the second vol. of the Fifth Queen.[1] I shall post you about 12,000 words of ms. I think it is coming out fairly good.

In revenge you will have to finance me, for I have exhausted every cent of ready money that I have. I suppose the 12,000 words to be worth about £50—for I think we agreed to put the book at about £300 for 70,000. You might, will you?, therefore pay that much to my bank. I left McClure's the proofs of several things & the first vol. of the V Queen—but I don't know what they will do with them. If they make me an offer I will cable the terms to you & ask you whether to accept them. What I have proposed to them to do is to publish the Soul of London, the Heart of the Country, and the Spirit of the People in one vol. called say: *The Anglo Saxons*.[2] And of course there is the Vth Queen—3 vols. I tell you this because S. S. McClure has started for Yurupp & if you see him, *you* might put it before him and blow my trumpet— wh. I can't do—tho' I'm well enough contented to have it done for me. Bradley is very amiable and well disposed—but I don't know what his powers are. We've seen practically nobody else in the 3 weeks we've been here—*everybody* being away in hills & woods where it seems impossible to follow—But I hope to see a number of people when we go back to New York—& of course I have got a good many ideas for "copy" of one kind & another. But I don't feel certain that the game is worth the candle. I mean that the U.S.A. will never appreciate *my* particular merits. —vast tho' they be. Well: farewell. [Illegible].   Yrs,

[1] The successful novel about Katharine Howard, *The Fifth Queen* (London, 1906), was followed by *Privy Seal* (London, 1907), and *The Fifth Queen Crowned* (London, 1908).

[2] McClure, Phillips & Co. published them in New York in 1907 under the title *England and the English*.

To R. A. Scott-James

Dear Mr. James:

Aldington, Hythe, Kent
[September? 1907]

Thank you for yr. letter: the exact circumstances were these: I was helping Marshall with the Mail Supplement, for fun more than anything else.[1] Soap[2] however has shut the Supplement down—the Mail seeking to gain respectability by abandoning its only respectable feature, after the manner of its kind.

I was doing one set of articles for it which however the Tribune snapped up before I cd. get into communication with you.[3] I should actually have preferred the News; but because I wanted to put the Harmsworthian nose out of joint I wanted to let the series go on in the Saturday of the suppression. (H. H. I mean wanted me to write in the Mail itself whereas I wanted to show him that I'd rather appear in a paper even of the Smallest Advertised Circulation! 56,000 copies per diem and so on.)

But, because I have the itch to discuss Literary Topics, I had also devised for the Supplement several sets of leaders and correspondences of kinds that appeared to me to be Popular and also Refined—such topics as "The Novel versus the Serious Book"; "How the Stage Influences Literature"; "The Relative Importance of Technique and Inspiration" with carefully devised contributions from such distinguished authors as myself, Conrad, Galsworthy, Wells and others of my intimates. The Mail want me to keep these over until such times as they shall be rich enough to restart their Supplement, but I haven't the least intention of depending on Soap and if you'd care to have them they'd be altogether at your service. I had proposed to run to a column a

[1] In 1906, Alfred Harmsworth, Viscount Northcliffe, owner of *The Daily Mail*, established a literary supplement called *Books* with Edmund Gosse as editor and Archibald Marshall as his assistant. After six months, Marshall took the editor's chair and commissioned a series of literary portraits by Ford, beginning April 20, 1907, and continuing for fourteen weeks, until Northcliffe abruptly closed down the supplement on July 20. R. A. Scott-James of *The Daily News* urged Ford to contribute to his literary columns.

[2] Possibly a nickname for Lord Northcliffe.

[3] *The Tribune* began the series on July 27 with a "portrait" of Hall Caine and continued for twenty-seven weeks. Not all of the essays are devoted to one writer; most of them are more acute criticism than *The Daily Mail* series.

week at, say, your ordinary review rates whatever they are—
because money is literally no object. If this idea appeals to you
I'd start at once with "The Novel versus Serious Books" for
which I've got some really good letters in hand. I should say that
I have enough matter to go on till Xmas when my holiday season's
coming to an end. I want to go on writing Books—a bad practice
which I have abandoned for this year in deference to the united
voice of the Press—which I declared I was ever writing. It is this
determined abstraction wh. has given me time for other things.

This is nearly all my tale—except that I want very much to
get a job for a man [. . . . .] whom we'd given a wretched job
as sub-editor in the Mail Supplement. He is really a novelist of
genius but, poor devil, has been living in doss houses for sometime.
We used him to collect Literary Notes and write them. But now
he's on the world again and it worries me to think of his Lan-
thorn-jawed starvation. If you cd. use him even at a pound a
week it wd. please me more—and do more real good, seeing his
real literary value, than anything else. And he can be most useful.

Yrs. sincerely,

To James B. Pinker

84 Holland Park Avenue
THE ENGLISH REVIEW
Oct 16th 1908

Dear Pinker,

My cousin Baron Ignatz von Aschendrof has been in communication with me about the M. S. called "The Psychology of
Crime" which you forwarded me. I have let him know that I may
probably publish it in a later number of the Review, upon the
same terms as H. G. Wells gets, & he agrees to this. He is also
willing that you should act as his agent.[1]

Would you kindly do what you can about the enclosed from

[1] Ford and his friend Arthur Marwood, a Yorkshire squire, pooled their
resources to found *The English Review*. The first issue appeared in December,
1908, and was instantly a *succès fou* since it printed Hardy, Galsworthy, Conrad,
Hudson, Tolstoi, Henry James, and the first installment of Wells' *Tono-Bungay*.
Ford wanted to use a story he and Conrad had written in collaboration several
years before, and for a pseudonym they chose a garbled Polish-German name,
either trying to deceive Pinker or merely jesting with him. In the April and May,
1909 issues the story appeared under the title "The Nature of a Crime."

Macmillan. I want to give the complete edition a long full-dress review in the second number, & as the second number is *considerably* stronger than the first, & more certain to attract attention, I think this ought to do the old man some good. If Macmillan's would only lend me copies, which I would return, it would suit me very well, as I cannot at this moment afford to buy them, practically every cent I have going into the Review.

It may interest you to know that the second number will contain a long unpublished poem by Rossetti, an unpublished short story by Anatole France, some Recollections by George Meredith, & several other plums. I suppose you will let me know who copyrights the various contributions that you are agent for in the United States.

Come and lunch with me one day at the Mont Blanc. I am there every day to lunch except Monday.   Yours,

To Edward Garnett

Dear Edward,

84 Holland Park Avenue
October 17th, '08

I was sorry you couldn't come. Shall I return Rudy to you, or where? I will take the Anatole France down to Conrad with me, & if he does not do it will forward it immediately to you. You can make it any length you like at the rate of £1.1.0 a page. For the second number, taking your advice, I have secured both Meredith and Rossetti.[1] I had to pay a high sum for the Rossetti, but am getting it all back but £5 from America. I quite realize the importance of the political articles and I fancy that my political articles will astonish even you. I quite realize what you say as to the awkwardness of the profit-sharing idea, but the only people who come into it are very intimate friends of mine and I have put the matter perfectly plainly to every contributor—"Will you

---

[1] In the January, 1909 issue of *The English Review*, Ford published Dante Gabriel Rossetti's "The Ballad of Jan Van Hunks" with a facsimile of the last three verses, holograph. George Meredith contributed "A Note on Cheyne Walk." Anatole France's "Les Etrennes de Mademoiselle de Ducine" was printed in French in the same issue, Ford apparently having been unsuccessful in persuading either Conrad or Garnett to translate it.

take £2 a 1000 words or will you take a sporting risk which might be estimated as a two to one chance against you, as a shareholder?"—and in order to avoid their incurring any liability I have added in a form of words to please Galsworthy "I do not undertake legally to pay you anything at all, but this is my private intention."

I know that inevitably there will be quarrels and recriminations, but in some things I am an idealist and my ideal is to run the "English Review" as far as possible as a socialistic undertaking. The kicks I shall get will be the price I shall pay for indulging my idealism and these I trust to bear with equanimity. I think Elsie would be glad if you would go down next Wednesday or Thursday rather than later.

Yours affectionately,

To H. G. Wells

84 Holland Park Avenue
Dear Wells,   Nov 20th 1908

If you insist, I must expend some of the intolerable supply of gold that overflows the coffers of the English Review on a detective and will trace down to his lair and cut the throat of the fool[1] in question, but I think that in that case you ought to indemnify the detective against any charge of murder incurred. Anyhow, does it really matter? *I* never have written a book that has not by someone or other been called autobiography. A Southend paper even said that what it considered the improper parts of my "Fifth Queen" must have been lived through by the author, as the descriptions were so vivid. What does it matter? Why I have even been accused of being my own grandfather and of starting the Plein Air School of Painting in France in 1821, but I never in my life wrote a letter to any newspaper to contradict anything that was said about me. Anyhow I am certain that I am not

---

[1] On November 14, 1908, the Glasgow *Herald* announced the founding of *The English Review* and the promise, for its first issue, of a long excerpt from Wells' *Tono-Bungay*. "The story," the column continues, "which is believed, like 'David Copperfield,' to be substantially autobiographical will be completed in four numbers." Wells ordered Ford to "trace the *Fool* who started this to his lair and cut his obscene throat."

responsible for the rumour. I sent out various proofs of the
Review, of the first number, to various papers so as to get what
is called publicity and part of the sheets of "Tono Bungay"
went to the Glasgow Herald. It—and this is part of its charm—
reads so like autobiography that the paragraphist may be pardoned
for jumping to that conclusion. Anyhow what is material is that
"Tono Bungay" really is a great book. It has all the qualities of
the traditional classical English novel and it is much better
handled than any of the British classical novels. The linking it
with Copperfield is rather a stroke of inspiration on the part
of the Glasgow Herald man, for it has most of the charm and
none of the foolishness of that book. I have just been reading it
for the second time and this is quite calm and deliberate judgment.

Yours always,

To Edward Garnett

Aldington, Hythe, Kent
Dear Edward: [December, 1908?]

Thanks for yr. letter: of course I understand yr. psychology &,
God forbid that you shd. restrain yr. irritation before men of
good will: but before capitalists and semi-strangers it is so
different. What I disliked in the review[1] was that, having praised
and appreciated the subordination of the figures to the central
figure, you say the book is a failure at the end because I have
resisted the temptation to bring in a Northcliffe 200 ft. high. It
seems to me to be a treachery to Form. I wanted to achieve a Greek
vase & you say it is spoilt because I have not turned it into a
Chinese dragon-pot with a black dragon, spouting fire, moulded
and engraved, as an excresence. I cut out three whole chapters
devoted to N. to avoid this and my conscience commends me
still. But then. . . .

Elsie says: won't you come down here for a day or two this
week whilst I am here. Do! And pray be irritated and jump on
me to any extent. I can't help my Olympian manner: it is due to
a consciousness of high aims defended by a defiance concerning

[1] Of *Mr. Apollo* (London, 1908), Ford's ninth novel.

a conviction of miserable achievements tempered by resignation to the inevitability of failure and yr. (is it?) Race, wh. won't believe in high aims, observes smallness of achievement & hates resignation of any kind. Yr. Race, naturally will be irritated. Only it ought not to choke off Capital. However, as you see, I don't bear resentment, or a shadow of it.

Yr.,

By the bye: Cd. Connie translate something short of Tolstoi for the second no. of the E. R.—to balance France.[2] I shd. prefer something not of a social propagandist kind, something like the sledge story in the Ivan Ilyitch vol., Master & Man I think it is called—but I do not want to bar out the other at all.

Apollo is being slated all round.

To Edward Garnett

84, Holland Park Avenue

Dear Edward,
[1909?]

I think I ought to tell you that I resent—and resent intensely— yr. telling people that I can't write. It does not matter before intimates but when it comes to a table full of comparative strangers I really think it is in distinctly bad taste. I don't use a stronger word. After all I am a writer as serious, as conscientious, & as earnest as yourself &, if our views of the functions of literature do not tally, that is not a reason for the denial of one's right to express one's views. I shd. never think of saying you cd. not write before business acquaintances: on the contrary I have always said exactly the reverse.

I don't say anything about the review of the Apollo: I know that that was intended to tease & to whatever extent it hits below the belt, it is no doubt part of the tournament & wd. not affect our personal relations. I don't know what you wish these to be: I imagine you know I do not resent the reviewing. I imagine you do not know that I resent the other as I have put remarks of the sort into my pipe about a hundred times already. But that,

<hr>

[2] Constance Garnett had translated Tolstoi's story "The Raid," for the first issue of *The English Review* (December, 1908). All that appeared from the Russian in January, however, was the second half of "The Raid."

as a rule, took place before a small circle of friends—on this occasion it was before two men whom I had invited to talk business with me. This one thing is bad enough: the other is too bad altogether. I can be as phlegmatic as I like when it comes to myself—but when it comes to an—I hope unconscious—crying down of the magazine wh. I am doing absolutely for the love of literature & without an idea of advancement or any profit at all for myself—a project wh. is intended to help so many people & causes wh. you desire yourself to help—I do think that it goes too far.

Yrs.,

To Mrs. H. G. Wells

Dear Mrs. Wells,

84 Holland Park Avenue
Jan 29th 1909

I have received a letter from Wells which I prefer not to answer for various reasons but I send you the following particulars which you can communicate to him or not as you please.

Last January Wells asked me to start the Review, saying that Tono-Bungay was not marketable & the Review would advertise him & do him good. His proposal was that he should share in the Editing & bear half the cost. A little later in conversation he said—I use his own words—that he wanted to back out of the Editing & that he felt like a worm for deserting me. I agreed to his backing out of the Editing. A week later he said that he desired to back out of contributing to the cost of the Review & that once more he felt like a worm. I agreed to his backing out of the cost of the Review. At the beginning of the negotiations Wells stipulated that he should have a fifth share of the profits of the Review as payment for Tono-Bungay. He was to have this fifth share, doing in addition half the work and contributing half the cost of the Review. When Wells drew back from performing either of these two duties I did not suggest that his share should be cut off. A little later Wells caused trouble about the date of publication which caused the appearance of the Review to be put off for six months & caused me also unheard of trouble. I did not remonstrate with Wells. A little later Wells made trouble as to the publication of Tono-Bungay with regard to Macmillan.

I then undertook that no copies of the Review should be sold as remainders. No copies have been or will be sold as remainders. A little later after the Review was started & printing had commenced Wells again refused to allow Tono-Bungay to appear, for no reason apparent to me at all. He withdrew his objection also for no apparent reason. The stipulation at that date was that Tono-Bungay was to be published as a book on the 15th of the month preceding the last issue of Tono-Bungay as a serial. Wells now announces that his book is to appear on the 2nd. This will be seriously detrimental to the Review but in spite of all the impediments that Wells has put in our way and in spite of all his breaches of agreement I have not once remonstrated with him. With regard to this final breach of trust it is of course my duty to remonstrate with him which I did in a perfectly formal manner. Wells is quite aware that as far as I am concerned he is at liberty to swindle or rob me or to do anything that he likes with my property. He knows that perfectly well but when it comes to damaging the Review it will be necessary to obtain some estimate of the damage he caused by his breach of trust. This damage I will make good to the Review out of my own pocket but it will have to be settled on a legal basis so that I am no way acting personally against Wells but against myself as I regard myself as being responsible for having introduced into the affairs of the Review a person whom I ought to have known, & indeed did know, could hardly be expected ever to keep to his engagements. In his letter to me Wells says that I am giving away copies of the Review although I have promised that no copies were to be given away. I never promised that no copies of the Review were to be given away; I promised no copies should be sold as remainders. A certain number of complimentary copies of every publication are given away & I have instructed Duckworth to give away a certain number of copies of the First Number but none of the subsequent numbers. To give away copies of the First Number can in no way interfere with the sale of Tono-Bungay as a book; on the contrary, each such number given away is an advertisement for Wells. In the course of the transaction Wells has broken his word innumerable times whereas as you know I am giving him more than he originally stipulated for, for whereas he only stipulated for a fifth share of the profits of the Review I have since stated to you personally that it was my intention to give him a share of the Goodwill proportionate to the length of his contribution. The reason why I have not put this into writing or made it the basis of a form of agreement with Wells is simply this: if the consideration that Wells received for Tono-Bungay was a share of the Goodwill, Wells would become responsible for the liabilities of the Review along with myself. As the liabilities of the firm are enormous—quite big enough to ruin both myself & Wells I have simply told you that it is my private intention to give Wells a share of the Goodwill, thus imposing no legal liability upon him at all. This is an arrangement for Wells of an entirely "Heads, I win. Tails, you lose," as he has every chance of becoming a part owner of valuable property with no risks of any kind, his only contribution being a piece of work which he himself declared to be unmarketable & his immediate & certain profit a much wider publicity than he has ever had in his life before. My own profits in the matter have been and will be nothing. I have most studiously avoided in any way advertising myself in connection with the Review. I have contributed very large sums in the way of capital & an enormous amount of work & as you know any profits from the Review are to be devoted to publishing books that would not otherwise be published, all the profits, that is to say, except those that go to Wells. Wells, as you must know, has behaved again & again most treacherously to me. I have always ignored the treacheries on account of his art which I admire sincerely & which I have continuously and always praised & tried to help forward. It is a great pity that Wells should give way to these panics and commit actions so questionable under their sway, but I am quite aware that these are the inevitable consequences of having anything to do with men of letters & regard them as being all in the day's journey. I would not write to Wells in any circumstances at all. His opinion of myself is of no consequence whatever, to me. Yours is however, & I think that my view of the matter ought to be put into black & white.

Yours always affectionately,

To Mrs. H. G. Wells

The English Review
84 Holland Park Avenue
Feb. 1st 1909

Dear Mrs. Wells,

Your statement of the final settlement arrived at strikes me as substantially correct and substantially in agreement with my letter of Friday but there *were* the two preliminary agreements in which Wells agreed to do half the Editing & find half the money. Your letter is substantially correct, this is to say if we substitute the word "profits" for the word "proceeds." I am perfectly willing to let it stand as "proceeds" but Wells ought to be aware that in that case he runs very considerable risks because he becomes a partner and liable for debts instead of a person being paid and I wish to avoid his incurring any liability whilst taking all the risks myself. I hope you understand this point. I repeat that, as I put it, it is my private intention to give Wells a share in the Goodwill of the Review. This means that Wells has no liability because he has no legal claim. If, on the other hand, Wells insists that he has a legal claim he must bear his share in the liabilities, &, not only that; if I were unable to meet them he being an unlimited partner would be liable for the whole sum. This I trust is now clear to you. The position is that I am risking large sums of money & am doing my best to prevent Wells having any kind of risks whilst assuring him of the full share of the money that I have expended; for there will obviously be no profits on the first four numbers whilst the Goodwill whatever it is worth is purchased with the money which I find. This of course is not exactly the agreement made with Wells but it is much more advantageous to him. If he wishes to stand on the footing of a partner I have no objection whatever, but he will have to bear his share of any losses. That is a matter entirely for him. But this stage is only the final one & I repeat that Wells made two other engagements; the one to do half the Editorial work, the other to find half the money. Both these he broke and at that time he was exceedingly apologetic. The date on which he agreed to publish 'Tono-Bungay' in book form was definitely stated in the letter that I possess to be February 15th but as I said before I am not anxious to press the point or to injure Wells; only, if the book is published before the agreed date there must be some sort of legal enquiry to ascertain what damage the publication will cause the Review. In that case I will pay my fellow-proprietors that damage out of my own pocket, as a punishment deserved by myself for introducing Wells into the affair at all.

Yours always,

P.S. Of course if you had arranged with Macmillan to postpone the publication *before* my letter it would materially change my view of the situation; in fact it would change it altogether, as being a proof that Wells had shewn *some* sort of consideration for the interests of the Review and I can only repeat that I am most anxious that Wells should in no way suffer. If the earlier publication of the books helps him, let it go at that; only somebody must be responsible for the damage to the Review & that person must of course be myself.

To H. G. Wells

84, Holland Park Avenue
[February, 1909]

Do *please* write a reasonably serious letter addressed to my proprietors: there is no need for you to read the rest of this—it is merely personal.

Dear Wells:

I am really exceedingly sorry if, by writing to Mrs. Wells, I have annoyed you. Nothing else wd. make me re-open the matter: but if in that way I have annoyed you I feel that I owe you an apology —as full as you like.

But I do wish you wd. understand that it is not I but my partners who are taking action in this matter. I am not hindering them because I think it my duty not to. But you have treated them all thru' with a levity that is perfectly appropriate to me: it is not however appropriate to people who are strangers to yourself to write depreciatory remarks outside envelopes and the like. Do, *pray*, revise the whole matter from that point of view. With regard to our personal relationship: you really ought to be aware of my extreme devotion to yr. interests. I don't mean to say that I have ever rendered you any particularly great services: it has not been necessary. But you will, if you consider it, see that I have, whenever occasions occurred, done my best to champion you: certainly, by word of mouth, I have told innumerable people that the possibilities of yr. work make you, as a writer, a figure of the utmost importance. And even in the matter of the Review— surely Mrs. Wharton's letter alone shd. shew you—that it has been the means of conferring on you all the credit of the enterprise, whilst all I have got have been the trouble & the expense. I am not grumbling at these: that is part of the day's journey. I am merely trying to make you see that I really do trouble about yr. interests. As to whether, as you express it in yr. last letter to me, I have "muffed" the Review commercially it is surely rather early days to say. I and my partners recognized quite composedly from the start that the chances of any commercial success were in-finitesimal & we agreed to drop a certain amount of money in the endeavor to establish a goodwill. That we are doing.

It became evident however from the start that it was impossible to run the Review on the original lines of paying the contributors in shares, simply because no one was willing to write under those conditions. We therefore decided to pay contributors in the ordinary way. This, however, does not alter yr. position with regard to the original arrangement. This original arrangement was this: that 2/5ths of the Review shd. be set aside for the con-tributors (including yrself) they to receive shares of the profits as per page contributed. This remains exactly the same. The 2/5ths are set aside & the persons providing the contributions will receive their share of the profits as per page contributed. It makes no difference to you whether the persons providing the contributions are the writers or ourselves. The only difference is that we have decided—as a piece of fairness, since the actual profits of the first four numbers will be non-existent—to give you a share of the goodwill wh. may be considerable if we can keep the Review running a little longer. You cd. of course have this made the basis of an agreement at any time—the only objection being, as I have pointed out, that you wd. then become liable for the debts of the Review. That we shall carry out this private intention you can, I shd. think, knowing me, rely upon.

All this is largely repetitious of previous letters but I rather think you have not read my previous letters with much attention. They are certainly long & troublesome to read, but since you resolutely refuse to come here there is no other way of communicating with you.

I wrote to Mrs. Wells merely because she conducted the final stages of the negotiations & in perfect good faith imagining, as I said, that she wd. communicate to you in a softened form any passages that she—knowing you—might consider wd. be irritating to you. I was most anxious not to irritate you: at the same time I am aware that there are so many possibilities of reading meanings into phrases of letters written—of necessity very hurriedly—that it seemed to me at the time to be a reasonable course to pursue. Perhaps it was not & so pray let me repeat my apologies.

The only sentences that I can recall with regret are those in answer to the letter in which you called me a swindler. I said then that I was indifferent as to what might be yr. opinion of me. But that was not—tho' it may have appeared—a particular insult to you. For the fact is that I am utterly indifferent to anyone's opinion of me except that I shd. be sorry that anyone I liked shd. think I disliked them. I never quarrelled with any of my friends however much they defamed me & I never will. As one's motives are known only to oneself, so one cannot quarrel with one's friends for misinterpreting them. But I shd. be sorry if you thought that my writing to Mrs. Wells arose out of any disrespect to her or desire to annoy you—or for any other disagreeable reason. My only desire was to clear up the matter with as little friction as might be—and, if you were annoyed by my writing as to yr. personal characteristics to yr. wife haven't you, upon innumerable occasions, dilated about me to mine? And Mrs. Wells is so entirely devoted to yr. interests. . . . However . . . there it is.

Yrs always,

To Mrs. H. G. Wells

The English Review
84 Holland Park Avenue
Feb. 23rd 1909

Dear Mrs. Wells,

I wish you would get Wells to take a more serious view of the position and to realise that he is dealing with a business affair called "The English Review" and not with me. Personally, I feel no animosity at all in the matter but you have to consider that there are in this affair several others besides myself and that it is not I that am taking the action, which is purely an automatic one. It was quite a different matter when I stood alone & as you know I will put up with anything but one cannot deliberately break one's engagements with a business firm & apart from the personal friendship for you and Wells, which you must know is very great, I have to do my duty. Indeed I have to do it all the more because of that personal friendship. We intend, therefore, deliberately to proceed against Wells, though as I have told you it is my intention to pay whatever damages are proved, to the Review out of my own pocket. This seems to be the only honourable course to pursue.

Yours always,

To James B. Pinker

84 Holland Park Ave.
March 24, 1909

Dear Pinker,

I cannot see that Nash is advertising "The Half Moon"[1] at all, though I see many papers, and as he doesn't appear to be sending out any copies for review, I cannot see what fun he gets out of publishing it at all. I suppose most of his finances are taken up by advertising his new magazine and I sympathize with him: but at the same time the book has so much chance of success if properly handled, that I think he might as well be touched up on the subject. Will you kindly do this, for it looks very much as if he intended to treat the book as Rivers treated "The Spirit of the People," and that, as you know, did me a great deal of harm.

By the bye, some devil or some angel has filled me with a

[1] In 1909, Eveleigh Nash published *The 'Half-Moon,'* a novel about Henry Hudson.

wild desire to write a series of articles on Music Hall Stars—for some of whom I have a great admiration—and on the Music Hall Stage as a factor in popular life. Do you think you could place this for me, or rather get them commissioned? I could do it myself but I always manage to extract such rotten low prices. "The Saturday [Review]" would take them but I am afraid that would upset Max [Beerbohm], which I don't want to do. What I want to do is, in my own matchless way, to visualise, say Victoria Monks and then point out why she is applauded and what light the applause casts on the circumstances and ideals of the lower middle class. The articles would be both beautiful and instructive. Do what you can, will you?

Yours,

To R. A. Scott-James

The English Review
84, Holland Park Avenue
[January? 1910]

Dear James,

I am sorry you appear to feel yourself aggrieved. Of course I should not have ordered an article from you if I had not intended to print or to pay for it and I should have put your review into the February number if you had answered me in time to have reserved the space for it. But you did not.

The Review was my property until some months ago when I considered that I had spent enough money on English literature and my friends. I then sold it to a Company[1] who proposed to retain my services, bought my serials and other matter but never paid me since, as it turned out, they had not the money. The fact that it was so sold appeared in the ordinary manner in the Press and the ordinary notice of liquidation must have been posted to you in due course. The Review was then sold in due course, too, to Alfred Mond[2] who undertook to pay the contributors or I should not have continued to edit it. Mr. Mond has now ejected me from the editorial chair because he is a Liberal which no one

[1] David Soskice, Ford's brother-in-law, tried unsuccessfully to form a syndicate to buy the *Review*, hoping that Ford, on salary, could continue as editor.

[2] Sir Alfred Mond, Lord Melchett, industrialist and financier. After buying the *Review*, he installed Austin Harrison as editor. The December, 1909 issue is the last one over which Ford had full control.

could accuse me of being. (And you might publish the facts in the Daily News as one more instance of political terrorism). But that is all in the day's work. The fact is that I stand here to be shot at and meekly ready to pay such contributors as Mond does not pay and I am perfectly ready to pay for your partly written article if you will send in a claim.

I should be extremely glad to see you if this explanation clears your mind of any feeling of grudge; if it does not I should prefer not to. And I must say that I resent your reference in the Daily News to the character of the Review. I spent a great deal of money on the Review with the definite design of giving imaginative literature a chance in England. It was my own money and I was not minded to spend twopence on the dull, badly written stuff that in this country passes for "serious" work. You have all the other Reviews for the display of such Pharisaism (I am not referring to you or your work which you must concede that I welcomed always—) and to cavil at a work of pure self-sacrifice because it was not something else is, as I said before, the sort of ungenerosity that I really resent. So that if you can not see the matter in that light I would really much rather not see you. This is being extremely frank but I think it is just as well. I don't want you to agree with me that imaginative literature is the only thing of any permanent worth in the world but I do expect you to realise that I have a right to do what I like with my own.

Yours,

To R. A. Scott-James

The English Review
84, Holland Park Avenue
[January, 1910]

My dear James,

Thanks. You have written a very nice letter and I am grateful to you. I wonder if it is true that I am troublesome and quarrelsome to such a degree. I daresay it is. But you see, I am a troublesomely solitary nature without the least desire for the companionship of my kind. . . . However, this is egotism, so I will not go on refining. Only, do get out of your head the British idea that the Serious Book is worth anything at all except for the moment's reference. It is a survival of the Nonconformist superstition that

Nuvvles are immoral, which again is a survival of the mediaeval idea that all knowledge was of the devil and ended in black art. It is a good theme, of course, for the Daily News but it should not be allowed to penetrate into one's private convictions or one will end on—let us say—the staff of the British Weekly, the Spectator, or the Athenaeum. Of which last Stevenson said, you will remember: "Golly, what a paper!"

No, I haven't had any business or other worries to make me irritable.[1] I have been latterly rather flourishing and cheerful. It is only the old Adam which renders me such a hell of a Tartar.

Yours,

You will find by the bye, reference to Adam in The Encyclopaedia Britannica, Muns[e]y's Enc. Amer., Sir Robertson Nicol[l]'s History of English Literature, Professor Flinders Petrie's Nova Egyptologia and other Serious Works. It is also flimsily and meretriciously treated of in a work of imaginative fiction. But no reliance can be placed upon these Hebrew novelists, and readers of the Daily News, members of the Y.M.C.A. and the Girls' Friendly Society are earnestly urged to abstain from the reading of the last-named collection of legends.

To James B. Pinker

84 Holland Park Avenue
March 30th 1910

Dear Pinker,

I shall be sending you in the course of a few days a manuscript called "The Simple Life, Limited," by a young author called Daniel Chaucer[1] in whose work I am exceedingly interested. I may say that I have not the slightest doubt that it is just as good or better than anything I could do myself. It will reach you as soon as it has had time to be typed. I write this now because I am going

---

[1] Considering that Ford had lost £2,800 on *The English Review*, his optimism is admirable.

[1] Ford used Fenil Haig as a pseudonym for his first volume of poetry, *The Questions at the Well* (1893). He chose to write two novels, *The Simple Life Limited* (1911) and *The New Humpty-Dumpty* (1912), under the name of Daniel Chaucer, perhaps because he had five other books appearing during these years.

away for a short holiday next week. The manuscript will reach
you as soon as it is typed. I feel sure that you will use your best
endeavours with it.

By the bye, did you do anything with the American edition of
"A Call" and have you done anything with "The Portrait"? Have
you, too, had any accounts as to the American sales of "The Half
Moon"? There ought to be something to come from that source,
I should think, by now.
                                                    Yours always,

To H. G. Wells

The English Review
84 Holland Park Avenue
Dear Wells,   2nd, April 1910

Thank you. The position of the above is as follows as far as I
know:

In November 1908 Marwood and I started the Review, he having a two-fifth share and I three-fifths. Of the £5,000 that we
spent on the Review he paid £2,200 and I £2,800, I being generally liable for the debts of the undertaking beyond that sum. I
consider that one fifth share should be set aside for contributors
who did not ask for payment, that share being taken from my
three. In August 1909, this sum being spent and feeling disinclined
to continue labours that were extremely arduous and unrequited
Marwood and I decided to discontinue the Review. After however I had given orders to the printers to discontinue, a speculator
who had been in waiting came forward and offered to continue it
upon exactly the same lines. The terms that he proposed were as
follows: Marwood received 800 one-pound shares and I nothing.
I was however to continue [as] editor at a nominal salary which,
by the bye, after a time was not paid. Before that, however, I re-
signed the editorship. I was dissatisfied with the sums that were
paid to contributors and still more dissatisfied with the party tone
that the new proprietors forced upon the periodical. Really needy
contributors I paid out of my own pocket sufficient sums to make
up what I considered fair payments. Of the business affairs of the
English Review Limited I have no cognisance at all. They wound
up on the 17th December last. I was at first informed that they

would pay twenty shillings in the pound, leaving a certain amount over for shareholders of whom you would rank as one. Marwood, that is to say, is—or was when I last heard of him, perfectly ready to make over to you his eight hundred pounds-worth of shares for what they would fetch. But absolutely the only evidence that I have of any activity on the part of the Liquidator is that he has stated to several persons that I owed a thousand pounds to contributors. You, I was told, were claiming £250. I know nothing at all more about the business. I owe nobody anything at all and have nothing at all to do with the Review. I am its principal creditor for salary and work done but I hardly expect to be paid for these things. The only motive that Marwood and I had for spending our money was the desire to establish an organ in which the better sort of work might see the light. This we have very efficiently done so our money was not spent in vain, for I understand that your new novel[1] is to appear in its pages.

The books of the Review as long as it was under my direction are open to you if you happen to doubt any of these statements though I hardly suppose you will.

Yours faithfully,

To James B. Pinker

Dear Pinker,

84 Holland Park Avenue
June 21st 1910

I am getting along with "The Novel for Constables." I understand that it was to be ready by six months from the date of signing the contract, but if they want it sooner I could manage it all right, but just let me know about this.

With regard to the title I cannot say very definitely. The story takes place about 1327. It might be called "The Cross of St. Joseph," or "The Tournament of Women," or if Constables could leave the Announcement until a little later, I might think of a more attractive title.[1] The second of these is fairly attractive, but it gives away the subject matter, which I think is not altogether desirable.

[1] The first chapters of *The New Machiavelli* began to appear in May, 1910.

[1] Constable & Co. published it in 1911 under the title *Ladies Whose Bright Eyes*.

The notices of "The Portrait" seem to be unusually laudatory. I suppose I shall have to stick to historical novels for the Constable Contract, though I hate writing them. "Such, however," as Solomon observes, "is Life!"

Yours sincerely,

To Edgar Jepson[1]

My dear Jepson,

29 Nordanlage
Giessen, 28th Oct 10

Your letter made me glad, glad, glad! In the language of our brethren across the Great Divide—or is it the Herring Pond?—you have handed me the glad hand and to answer you I put on my glad rags.[2]

I am glad that H. G. [Wells] is troubling so many dovecotes; but I do not agree with you that his end will be blood. I think it will either be a country-house with a Tory Seat attached to it. Or else it will be the chains and straw of Bedlam. At one time I thought very strongly it would be the former, now I would put one hundred to thirty three upon the latter. Good Lord, I remember years ago advising H. G. not to be afraid of using personalities in his work—to sacrifice all the scruples to the desire to be vivid. What a dangerous animal I begin to think myself. Mr. Jepson, sir, I am a high minded Idealist, sans peur et sans reproche. You are on the other hand an unprincipled villain. I have never, that is to say, been able to discover in your writings or in your conversation one word that showed you to be possessed of any principles whatever. I do not believe that if the Daily News knew what you really are that they would permit the pure-souled Scottie[3] to put his knees for one moment under the same table with you. Under, I mean, the bounties and the sparkling wit that adorn the round mahogany of the Square Club[4] (This sentence has gone slightly astray because my secretary being unacquainted with the

[1] English novelist, author of *The Admirable Tinker* (1904) and *The Four Philanthropists* (1907).

[2] Ford had set up residence in Giessen in order to seek a divorce, under German law, from Elsie Hueffer.

[3] R. A. Scott-James.

[4] Founded by G. K. Chesterton and Conal O'Riordan. John Masefield, Walter de la Mare, John Galsworthy, and later Ford and Ezra Pound were among the members who attended monthly dinners to discuss new books.

real deep mysteries of the English tongue has introduced some
words that I did not intend and that I will not cross out because
I hate the sight of erasures upon a page. But you will understand,
who search all hearts).

I am glad your Non-Conformist friends so loved me. When
you—the unscrupulous villain and I, the pure-souled Idealist join
forces how *that* dovecote will flutter! And I see no reason why you
should desire to cut my throat, blast my reputation, reveal what
you think to be my secrets or throw vitriol upon me. I never discovered your first work, offered you shelter, food, clothing or
encouragement when you were starving. I never lent you money,
wrote in praise of your writing or committed against you any of
the twenty-seven Nonconformist Deadly Sins.

I am glad too that May Sinclair has put me into a book. The last
person who did it was the brother of William James; I am glad
too that I do not feel the least inclination to read Miss Sinclair's
book.[5] And oh I am very glad, very glad, indeed that you accuse
me of imitating the brother of William James. Mr. Jepson, sir,
nothing gives one a greater pleasure than to discover in one's most
cherished and penetrating friends—than discovering in them a
capacity for uttering the purely obvious. Observe with what a
Jacobian lightness I dance round this cobwebby theme. I might
have said that you exhibited a perspicacity worthy of Mr. Clement
Shorter who has made the same remark about every one of my
last thirty books. I might have said so but you will observe that I
have carefully refrained. I am glad too that you have been writing
on the *Future of Love*. It sounds a promising subject for your pen
which is so unlike that of Aretino, Mr. Edmund Gosse, Mr. Edmund [*sic*] Garnett or Sir Something Robertson Nicholl [*sic*]
and Mr. John Galsworthy. (These are, are they not, the principal
ornaments of the Royal British Academy of Letters, Aretino being
of course elected honoris causa?) Do send me a copy! I will froth
too before I die!

Sir, it is my intention to deliver that paper. I should be glad to
take the chances of vitriol. It cannot be delivered from any in-

[5] Henry James is said to have modeled Merton Densher (*The Wings of the
Dove*) on Ford. May Sinclair could have had Ford in mind while writing *The
Creators: A Comedy* (London, 1910).

strument of precision and the fun would be huge. Please thank Mrs. Jepson: Yes I will soon be supping with you again. I am, thank you, well, prosperous and occupied. With my right hand I am writing a history of cholera in Ireland; with my left an historical novel dealing with the divorce of Anne Boleyn, using it as a peg on which to hang many disquisitions on Divorce in general. My feet are dealing with the treadles of a type-writing machine that pours out the history of literature in England during the last two years, whilst my eyes are engaged in perusing the materials for my gigantic life of Sejanus. Good bye; may you occupy the blind spot in the eyes of God. Then you will prosper.

Yrs.

If you think this commun. worthy of one of the feasts of the S. C. pray read it them with all my love.

To James B. Pinker

29 Nordanlage
Giessen
31st Jan 1911

Dear Pinker:

Would you care to attempt to arrange for me the whole rights of a book I want to write called "Men and Women"?[1] This would be a sort of philosophical discussion on the relations and the differences between the sexes—something in the note of my Soul of London. Or equally something in the note of my Reminiscences —You know the sort of nonsense, a mix-up of anecdotes and fatuous moralizing. I reckon it to take about fourteen chapters of 5000 words each, each chapter to be capable of appearing as a separate article—or say ten of them. I want to make about £500 out of the book all out—say ten articles at £30 a piece and £200 advance royalties in England and the U. S. A. The point is, do you think you could reasonably expect to make this? I have made about as much by the Reminiscences in one way or another at the cost of a certain amount of bother and pushing. I'd be glad to get rid of this last in the second case. Just let me know what you think

[1] Not published until 1923, as *Women and Men*, at Three Mountains Press, Paris. The essays had previously appeared in four issues of *The Little Review* (1918).

and I will send you a synopsis. The point is that the book would be really Reminiscences of undistinguished people I have met in the course of my varied career, always keeping in mind the main thread of the differences between the sexes. Thus as undistinguished people are odder and more amusing than distinguished people, you would get a more amusing book than the Reminiscences actually are. I don't suppose you will see anything in the idea but you may trust the cavernous recesses of my brain do contain something worthwhile.

I am beginning the second novel for Constable tomorrow.[2]

Yours always,

To the Editor of *The New Age*[1]

Dear Sir:

[Giessen]
[February, 1911]

You ask me what is my chief reason for being the ardent advocate that I am of the cause of Woman's Suffrage. It is like asking a man who is being stung to death by bees which bee most incommodes him. For the reasons for giving women the vote—for encouraging women, that is to say, to take interest in public questions and to regard themselves as members of a State rather than as the scavengers of isolated households—the reasons for this assail me on every side. But I suppose my chief reason for desiring that women should have the vote—for desiring it rather than for saying that it is right and just that they should have it—for there is no man that denies that it is right and just, every man basing his denial on, and taking refuge behind, expediency!—and you will observe that my emotions upon this subject are so keen that my English has become complicated and incomprehensible;—my chief reason for desiring it is personal. I have, sir, in common with most men, suffered enormously at the hands of women. I have suffered a good deal at the hands of men, but men I have been able to get rid of. But the poor are always with us—and so are women, because they are poor. You will observe that I am taking the ground of the usual opponent of the cause. The usual opponent

[2] *The Panel* (London, 1912).

[1] See vol. VIII (February 9, 1911), 356-357.

of the cause says that woman is an inferior, is a mendacious—
let us say a generally bothersome animal. Therefore, she should
not be allowed to exercise public privileges which are accorded
to senile imbeciles and such reprieved murderers as have served
twenty years in one of his Majesty's prisons. As a general rule I
am accustomed to say and to believe that there is really no essential
difference between man as man and woman as woman. I have
written a great deal upon this theme, but it is one of some complication, and one which admits of dispute. Let me, then, take up
my stand upon the ground that woman *is* the inferior, *is* the
bothersome animal. Let that be conceded and we have at once the
most powerful reason in the world for giving her a sense of her
civic responsibilities. I have been persistently nagged, swindled,
worried out of my life, and distracted during the course of my
existence by some five or six women. I have been nagged at, betrayed, swindled and worried in one way or another during the
course of that existence by perhaps fifty men. The men were inter-
mittent pests, the women were there all the time. I do not mean
to claim for myself any special experience in the matter of women.
Most middle-class men approaching middle age support at least
five women and are worried by them in one way or another. Most
working-men support from two to three women, and are equally
worried *pro rata*. I was talking the other day to a prominent Tory
gentleman about the Chancellor of the Exchequer. But did this
Tory and gentleman abuse that much-abused person? Not a bit
of it. He sighed:

"Ah! We ought to have had Lloyd George! We have always
had to have someone to do our dirty work. We had Disraeli, we
had Chamberlain; we ought to have had Lloyd George."

Sir, man in these islands—man throughout Christendom—is
like my Tory friend: is like the Tory party in miniature. No sooner
does he set up for himself; no sooner does he determine, with
head erect and with courageous eyes, to face the world, than he
looks round for someone—to do his dirty work! And that someone is a woman. Sir, I have been through it—moi qui vous parle.
Sir, I am a thoroughly manly person. Sir, I am noble and generous;
I throw my money about in restaurants, I tip porters with enor-

mous lavishness, I get into splendid troubles through my chival-
rous behaviour.

I am talking not, of course, of myself as a person but of myself
as a man. All men, as distinguished from all women, are such fine
creatures. That is why they have the vote. [. . . . .]

As for the question of militant tactics, I am certainly in favour
of them. It is the business of these women to call attention to their
wrongs, not to emphasise the fact that they are pure as the skies,
candid as the cliffs of chalk, unsullied as the streams, or virginal
as spring daffodils. They are, of course, all that—but only in novels. This is politics, and politics is a dirty business. They have to
call attention to their wrongs, and they will not do that by being
"womanly." Why should we ask them to be? We cannot ourselves make omelettes without breaking eggs. Why should we ask
them to? Sir, there is a Chinese proverb which says: "It is hypoc-
risy to seek for the person of the Sacred Emperor in a low tea-
house." Sir, politics is a low tea-house from which, in His mysterious way, God slowly grinds out some good small flour. When
they have got that, the women can afford to come out and bake
tea-cakes. Of course, if someone can point out a better way than
kicking policemen, no one would be better pleased than I, but
since Joan the Maid helped the King of France to his sacring at
Reims, there was no action which has so called public attention
to the capabilities of women as that memorable moment when a
journalist invented the helpful lie that Miss Pankhurst spat in a
policeman's face. Miss Pankhurst did not do it, but the journalist
knew what our public wanted.

To Violet Hunt[1]

15 Friedrichstrasse
Giessen
9th Apr. 1911

Dear Miss Hunt,

   With regard to Mr. John Lane's[2] letter of the 29th March re-
questing details of my biography.[3]

[1] English novelist, author of *The Wife of Altamont* (London, 1910), and intimate friend of Ford.

[2] The London publisher.

[3] Ford may well have had good reasons for publishing his anti-utopian satire,

The family of Chaucer is ancient and respectable having, from
time immemorial, had its seat in the County of Kent. The most
distinguished member of the family was the poet Geoffrey Chaucer
of the 14th century. Geoffrey Chaucer as Lord of the Manor of
Bilsington near New Romney in that County was invested with
the Grand Serjantry [*sic*] of England by right of which he presented to the King upon his coronation, two boxwood cups, receiving in return two cups of gold. This right passed into the
hands of the family of Halliday of Glenthorne in North Devon in
whose hands it remained until the year 1904. In 1896 I attempted
to purchase Biltington [*sic*] priory along with the Lordship of the
Manor, carrying with it the Grand Sergantry [*sic*]. The then Mr.
Halliday was unwilling to sell but the estate together with privileges passed in 1906 into the hands of Mr. Balston, a most disagreeable man who is I understand the proprietor of large paper
mills in the neighbourhood of Maidstone. With Mr. Balston I
was for several years at law about the boundaries and rights of
way and I once revenged myself upon him by "kiting" over his
land which my land commanded. As Mr. Balston was on that date
giving a large shoot to which he had invited members of the nobility and gentry, and as not a single bird rose on that occasion, Mr.
Balston was very properly enraged. This is the most exciting incident of my career which has been otherwise that of a quiet
country gentleman of ancient but impoverished lineage. The
Mr. Balston of whom I have written above has no merits except
that he is the cousin of Mr. Geoffrey Robinson at present tutor in
the family of Constance, Lady De la Warr, an agreeable gentleman whom you will remember to have met at Inchnary. As for
any further information concerning myself perhaps you would
like to forward for Mr. John Lane's instruction the following note

---

The Simple Life Limited, under the name Daniel Chaucer since several of the
characters are less than flattering portraits of contemporaries. Frank Harris appears as the theatre-manager, George Everhard. Edward Garnett is the tired
critic, Mr. Parment, who discovers Simeon Brandetski (Joseph Conrad), a writer
who changes his name to Simon Bransdon before publishing his first novel,
Clotted Vapours. But more important than the satire is the portrait of Gerald
Luscombe, the Tory landlord, scholar, and athlete, perhaps a mirror to Arthur
Marwood, Ford's Yorkshire friend and eventual model for Christopher Tietjens.

which I am just sending to the editor of "Who's Who." *Chaucer*, Geoffrey [Daniel?] born 1869 the son of W. Chaucer Esq of Poultney Wick, Kent, and of Muriel daughter of Launcelot Kirby. *Educated* privately and at Trin Col. Cam. *married* 1891 Eugenia Blossom, the champion barefoot sandal wearer of the world, whom he divorced 1910. Publications *"How to live healthily on nuts,"* 1907. *"Why I wear vegetarian sandals,"* 1909. *"The Simple Life Limited,"* 1911. *Recreations* hunting, shooting, fishing and stamp collecting. *Clubs*: Thatched House. *Address* The Manor House, Poultney Wick, Kent. Telephone 190 Ightham.

It may be well understood that the unfortunate event of 1910 together with the connection which preceded it accounts at once for my knowledge of and my repulsion from all forms of the "Simple Life Limited" or Unlimited.

Believe me, my dear Miss Hunt

Yours very sincerely,[4]

To R. A. Scott-James

15 Friedrichstrasse
Giessen
11. V. 1911

My dear James,

Of course I am going to write the articles for you. But I have been busy and lazy and unable to make the mental effort of turning my thoughts into channels other than the work I had in hand. However, I will begin upon the articles to-morrow and will send you three or four in a day or two so that you may publish them at your convenience. Your notice of "Ancient Lights" was very touching.[1] I called at your office on the day it appeared and was told that you had left for the centre of Africa or some such improbable place. But you need not have been so alarmed. The large pistol that was sticking out of my pocket was not really loaded. I was in a state more of sorrow than of anger—though you are the first man who has called me a liar in print and lived to tell the tale.

I shall be returning to Town for the season on the 27th or 28th

---

[4] Signed Daniel Chaucer.

[1] *The Daily News*, March 24, 1911, p. 3.

and I hope I shall find you and Mrs. James more successfully than was the case with my last efforts.

By the bye: Wagner's "Memoires" have been published quite lately here by Brockhaus of Leipzig. If they should happen to send a copy to you you might let me have it for review.

Yours always,

To R. A. Scott-James

Authors' Club
2, Whitehall Court,

Dear James,
June 30th 1911

I've cut this blessed thing with coolness and ferocity.[1] But I really can't judge of lengths a bit so that I have marked with a blue pencil along the margin of other passages that you might cut if it is still too long. These passages are in my own autograph so if you tear them out you had better keep them as a valuable M. S. for as my writer's cramp goes on getting worse it is probably the last piece of my M. S. that the world will ever see, that is why the printers are cheering (you understand, as Lord Tennyson said about the egg, this is a joke, the market value of my autograph being exactly 6d according to the catalogue of such things that get sent to me.) I am afraid I treated you with shameful neglect last night but I had to gallop round and talk to so many people that I simply don't know whom I talked to and whom I neglected.

Yours very sincerely,

To Edward Jepson

South Lodge
Campden Hill Road

My dear Jepson,
August 8th, 1912

I cannot sufficiently say how much I admire your new romance[1] —religious tract I fear you will not permit me to call it. Where all is so good it is difficult to pitch upon any scene for a special commendation, but perhaps the palm should be given to the deathless episode where your eponymous hero discovers the black man's

---

[1] Probably his review of five German novels, *The Daily News* (July 2, 1911), p. 3.

[1] Probably *The House on the Mall*, published in March.

footprint in the sand. Marvellous also are the conversations in which he tries to induce his man Friday to embrace the true religion. I don't know how you do it.

Indeed now that you have placed this work to your credit I begin to fear that your name will live longer than mine in the annals of fame. As long as you had only written the "Old Curiosity Shop," "Othello," the poem beginning "Little drops of water," and the "Shorter Catechism," I felt fairly safe; for, could I not point to the English Bible, the Novum Organum, Webster's Dictionary, the Christian Science Testament, the Master Christian and the New Machiavelli as works of mine that will live for ever? But now that you have given us Robinson Crusoe, imagination fairly reels. . . .

Anyhow what is this new joke? I am absolutely mystified. And why drag in Wells?

Our kind regards to you both. We go to Selsey[2] on Saturday.

Yrs,

To Lucy Masterman[1]

South Lodge
Campden Hill, W.

Dear Mrs. Masterman,

Jan. 23d, 1913

Forgive my having taken so long about thanking you for your poems; I have been very busy and fussed with one thing and another and moreover my doctor forbade me to read or write at all. Still, here I am.

It is, you know, so difficult to write anything but banalities about one's friends' poems unless one takes them seriously, criticises them and propagandises along the lines of one's own particular critical fads or canons.

Let me do this last. I don't know whether you in the least want it. You may be satisfied that you have said your last word and that no suggestions will be of any service. In that case, accept what I am going to say merely as a token that I have taken your gift seriously.

[2] Violet Hunt owned The Knap Cottage in this Sussex village. Her London house, South Lodge, was in Kensington.

[1] Wife of C. F. G. Masterman, the Liberal politician and author of *The Condition of England*.

In the first place, then, I began to read, and read about the first half of the book with pleasure—at a gulp as you might say. I liked QUOD SEMPER very much and VENI CREATOR & SONG OF REVOLUTION & THE SPHINX & HE SHALL GATHER THEM IN & particularly VICTORIA STREET. I had the emotions that I have when I am reading poetry that is more than mere verse. That is as much as to say that I felt really in contact with a poetic temperament, aloof, pleasant and not common. It is a good idea in WESTMINSTER ABBEY; it is a good mental vignette in the TRAMP's SONG; the first page of IN TIME OF DEFEAT is heavy, bitter, ponderous and authentic in a way that one wants.

But, after I had read a certain distance I became conscious of a certain heaviness. It was not that the personality seemed any less pleasant but simply that the method, the wording was always so much on the same note. To jump quickly to what I want to say— to what I am always wanting to say—the note is too refined, too remote, too LITERARY. My dear lady, your poems in the future must not be written in that pleasant and sheltered verandah with the grey sea and the grey sky and all the chastened romance of it. That is holiday time. Your poetry should be your workaday life. That is what is the matter with all the verse of to-day; it is too much practised in temples and too little in motorbuses—LITERARY! LIT-ERARY! Now that is the last thing that verse should ever be, for the moment a medium becomes literary it is remote from the life of the people, it is dulled, languishing, moribund and at last dead.

(I would not write to you in this strain if I did not imagine myself to perceive in you a certain preoccupation with actuality— the EVENING HYMN IN A CITY, the WESTMINSTER ABBEY, and IN VIC-TORIA STREET have something of the note that I want to find. I like too the religious note for in a Papist sort of way I am a tempestu-ously religious person and I do not think that any clearness of thought is possible unless one either is or has been intensely reli-gious. But I should like you to probe yourself much more deeply and harshly. Don't in any region of thought let any single accepted idea be your final end. It is necessary to get even further than the proposition that God is of necessity brutal as often as benevolent or that the poor are only the stuff to fill the cemeteries with, just as the function of autumn foliage is to be trodden into clay.)

You will, I hope, understand what I mean—it is that roughly, your work—like most work of to-day—suffers a little from the want of the quality of surprise, which in the end is the supreme quality and necessity of art. You ought to search your mind and your vocabulary much more thoroughly. The TRAMP'S SONG, for instance, has its idea—but would it not be better if its phraseology were nearer that of a tramp: why drag in "Hey." George V and your husband reign over us today, not Elizabeth and Burleigh.

Yes, remember that when next you sit down to write. And sit down to write, metaphorically speaking, in a railway waiting room, or in a wet street, or in your own kitchen (not in your nursery, that would be too idyllic) or in the lobby of the House of Commons, I was going to say, but the jobs that are perpetrated there are too artificial. But go where something real is doing and let your language be that of the more serious witnesses in Blue Books. My father once wrote of Rossetti that he set down the mind of Dante in the language of Shakespeare. That was clever of my father, but could there have been a greater combination of that magic Amateur—for what the poet ought to do is to write his own mind in the language of his day.

Forget about Piers Plowman, forget about Shakespeare, Keats, Yeats, Morris, the English Bible and remember only that you live in our terrific, untidy, indifferent empirical age, where not one single problem is solved and not one single Accepted Idea from the past has any more any magic. Our Lord and his teachings are dead; and the late [Samuel] Smiles and his, and the late William Morris and John Ruskin and Newman and Froude—only that Newman was a very beautiful, unadjectival writer. It is for us to get at the new truths or to give new life to such of the old as will appeal hominibus bonae voluntatis. Only to do that we must do it in the clear pure language of our own day and with what is clear and new in our own individualities.

This is a terrific sermon, but it does at any rate show that I have taken you, as I said, seriously enough to want to bend you to my own purposes which I believe are the purposes of this age if we could only get a clearer view of it.

Tell your husband to come and play golf with me at Le Toucquet where I am going shortly. I will then sermonise him too with the utmost ferocity about the nature of things and he can listen with that splendid air of attention and respect which always does me as much good as attending at a first-rate farce. In fact, it must be good practice for him too, to listen to such huge dogmatism with an air of attention. I see it leading him, swiftly and remorselessly, to the highest office of the State.

Do you know that, five years ago—and it is on record—I prophesied that Mr. Bonar Law would be Leader of the Opposition; H. G. Wells a country Tory landowner; and your husband next Liberal Prime Minister, but one. But he is a good fellow all the same and you are a poet which is more valuable—if you will pardon the familiarity of address.

Yours sincerely,

To James B. Pinker

Hotel de Provence
St. Rémy-de-Provence
March 17 [1913]

Dear Pinker:

The title of the book is, for the time being, "The Young Lovell,"[1] a Romance of the Borders. The date is towards the end of the XVth Century, running up to the beginnings of the Reformation, though it isn't in that sense concerned with religion. The action takes place in Northumberland and the story contains any number of things concerning "The Percy out of Northumberland," the Bishops Palatine of Durham, the besieging of castles, border raids, and so on with what is called "a strong element of the supernatural" and a vigorous love interest.

This is rather putting the matter in terms of advertisement, but the book will be, when it is done, a pretty big and serious historical work, rather like "The Fifth Queen," but, in a sense, more romantic. I don't want to let it go to just any publisher, because, if it is anything at all, it is really literature and I have spread myself enormously over it, but of course I leave that to your discretion.

Yours,

[1] Chatto and Windus published it in the fall of 1913, the second of three books they published for Ford.

To James B. Pinker

South Lodge
Campden Hill Road
May 6th 1913

Dear Pinker,

I enclose a biography of myself which contains everything that I can think of that is likely to amuse and instruct the American public. With regard to photographs, I really have none at all. Would you write to Hoppe of Baker Street and Elliot & Fry who are the only people that have ever taken me.—I suppose Bobbs Merrill will pay, as I believe the question of rights of reproduction will arise and have to be met and Mr. Merrill is no doubt a wealthy man whereas, bother you, you keep me so confoundedly poor that I couldn't afford, if I wanted to, to buy photographs for my favourite actresses, let alone for myself (the insulting portions of this sentence are *jokes*). I have no objection to Mr. Bobbs Merrill doing anything he likes with "The Panel." He may change the title, rewrite the dedication, alter the end into a Tragedy in which all the people stab each other or do anything else that pleases him.[1]

Yours,

P.S. Why shouldn't he call it "The Bedroom Comedy" once for all?

To James B. Pinker

South Lodge
Campden Hill Road
21/11/13

Dear Pinker:

Yes, it is not a gay report. But, if you will remember, years ago I prophesied that the bottom of my vogue, such as it was, as a novelist would fall out. You, on the other hand, took all the heavy responsibility of saying that it would not. You, in fact, took the burden of my fate on your shoulders. I might, but for that, by now have been a be-diamonded stockbroker selling Marconi's to Cabinet Ministers. (I write this more in sorrow than in anger.) Of course you will reply that "Mr. Fleight" is my own fault—and so it is.[1]

[1] Constable & Co. published *The Panel* in 1912. Ford slightly revised and expanded the novel before the Bobbs-Merrill Company published it as *Ring for Nancy* (Indianapolis, 1913).

[1] *Mr. Fleight* (London, 1913) was Ford's seventeenth novel. Though not wholly enthusiastic, the reviews did not damn the book.

But the slump had been going on for years. For years and aching years as the poets say, witness my hollow flanks and gaunt eyes of famine!

Have you any contract for me, now, or have you any in sight? If not I seriously think of taking a contract with one of the more ancient firms to give them all my work for the rest of my life on a basis of a 20% royalty on sales and no advance. Of course, if you have a really good contract I should not refuse it—I mean that I do not wish to force your hand. But I really should prefer a settled contract.

The New Year, you know, is approaching, when one takes resolves and looks back upon one's past career and so on. I should like to fix it up one way or another by the New Year. I met, the other day at lunch, Stanley Paul who told me a sad story and suggested he wanted a contract with me. I do not know how much truth there was in either suggestion; but you might approach him; for an extended contract at a good price I might sell him my soul —say six novels at £250.

Reflect upon these matters will you and let me know the fruits of your reflections at once.

Yours,

P.S. Have you had a cheque from the Outlook for £5 for Galsworthy? He asked me to tell them to send it to you; but I rather think I forgot, which would be just like me.

To R. A. Scott-James

The Knap Cottage
Selsey, Sussex
[January, 1914?]

My dear Scotty,

I suppose I may now congratulate you, as I do very heartily at having again got your foot into what appears to be such a very gold-plated stirrup.[1] Violet [Hunt] told me all about it some time ago; but she forbade me to write to you congratulatorily, saying that you had told her in confidence, so that presumably I was not to know anything about it. I really am as sincerely glad about it as you can be yourself; do believe that. I think the programme

[1] R. A. Scott-James founded *The New Weekly* early in 1914 and began publishing on March 21.

looks excellent from a solid paying point of view and you can rely on V and myself doing all that we can to spread your fame.

I do hope you will not forget les jeunes—the quite young and extravagant; it is only on them that you can put your trust. And I daresay you will not. Your list of extinct and semi-extinct volcanoes,[2] alarming though it be, is I know only window dressing. But you *cannot* go too far in the other direction, simply because your fat tol-lol goshawks will give you tired stuff, and tired stuff and again tired stuff; whereas the tassel-gentles, though they may fly at the moon—and very probably will fly at the moon—will yet give you the only casts that in ten years' time you will not be ashamed of having promoted.

However, you will not want to be preached to, like this. Anyhow, all good luck go with you.

Yrs.,

To James B. Pinker

The Knap Cottage
Selsey, Sussex
Feb. 13, 1914

Dear Pinker,

The view I like of it is that I don't want to deal with Stanley Paul at all, & if he wants my name he must just pay for it.

I have worked damned hard for many years to establish my name as a good-will & that's all there is to it—conceit or no conceit. I don't need money &, unless I can get a good price, I won't sell my immortal soul to any of your blooming devils.

I want also stability; I can't think it to be either good or gracious to go jumping about from publisher to publisher as I have done in the past. If Paul wants to attain to respectability by publishing me, he must give me my own terms. He must pay me £300 on receipt of the manuscript of a first novel & after that what any book earns on subscription, & must make up accounts & pay them on the 1st of each subsequent month. He must contract to publish twelve novels from me on these terms & I must be at liberty, if I want to oblige a friend, to give an occasional novel to someone else—not that I am very likely to want to do so.

[2] Probably Edmund Gosse, G. K. Chesterton, and Thomas Hardy, among the contributors to the first three issues.

Paul may answer that this means that he is tied & that I am not tied, but such, my Pinker, is my arrogance that that is what I want.

Other books, not novels, to be a matter of ordinary negotiation. I think that is fairly clear. These are the lowest terms I will take; of course, if you can get any better I shall be better pleased.

Yours faithfully,

To James B. Pinker

Confidential   South Lodge
Dear Pinker,   Campden Hill Road
[. . . . .]   22/12/14

Re Cinema Rights of "Romance"

As far as I am concerned I am ready to agree to the terms you mention. But I should like to make a preliminary query as to the respective shares of myself & Conrad. On the original we shared equally but on the rights of the cheap editions Conrad took two thirds to my one. I did not much mind this at that time because Conrad was very hard up. If his financial position is now secure —as to which you must be better posted than anyone else—I think we ought to revert to the original shares, since C. does owe me a certain amount of money & I am not a millionaire, and have a good many people dependent on me. Of course if Conrad is not yet straight I don't want to exact this but, if he is, I think I ought to. This, of course, is in strict confidence & I am quite ready to leave the decision to you, but, of course, you can cable to the people in the U. S. A. that I accept the terms & we can settle the other matter afterwards.

Yrs.,

To Lucy Masterman   South Lodge
Campden Hill Road
My dear Lucy,   31/7/15

You may like to know that I went round to the W[ar] O[ffice] after seeing you and got thrown into a commission in under a minute—the quickest process I have ever known. I am to go to Tenby to school on the 15th so I suppose I shall get to Porthcawl in time. I can assure you, for what it is worth, that it is as if the peace of God had descended on me—that sounds absurd—but there it is! Man is a curious animal.

Have a good holiday, both of you.

Yours affectionately,

To John Lane

South Lodge
Campden Hill Road
12 August 1915

Dear Lane:

I should be obliged if you could pay me the fifty pounds that became due to me on the delivery of the ms. of the "Saddest Story."[1] These are, I know, hard up times but I guess I am harder up than you as I have had to give up literature and offer myself for service to George Five; so shortly you may expect to see me pantingly popping cartridges into garrison guns directed against my uncles, cousins and aunts advancing in pickelhaubes.[2] And presumably if the said uncles cousins and aunts penetrate behind said garrison guns they will suspend me on high. Whereas, though I daresay you deserve it quite as much, I do not believe they would hang you. So you will perceive the equity of my request.

Yours,

To C. F. G. Masterman

3d Bn. Welch Regt.
Tenby
28 Aug. 1915

My dear C. F. G.

Here I am and hard at it—6 a.m. to 7 p.m. everyday, like any V form boy & at about the same sort of stuff. Literature seems to have died out of a world that is mostly interesting from its contours. (A contour is an imaginary line etc.) But I am really quite happy except for an absolute lack of social life. I suppose you or Lucy don't know anyone hereabouts to whom you cd. give me an introduction?

[1] "The Saddest Story" first appeared, in part, in *Blast* (June, 1914), the Vorticist magazine founded by Ezra Pound and Wyndham Lewis. It would have been continued in the second issue of *Blast* (July, 1915) but by then John Lane had published the whole novel under the title *The Good Soldier*.

[2] Spiked helmets.

By the bye: pay some attention, will you, to the reviews of "Between St. D." etc. The more I think about it the more certain I feel that it is more valuable than "When Blood," etc.[1]

Give my love to Lucy: I hope she goes on writing poems.

Yrs. always,

To Lucy Masterman

3rd Batt, The Welch Regt.
Cardiff Castle

Dearest Lucy,   25th Jan 1916

I rang you up to say goodbye, but could not get at you—so you get a stupid letter instead. I have just slipped back here as if I had never been away, but I have profited, of course, by various knowledges that I had not before.

It's perhaps no business of mine—but I do hope C. F. G. will stick to the job that he does so well & not, out of restlessness—tho' I know what it is to be restless—plunge into unsoundable depths. I don't see that, now, in the Political World, he can form any alliances that won't be kaleidoscopic or of sand foundations. But maybe you will think I am talking nonsense or about what doesn't concern me. All the same I know you will believe that I am very concerned, always, about yr. destiny—or at any rate that I do care for you very much.

Goodbye, my dear: keep in your heart a warm corner for

Yr.

By the bye: don't mention to Sixtus[1] about the gent who [illegible] in the street. As he is in Sixtus' command, S. will either hear of it in due course or it will pass over—wh. I hope it will.

---

[1] In March, 1915, Ford published a volume of war propaganda essays, *When Blood Is Their Argument: An Analysis of Prussian Culture.* Six months later a second volume appeared, *Between St. Denis and St. George: A Sketch of Three Civilisations.* Both books were written at the request of C. F. G. Masterman who, at Wellington House, was in charge of a counter-propaganda office.

[1] C. F. G. Masterman's younger brother.

To Lucy Masterman

3rd Batt, The Welch Regt.
Cardiff Castle,
15 Feb. 1916

My dear Lucy,

I haven't a bit forgotten you—& never do, you know—but I have had very little time to write, even to you. Now, however, I am transferred to a Coy. where there is very little to do & I ought to be able to write more: so indeed I am.

But I have nothing, really, to write. It is astonishing how the day slips round from coy. 6/R to dinner and bed and back again, as if one were in a sort of closed ball of dreams. It is probably very good for me—a sort of progression of little incidents that suggest nothing so much as a mist of bluebells in a wood. That may seem a queer simile, but it is fairly exact.

Sixtus, I suppose, will be coming back some time. I go down to Porthcawl every Sunday to play golf with an old major who is a soothing person. I wish you wd. come down there. Couldn't you? & we cd. have a day or two together. Some of these places are *wonderfully* beautiful just now: if I ever wrote poems now they wd. be full of Celtic twilight—with your beautiful hair to give them color.

Goodbye, my dear; think of me now & then & give my love to Margaret & C. F. G.

Yrs,

To H. G. Wells

3rd Batt., The Welch Regt.
Cardiff Castle,
22. 3. 16

My dear H. G.,

I am much touched by your letter—tho' I do not really know what to make of it. I hadn't the least idea that there was any difference between Violet & myself—or at least anything to make her face the necessity of talking about it. I, at any rate, haven't any grievance against her & want nothing better than to live with her the life of a peaceable regimental officer with a peaceable wife.[1] Of course that is not very exciting for her & her enjoyment of life depends so much on excitement. But one's preoccupations can't, now, be what they were in the 90's—or even three or two years ago.

---

[1] Ford and Violet Hunt were never married under English law.

That, I suppose, is the tragedy—but it is the tragedy,—isn't it?—of the whole of Europe. At any rate, if you see V., do impress her with the fact that, short of absence without leave or cutting parades, I shall always be & am [illegible] at her disposal. I have the greatest possible affection & esteem for her; there isn't anyone else (but I don't know what she has got into her always romantic head) and I am frightfully sorry that these bad years are such bad years for her. Anyhow there I am, expressed to the absolute mot juste.

We are frightfully busy here—what with sending out drafts and an inspection on Friday by the Commander in Chief—wh. is a fairly nervous affair, I can tell you. It is rather fidgetting work—but no doubt it will be serene enough in the retrospect. Standing at attention in front of a battalion is, I mean, for a full twenty minutes, the devil of an affair. You try doing it in your study & see. But it melts away as an experience in a few minutes—& it is useful enough for the men & one's poor soul too.

Well, God bless you and give my love to Jane.   Yrs.

To Lucy Masterman

3rd Batt, The Welch Regt.
Cardiff Castle,
13/5/16

My dear Lucy,

I was very glad to hear from you again, at last—for I have not had a letter from a soul for ages. Literally no one writes to me.

But I am a dull creature with nothing to write to anyone but the happenings here—wh. are interesting enough when you are inside the shell but will not thrill the outsider. As thus:

The day before yesterday I was set to write a long memorandum about a lady who got into the Rink at night & was chased round and round by sergeants, over the men's beds and the like & then, quite illegally, handed over to the police on an impossible charge. I had to exercise a good deal of ingenuity to get our people out of quite a nasty scrape and composed a forcible document wh. went up to H. Q. It was returned with the comment from the Garrison Commander that the document of the subaltern, name undecipherable, was illegible & *illiterate* & must be written over again. I had worried the good gentleman by using the words *proprio motu—*

'the charge wd. not lie because the lady had not come into the Rink *proprio motu* but had been introduced by Cpl. Plant, 5th Welch, etc.'

And so everybody strafes everybody else in this microcosm & without doubt discipline is maintained.

I do not seem to get much nearer the fields of France—but I may go suddenly. I devoutly hope so. Sixtus—of whom I see a good deal —says it is because the Adjutant hates him & so keeps me back: but I shd. think that is probably Sixtian nonsense. He seems to be pretty well, but is generally dissatisfied & uproarious. I fancy you will be seeing him on Monday. All leave has been stopped here for some months past on account of three Hun cruisers & we have had many alarums & excursions. But I shall try for a weekend, next week, and will come to you & Charlie, then, if I may.

I don't know: one can't comment on Ireland. At least I can't. As for shooting the rebels: I wish it had been done *in situ*; I suppose it had to be done, tho' I don't know why. . . . But at any rate it is no business, thank God, of mine to worry about these affairs.

Sixtus has just come in today to say he is going up on leave— so I entrust this to him. May it reach you, my dear, with all sorts of cordialities & affection implied.

I'm so sorry C. F. G. has had flu. I hope it will exorcise the Hay Fever. I sent him a wire that I had received the other day.

Yrs. always,

To Lucy Masterman

5/Welch
The Castle, Cardiff
My dear Lucy:
11. 7. 16

We are still here, balancing & delayed—wh. is eminently disagreeable since one hasn't the very slightest idea as to when the trumpet will sound, or the 'phone ring—& Coy. work seems eminently dull & nothing very interesting: & I am desperately hard up —so hard up that I can't stir out of the Castle.

Pardon these groans: one requires a sympathetic ear now & then. I guess I shall pick up some resiliency in a day or two—for, seriously I don't imagine we shall start for a month, if then.

I thought C. F. G. looked well & cheerful wh. pleased us—

& as for Sir Gilbert P. he looked like a blossoming May tree. I have been writing silly little lyrics wh. no one will print.

I wonder what you are doing? I have also been correcting the proofs of V[iolet Hunt]'s novel wh. is really very good.[1] She seems to be absolutely untouched, mentally, by the war—wh. is no doubt a blessed state.

I am writing in the coy. office with a number of people telling indecent stories wh. is trying to a letter-writer—so, in the Tommies' way, I shall conclude.

Goodbye, my dear. God bless you.

                                                    Yrs,

To Lucy Masterman

                                        3d. Attd. 9th Welch
                                           B. E. F., Rouen,
Dear old Lucy,   18. 7. 16

We leave here today to join our various units—presumably in the firing line: I don't know where. We are all scattered—wh. is disagreeable, but, as jollities go, we have had a jolly time till now, on the boat & so on—but I haven't much to write about—or too much, to get in. So this is only a friendly hail. Sixtus, who is sitting beside me, sends you his love—& you have all mine, as you know.

                                                    Yrs,

Love to C. F. G. too and the children.

To Lucy Masterman

                                          Attd. 9/Welch
Dear Lucy,   28. 7. 16

Thanks so much for your letter which reached me today—letters taking, it seems, nearly a week. We are right up in the middle of the strafe, but only with the 1st line transport. We get shelled two or three times a day, otherwise it is fairly dull—indeed, being shelled is fairly dull, after the first once or twice. Otherwise it is all very interesting—filling in patches of one's knowledge & so on, but it isn't more than interesting, because one gets no news. Absolutely none, except gossip. One hears that such & such a

[1] Probably *Their Lives* (London, 1916).

division has taken such & such a place—then that it hasn't; such & such a regiment has been wiped out, then that its casualties are one accident. The landscape here is long downland, the sun blazes down & then gets obscured by haze, blazes down & is then obscured again; there are trees in rows; in little copses—each copse with a name—La Boiselle, Mamets, Pozières, & so on. But there isn't any village any more to bear any of the names. The air is full of sausage balloons, swallows, larks & occasional aeroplanes. The Germans do not seem very enterprising in this department & rarely come over our lines. I have only seen three since I have been here & one was brought down. The noise of the bombardment is continuous—so continuous that one gets used to it, as one gets used to the noise in a train and the ear picks out the singing of the innumerable larks. . . .

The Daily Mail has just come in & I see that we have taken Pozières & that the Rt. Hon. D[avid] L[loyd] G[eorge] still has his back to the wall & will fight to the last drop of our blood. I wonder what he wd. say if he were out here for a week!

Poor V[iolet Hunt]. I wonder what is happening to her. I have not had a line from her since I started; I don't know what psychological vagary or manoeuvre it implies. But it is a queer way to set to work.

Well, goodbye, my dear. I hope you are really over the flu & C. F. G. over the hay fever. I am fairly fit—but the off'rs here are a terrible lot, without a soul that one can really talk to except the little boys. I have heard nothing from Sixtus since we have parted at Rouen.

Yrs,

To Lucy Masterman

9/Welch
19th Div., B. E. F.
[August? 1916]

Dearest Lucy,

As I worried you with my depressed mood the other day, I ought in duty bound to share my comparative gaiety with you. I don't know why I am gay—except perhaps that the whole army is gayer. Anyhow, there it is. I have got plenty to do & have been rather commended. Bridges, so I hear from his staff capt., has written to Plumer to suggest that I ought to be given a staff job.

I didn't know he knew of my existence as a name, tho' he has talked to me once or twice—once on parade & once when I was marching a draft along a very filthy road & once I ran into him at an O. P. O.—tho' he never ask'd my name. Of course it does not mean that Plumer will do anything—& I wd. really rather stop here. The work is interesting in the extreme & one gets a certain amount of fun out of oneself. This morning, for instance, I was standing in a pail like Adam before the fall when some shrapnel burst overhead—& I was amused to discover that I grabbed for a shirt before a tin hat.

Goodbye, my dear—this is just a friendly hail—not a [illegible].

Yrs,

To Lucy Masterman

Attd. 9/Welch, 19th Div.
B. E. F., Belgium
[August? 1916]

Dear old Lucy,

Using a good deal of determination, I have got out of the muses' hands & back to duty, after an incredibly tortuous struggle across France. I rather began to think that I shall not be able to "stick it"—the conditions of life are too hard and the endless waitings too enervating. However, that is on the knees of the Gods. It is extraordinarily quiet here, compared with the other front: the Germans seem to have nothing but minenwerfers & little or no artillery—only occasionally a shell comes over here—so that it seems wonderfully like Heaven. I have had no news of Sixtus & am not vastly happy with the people here—can't get on with the C. O. or the adjt.—wh. is disagreeable. However, it is very interesting, all of it—if not gay.

Love to C. F. G.

Yrs,

To Lucy Masterman

Attd. 9/Welch
19th Div., B. E. F.
23. 8. 16

Dearest Lucy;

I am fairly cheerful again, thank you—tho' I do not get on with the C. O., & the Adjt. overworks me because I talk Flemish. So I have to buy straw and pacify infuriated farmers as well as attending all parades & fatigues. Still it is all very interesting & one learns a little more everyday. We have been out of the trenches since Monday & go in again almost immediately—but it is quiet here at its most violent compared with the Somme. Even the strafe that the artillery got up for George V—wh. the artillery off'rs called "great" or "huge" according to their temperaments— wd., for sound, have gone into an old woman's thimble in Albert, not to speak of Bécourt or Fricourt. George V—whom I saw strolling about among the Cheshires—really was in some danger. At least he was in an O. P. that was being shelled fairly heavily when I was in it "for instruction." But I guess they squashed the Bosche fire fairly effectually while he was here. Still he gave the impression of a "good plucked 'un"—& the P. O. W.—who was quite unrecognizable, was perfectly businesslike. I rather think the staff is nibbling at me—at any rate Bridges rode up beside me the other day & talked about *Entre St. Denis* etc. I shd. not be really sorry—because I have had my week in the Somme & three weeks here & a week in Field Ambulance & a week draft con- ducting. I shd. naturally prefer going on as a regimental off'r— but the C. O.—an ex-Eastbourne Town Councillor & the adjt., an ex-P. O. clerk—annoy me—the C. O. says I am too old & the adjt. thanks me all day long for saving the H. Q. Mess 2 frs. 22 on turnips & the like. I don't know which I dislike most.

Still, otherwise, it is—tho' you won't believe it—a dreamy sort of life in a grey green country & even the shells as they set out on their long journeys seem tired. It is rather curious, the extra senses one develops here. I sit writing in the twilight &, even as I write, I hear the shells whine & the M. G.'s crepitate & I see (tho' it is hidden by a hill) the grey, flat land below & the shells bursting & I know that in all probability W. 63 or some such section has just phoned to the H. A. & that the Bosche are getting cheeky with [illegible] & need suppressing. . . . Thanks so very much for the Echo de Paris. It has pleased me vastly— & for ten minutes at least I remembered that "atque ego in arcadia vixi,"—with you my dear. Love to C. F. G. I suppose he cd. not get me sent to Paris. I shd. like a weekend there and cd. spout about the Somme and here.

Yrs.

V[iolet Hunt] seems very queer; *don't* tell her anything that I tell you, because she does so worry.

To Lucy Masterman

Attd. 9/Welch
19th Div., B. E. F.

Dear Lucy,
25. 8. 16

You may be glad to hear—tho' I dare say you know already—that M. Gérard, "Ambassadeur de France" & Gabriel Hannotaux are writing about "Entre St. D. et St. G." &, according to the pub[r], the book ought to make me famous in France.[1] Isn't it rather queer & bitter to think that no one—according to V[iolet Hunt] at least—will publish my poems—of wh. I have written several out here? I wish C. F. G. wd. make some of his editors put them in—for I rather suspect V. (tho' I may be unjust) of suppressing them for ends of her own.[2]

With the labour of 184 men I have today drained a considerable portion of this country & I have also marched 12 miles to bring up a draft. So I have not been idle. But the C. O. continues to impress on me that I am too old for this job. I think he wants to force me to relinquish my commission. I suppose you do not know anybody who cd. impress on Gen[l] Bridges the desirability of having me in his In[tgce] Dept? It wd. be a good action—because I am sure I deserve better—even in a military sense—than to be harassed by a rather doting Lt. Col. of C. A. who cherishes a special dislike for the Special Reserve.

I suppose I am a bore: I am terribly afraid of becoming a bore with a grievance. I shd. certainly not write about it to anyone else. But I really am rather considerate about this & I know you suffer fools, if not gladly, then at least more patiently than most people.
Yrs. always,

[1] Marie Butts translated *Between St. Dennis and St. George* into French; Payot & Cie published it in Paris in 1916.

[2] In September, *The Westminster Gazette* published "Nostalgia," and in March, 1917, *Poetry* published "What the Orderly Dog Saw," followed by a poem by Violet Hunt, "What the Civilian Saw."

To Joseph Conrad

Attd. 9/Welch
19th Div., B. E. F.
[September, 1916]

My dear Conrad:

I have just had a curious opportunity with regard to sound wh. I hasten to communicate to you—tho' indeed I was anyhow going to write to you today.

This aftn then, we have a *very* big artillery strafe on—not, of course as big as others I have experienced—but still *very* big. I happened to be in the very middle—the centre of a circle—of H. A. and quite close to a converted, naval how[itzer]. The [illegible] last for about an hour—incessant and to all intents and purposes at a level pitch of sound. I was under cover filling up some of the innumerable A. F.'s that one fills up all day long even here—& I did not notice that it was raining and suddenly and automatically I got under the table on the way to my tin hat.— Out here, you know, you see men going about daily avocations, carrying buckets, being shaved or reading the D'ly Mail &, quite suddenly, they all appear to be pulled sideways off their biscuit boxes or wagon shafts. I mean of course shrapnel or minen.

Well I was under the table and frightened out of my life—so indeed was the other man with me. There was shelling just over-head—apparently thousands of shells bursting for miles around and overhead. I was convinced that it was all up with the XIX Div. because the Huns had got note of a new & absolutely devilish shell or gun.

It was of course thunder. It completely extinguished the sound of the heavy art[iller]y, and even the how[itzer] about 50 yds. away was inaudible during the actual peals and sounded like *stage thunder* in the intervals. Of course we were in the very vortex of the storm, the lightning being followed by thunder before one cd. count two—but there we were right among the guns too.

I thought this might interest you as a constatation of some exactness. And, for the matter of that, when the rain did come down the sound of it on the corrugated iron roof of the dugout also extinguished the sound of gun-fire tho' that is not so remarkable. It probably stopped the guns too, but that I don't know. At any rate they are quiet now, but the rain isn't.

The mud and rain here are pretty bad—after about a fortnight of wet—but they are not really much worse than Stocks Hall[1]—*t'en souviens tu?*—used to be and I bear them with more equanimity than most of my brothers in arms—I daresay because of that early training. I certainly remember worse weather experiences between the Pent & Aldington. But I have lain down wet in the wet for the last three nights and do not seem to have taken any harm except for a touch of toothache. And I am certainly in excellent spirits tho' of course it is not yet cold and that may prove too much for me. I daresay eulogia of the French Press which continues to blaze and coruscate about my gifts has remonté my morale. It *is* gratifying, you know, to feel that even if one dies among the rats in these drains one won't be—if only for nine days—just like the other rats. Of course these salvos are a little machined by the French Govt—but still, some of them are genuine—and Genl Bridges who kindly commended me on Bn parade the other day—tho' God knows my [illegible] was dilapidated enough with seven smoke helmet buttons and three cap badges missing!!—tells me that he has written to Genl Plumer to say that I ought to have a staff job so I may get one—and I don't know *what* I should be sorry. I have been for six weeks— with the exception of 24 hours—continuously within reach of German missiles &, altho' one gets absolutely to ignore them, consciously, I imagine that subconsciously one is suffering. I know that if one of the cooks suddenly opens, with a hammer, a chest close at hand, one jumps in a way one doesn't use when the "dirt" is coming over fairly heavily.

An R. F. A. man has just come along & explained that the "rain has put the kybosh on the strafe"—so there, my dear, you have the mot juste. But it is fairly sickening all the same.

I hope you are all right: Drop me a line now & then. There are no goats here—but 40,000 mules—mostly from Costaguana![2]

Yrs always,

[1] Early in November, 1898, Joseph and Jessie Conrad rented from Ford an old Kentish farmhouse, Pent Farm, near Postling and Sandling Junction. Ford and Elsie Hueffer occupied Stocks Hall, a smallholder's cottage at Aldington.
[2] Conrad's *Nostromo* is set in the imaginary province of Costaguana.

I have been re-reading *Pierre Nozière*[3] at intervals: it's thin; it's *thin,* my dear. I wonder the old man won't appear like thread paper after all this. C'est là son danger, as far as the future is concerned.

To Joseph Conrad

My dear,

9/Welch
19th Div., B. E. F.
6. 9. 16

I will continue, "for yr information and necessary action, please," my notes upon sounds.

In woody country heavy artillery makes *most* noise, because of the echoes—and most prolonged in a *diluted* way.

On marshland—like the Romney Marsh—the *sound* seems alarmingly close: I have seldom heard the *Hun* artillery in the middle of a strafe except on marshy land. The *sound,* not the diluted sound, is also at its longest in the air. [An arrow is drawn from the "e" in the following paragraph to the "e" in this paragraph.]

On dry down land the sound is much *sharper*; it hits *you* & shakes *you.* On clay land it shakes the ground & shakes you thro' the ground. A big naval (let us say) gun, fired, unsuspected by us out of what resembled (let us say) a dead mule produced the "e" that I have marked with an arrow.

In hot, dry weather, sounds give me a headache—over the brows & across the skull, inside, like migraine. In wet weather one minds them less, tho' dampness of the air makes them seem nearer.

Shells falling on a church: these make a huge *"corump"* sound, followed by a noise like crockery falling off a tray—as the roof tiles fall off. If the roof is not tiled you can hear the stained glass, sifting mechanically until the next shell. (Heard in a church square, on each occasion, about 90 yds away). Screams of women penetrate all these sounds—but I do not find that they agitate me as they have done at home. (Women in cellars round the square. Oneself running thro' fast.)

Emotions again: I saw two men and three mules (the first time I saw a casualty) killed by one shell. A piece the size of a pair

[3] Anatole France's second autobiographical volume.

of corsets went clear thro' one man, the other just fell—the
mules hardly any visible mark. These things gave me no *emotion*
at all—they seemed *obvious*; rather as it wd. be. A great many
patients on stretchers—a thousand or so in a long stream is very
depressing—but, I fancy, mostly because one thinks one will be
going back into it.

When I was in hospital a man three beds from me died *very*
hard, blood passing thro' bandages and he himself crying perpetually, "Faith! Faith! Faith!" It was very disagreeable as long
as he had a chance of life—but one lost all interest and forgot
him when one heard he had none.

Fear;

This of course is the devil—& worst because it is so very capri-
cious. Yesterday I was buying—or rather not buying—flypapers
in a shop under a heap of rubbish. The woman was laughing &
saying that all the flies came from England. A shell landed in
the chateau into whose wall the shop was built. One Tommie
said, "Crump!" Another: "Bugger the flies" & slapped himself.
The woman—about thirty, quick, & rather jewish—went on
laughing. I said, "Mais je vous assure, Madame, qu'il n'y a plus
comme ça de mouches chez nous." No interruption, emotion,
vexed at getting no flypapers. Subconscious emotion, "thank God
the damn thing's burst."

Yet today, passing the place, I wanted to gallop past it & positively trembled on my horse. Of course I cdnt. gallop because
there were Tommies in the street.

Yrs,

To Lucy Masterman

9/Welch, 19/Divn.
B. E. F., France
6. 9. 16

Dearest Lucy,

Why does *no*body write to me? Does one so quickly become a
ghost, alas!

I have had nothing for a week but notes from V[iolet Hunt]
deploring the fact that I have lost my bicycle & the like—wh. of
course takes one's mind off oneself—& before then no one wrote
to me for ever so long except French ministers of sorts. We are
in a h-ll of a noise, just now—my hand is shaking badly—our

guns are too inconsiderate—they pop up out of baby's rattles & tea
cosy & shake the rats thro' the earth.

Goodbye my dear

To Joseph Conrad

Attd. 9/Welch
19th Div., B. E. F.
7/9/16

Dear Conrad,

    I wrote these rather hurried notes yesterday because we were
being shelled to hell and I did not expect to get thro' the night.
I wonder if it is just vanity that in these cataclysmic moments
makes one desire to *record.* I hope it is, rather, the annalist's wish
to help the historian—or, in a humble sort of way, my desire
to help you, cher maître!—if you ever wanted to do anything in
"this line." Of course you wd. not ever want to do anything in
this line,—but a pocketful of coins of a foreign country may sometimes come in handy. You might want to put a phrase into the
mouth of someone in Bangkok who had been, say, to Bécourt.
There you wd. be! And I, to that extent, shd. once more have
collaborated.

    This is a rather more accidenté portion of the world: things in
every sense "stick out" more in the September sunlight. The Big
Push was too overwhelming for one to notice details; it was like
an immense wave full of debris. It was France, of course—and
this too is France. But this is France of tapestries—immense ave-
nues along the road, all blue in the September twilight & the
pleasant air that gives one feelings of bienaise. It is curious—but,
in the evenings here, I always feel myself happier than I have
ever felt in my life.—Indeed, except for worries, I am really very
happy—but I don't get on with my superior officers here & that
means that they can worry me a good deal in details—there are
almost endless openings for the polite taquineries called "strafing"
in a regiment—especially if one has had a Regular training & gets
attached to R. A. Bn, where all the details are different. However,
these things, except in moments of irritation, are quite super-
ficial—and it is all matter for observation. One of these days I
daresay I shall fly out at someone & get into trouble—tho' not
the sort of "trouble" one minds. But indeed I hope I shan't—

because discipline is after all discipline & [I] begin to believe it is the first thing in the world.

God bless you, my dear. Love to Jessie. I hope you have good news of Borys.[1]

Yrs,

To C. F. G. Masterman

9/Welch
19th Div.
B. E. F.

Dear C. F. G.,

13. 9. 16

The minister "of Instruction and of Inventions useful to the War" asked me to come and see him—merely as a vague politeness, I suppose—so, armed with the letter I extracted W. E. leave from the authorities & went to Paris, where H. E. thanked me very prettily. *Entre St. D[enis et St. George]* is really rather booming among the lit. gents & official world of Paris &, to please Payot, I spent 36 hours in strenuous work, cutting it down & writing into it in French—a rather pretty epilogue wh. pleased Payot. The writing rather exhausted me—& indeed I collapsed & was made to see the M. O. who said I was suffering from specific shell-shock & ought to go to hospital. However, I wdn't. & got back here.

I wired to you about yr. representative in Paris because I wanted to know how I shd. stand with regard to the Censure & King's Regs. par. 493-4 in making the alterations. I suppose it will be all right? I haven't said anything "that cd. convey military information"—only stuff about *Lakmé* at the Opéra Comique & the like.

Yrs.,

To C. F. G. Masterman

3rd Batt. Welch Regt.
Rhyl, North Wales

Dear C. F. G.,

12. 10. 16

I seem to be destined to be stuck down here & am posted to a Coy—wh. does seem to be a waste of my abilities—otherwise I wd. not worry you. Moreover I can't afford it—wh. is also a motive—whereas in France I c'd. be really useful in a dozen ways

---

[1] Conrad's elder son.

and could just live. So if Braid wd. play Perseus to this Andromeda it wd. be what the French call une bonne action. I have been trying to write that article for Randall—but it is rather difficult to write in an anteroom with 40 officers. However, it will get itself done. I hope you have better news of Sixtus. They don't here, regards

Yrs.

To C. F. G. Masterman

3rd Batt., The Welch Regt.
Denbighshire, N. Wales
25. 10. 16

Dear C. F. G.

No: I have not heard anything at this end &, knowing the W. O. as I do, I don't suppose I shall. I wish you cd. have done something—but never really expected that you cd. My luck is too much out.

As things are I see nothing for it but to relinquish my comm^n—wh. I shall do on 1.11.16—& to disappear into a decent obscurity. I am doing no good here, either to myself or to anyone else—& the training we give the men here seems ridiculously ineffective—so I can't even console myself with the idea that I am doing useful work.

No: I am not doing any writing; to write one must have some purpose in life—& I simply haven't any. You see one has phases of misfortune that get too heavy for one as one gradually loses resiliency & I am too bored now to keep [illegible].

But God bless you just the same. Give my love to Lucy: I hope she will soon be all right again. There seems to be a great deal of flu about. I wrote to her about a matter that has worried me a good deal, the day before yesterday; but please impress on her that I don't—& I didn't mean to express anything approaching resentment. I guess I am fair game!

Yrs. always,

To Lucy Masterman

3rd Batt., The Welch Regt.
Kinmel Park, Denbighshire
27. 10. 16

[Dear Lucy,]

All right, my dear, call it a wash out. The point was that V[iolet Hunt] recounted this history to me with great minuteness, as coming from you—& has since related it to half London & half Cardiff & so on. But it doesn't matter.

As for my position here—it is very simple. I can't meet my liabilities any more—& it is better to apply to relinquish one's comm. than to be forced to for that sort of reason, even if one sets aside the question of honesty. One can't, with my age & disposition, run up bills at shops without any possibility of meeting them & so on. I cd. get along personally on my pay—but I have outside liabilities too, you see. And V's campaign of vilification makes people very shy of publishing my work, even if I cd. write, so I shd. really be much better off if I relinquished my comm^n. & enlisted. It isn't depression, or pique, but just common sense.

Yrs. always,

To C. F. G. Masterman

3rd Batt. Welch Regt.
Kinmel Park, near Rhyl

Dear C. F. G.

29. 11. 16

The Adjutant tells me to-day that the W. O. has sent down imperative orders that I am to be sent to France!!! So I suppose I shall go in a day or two.

All I am really anxious about is that I sh. not go back to the IX Welch. Wd. it be too much to ask you to ask Genl. Braid to suggest to Col. Dickinson at the Base camp at Rouen that this wd. be inconsiderate. I don't at all want not to be killed—but I don't want to be strafed unjustly as well.

France in the meantime continues to honour me. Academies & things offering me ribbons & so on—from the Academie Internationale Historique—wh. is probably a bum show—up to the Institut de France—which isn't! Also I have found a considerable portion of my Mess Bill out of Auction [Bridge]—wh. shows that God is on my side!

Love to Lucy,

To Joseph Conrad

3/Attd IX Welch
No ii Red X Hospital
Rouen, 19. 12. 16

My dear:

It must be all of five months since I heard from you—tho' I heard from you thro' Jessie later than that. I hope you continue

the victorious career in various elements that she then spoke of.
. . . But it is miserable business, really, wishing anybody who has
anybody out here anything. Only I do hope Borys is all right—
& probably back? The trenches are not gay in this weather.

As for me, c'est fini de moi, I believe, at least as far as fighting
is concerned—my lungs are all charred up & gone—they appeared
to be quite healed but exposure day after day has ended in the
usual stretchers and ambulance trains—& this rather queer Rouen
—wh. for its queerness wd. delight you—but I am too stupid to
explain. But I saw the trésors[?] of Flaubert & the whole monument of Bouilhet[1] thro' the tail of the ambulance that brought me
here, in the Rue Thiers.

I have been reading—rather deliriously—"Chance" since I have
been in this nice kind place. The end is odd, you know, old boy.
It's like a bit of Maupassant tacked onto a Flaubert facade.[2]

Pardon me if that sounds inept: I think still a good deal about
these things—but not cleverly!—And one lives under the shadow
of G[ustave] F[laubert] here. After all you began yr. literary
career here—and I jolly nearly ended mine here too—And I assure
you I haven't lost a jot of the immense wonder at the immensities
you bring down onto paper. You are a blooming old Titan,
really—or do I mean Nibelung? At any rate even in comparatively loose work like "Chance" there is a sense of cavernous
gloom, lit up by sparks from pickaxes. But that's stupid too. . . .

But this is rather queer: the last active military duty I performed
was to mount guard over some wounded Germans in hospital
huts. As I had to wait for some papers and it was snowing I went
into a tent. I asked one of the prisoners—who was beautifully
warm in bed, where he came from and what he did before the
war. I was wet thro' and coughing my head off—not in the least
interested anyhow. So I don't know where he came from—somewhere in Bavaria. But as for his occupation, he said, "Herr Offizier,
Geisenhirt!" So there was our: "Excellency, a few goats!" quite

[1] Louis Hyacinthe Bouilhet, poet and dramatist, died in Rouen in 1869. He
was a schoolfellow of Flaubert.

[2] Surely one of Conrad's most cumbersome novels, *Chance* was nevertheless a
best-seller in 1913 and the turning-point in his career, financially. Ford's diag-
nosis is unusually apt, for Conrad had written to Pinker in 1912 that he was
thinking of the public when he altered the ending to make it "nicer."

startlingly jumped at me.³ And then, it may interest you to know, he smiled a fatuous and ecstatic peasant boy's smile and remarked: "But it is heaven here!"

I suppose he took me to be friendly and benevolent,—but as things drag on & all one's best friends go—(of fourteen who came out with me in July I am the only one here and of sixty who came from 3/W since, eleven are killed & one gets very fond of these poor boys!)—one gets a feeling of sombre resentment against the nightmare population that persists beyond No Man's Land. At any rate it is horrible—it arouses in me a rage un-expressed and not easily comprehensible—to see, or even to think about, the dead of one's own regt, whether it is just the Tommies or the NCO's or one's fellow officers.

But anyhow: the few goats turned up again!

However, perhaps all this does not interest you: I can't tell. Since I have been out here this time I have not had one letter from one living soul. So one's conviction does not get much from wh. to gain anything!

The M. O. who has just sounded my poor old lungs again says I am to be sent to Nice as soon as they can move me. God bless you, my dear, and may Xmas be a propitious season to all of you.

Yrs.

It is not much use writing to me because, after Nice, I shall very likely be transferred to one of the regular Bns. in the East or some other non-pulmonary district of the war—but wireless me a kind thought.

---

³ An old joke between Ford and Conrad. While writing *Romance* together in 1901-02, Ford gave to an obscure *Lugareño* a line of dialogue which for some inexplicable reason delighted Conrad for years afterward. When questioned by the judge as to his occupation, the ruffian answers evasively, "Excellency—a few goats. . . ." Ford recalls that "no sooner had [I] got the words on paper than Conrad burst into one of his roars of ecstasy. 'This,' he shouted when he was in a condition to speak, 'is genius!' "

To F. S. Flint[1]

IX Welch Regt
II Red X Hospital, Rouen

My dear Flint: 1. 1. 17

A note to wish yr. poetic elbow all the power in the world from
1.1.17 to 31.12.17 et in saeculum saeculûm. I am much outside
Poetry (even of Chicago)[2] in these days—but I do often think of
yr. power of evoking the beautiful—if it isn't offensive to call
it that. You see I am become timid in writing to poets & don't
any more know what to say. I don't even know if this will
reach you—but I hope it may. If it does, send me, will you?, anything—everything—you have done lately & I will read them
amongst stone pines and cypresses—for I understand I am to be
evacuated to a hospital on the Mediterranean as soon as I can be
moved. From there I hope to get to Mesopotamia as I am not
fit for the front line—or shan't be till the summer. It is annoying
—but still it will be pleasant to see some dry fighting. Give my
love to yr. children & to any who, for me, *hominibus bonae
voluntatis.*

Yrs always,

This is a perfectly stupid letter—but my temperature is normal
today for the first time for a long spell so I thought I'd let you
know that I hadn't forgotten you.

To C. F. G. Masterman

No. II Red X Hospital
Rouen, BEF

My dear C. F. G.   5. 1. 17

I haven't written before, partly because of unsettlement & partly
because I have been too ill for some time to write cheerfully—&
I am tired of writing uncheerfully.

I got to the base camp & was greeted with the news that I was
re-attached to the IX Welch—wh., I am informed, was meant
amiably!—But it did not seem to me to be very tactful; for, if
that particular C. O. didn't want me, I still more actively didn't
want that C. O. So I protested rather vigourously, though un-
officially. En attendant they—I don't really know who, as things

[1] English poet, critic, translator, and one of the early Imagists.
[2] *Poetry: A Magazine of Verse*, published in Chicago.

are confused here—gave me various polyglot jobs that rather amused me—writing proclamations in French about thefts of rations issued to H. B. M.'s forces & mounting guards over German sick. In the meantime my lungs intervened, wh. is not to be wondered at as what I was doing meant getting wet thro' & coming in to write for a couple of hours in a stifling room, often getting wet through some more & then sleeping in a dripping hut. So, when it came to being really examined my lungs were found to be in a devil of a way, with extensions at the bases & solidifications & all sorts of things—partly due to a slight touch of gas I got in the summer & partly to sheer weather. So they shoved me in here, where I seemed to be doing very nicely till I had a sudden relapse on Xmas Eve. However, my temperature has been normal since yesterday, tho' I am jolly weak.

Such is my short & simple story: I think I shall be sent to Menton pretty soon & I shd. be fairly contented if I didn't chafe at the inactivity. But of course I couldn't very well be active— even at writing proclamations because all day I am as stupid as an owl & all night I lie awake & perceive the ward full of Huns of forbidding aspect—except when they give me a sleeping draft.

I am in short rather ill still & sometimes doubt my own sanity— indeed, quite frequently I do. I suppose that, really, the Somme was a pretty severe ordeal, though I wasn't conscious of it at the time. Now, however, I find myself suddenly waking up in a hell of a funk—& going on being in a hell of a funk till morning. And that is pretty well the condition of a number of men here. I wonder what the effect of it will be on us all, after the war— & on national life and the like. I fancy amenity of manners will suffer a good deal—for most of us who were once civil spoken enough have become arrogant & intolerant. Well, *qui vivra verra*!

What a Ministry! Everything one has fought against all one's life. Northcliffism, Georgeism, Mondism, Balliolism! If it weren't for [Arthur] Balfour and Robert Cecil—& I don't suppose they cut much ice *dans ces parages*. . . . If I only had a pen & could still use it & it wasn't war time & I wasn't a bit dotty, I wd. shew you, my dear, what I cd. do as a political writer!

And you? I wonder where you stand in all these earthquakes? I hope you haven't lost Wellington House—for I am sure you could not have done a better "bit" during Armageddon—& no one else cd. have done it better, either.

Well, God bless you, mon vieux! May MCMXVII give you all you want. Give my love to Lucy & thank her, will you, for her p. c. What nice kids! I wish I had a son.

Yrs.,

To F. S. Flint

Attd. IX Welch, No. 6, I. B. D.
B. E. F., France
19. 2. 17

My dear Flint:

I very ungraciously didn't answer yr. letter—wh. reached me in the far South. However, I was lazy there—where the Mediterranean spurts up into the rosemary & lavender.

But this is the bare, cold & trampled North, with nothing but khaki for miles & miles . . . Bare downs . . . & tents . . . & wet valleys . . . & tents . . . & AAC guns . . . & mud . . . & bare downs . . . & huts . . . & bare downs . . . & RFC . . . & mud . . . & motor lorries . . . & mud . . . & bare downs.

And I am promoted to Adj.—& run a Bn. much as I used to run the *Eng[lish] Rev[iew]*—It's the same frame of mind, you know, & much, much easier—or more more difficult, according to one's mood. . . .

I want to ask you a favour: I somehow pine to publish a vol. of poems before the war ends or I am killed. Cd. you, do you think?, arrange for someone to publish:

Antwerp
The Old Houses
Two or three poems written in the trenches & other nasty places
& Heaven

in one volume? And could you collect & arrange them, somewhat in that order?

I have the m. s. of one or two here & wd. send them to you & I daresay you could gather up some more in one way or another. Mrs. Jackson has one & Mrs. Masterman & Mrs. Wells some. If you'd do this I shd. be really very grateful to you & I fancy it wd. make a pretty good volume. I have got rather a good one written to the dead of the Welch Regt & so on. . . . Let me know?

I do admire yr. work very much—you know. "Cadences" is an ever so beautiful volume. I gave it to some people in Mentone—not because I did not value the gift, but because it wd. spread yr. fame a little—& because in my valise here it wd. only disintegrate amongst revolvers & straps & the mud in wh. one lives.

Goodbye, my dear.

I am personally very happy in this sort of life: in the end it suits me better to write:

"*O. C. Canadaous will detail a fatigue party of 1 NCO & 10 men at 4:30 a. m. . . .*" than to watch the Mediterranean foam spattering over rosemary & lavender—for I don't believe I am really, really Highbrow—as you truly *are*.

But God bless you, all the same.   Yrs,

There is a rather funny article of mine in the *"Bibliothèque Universelle et Revue Suisse"* for Jan. in French, if you can get hold of it.[1]

To Lucy Masterman

3rd Battalion
The Welch Regiment
8. 9. 17

Dear Lucy:

Could you kindly let me have a copy of that poem about M[achine] G[un]s that I sent you from Nieppe?[1] I am trying to get together, languidly, a small volume—that no one, probably, will want to publish.[2]

I haven't had any news of you for a long time—or indeed from anybody: it is like being a ghost, rather. I am pretty hard-worked but not yet passed fit—wh. is vexing as I suppose I shall get shoved out in December again & I rather dread the bad weather out there.

I hope you all flourish & that C. F. G.'s affairs prosper—but no one seems to prosper much except the civilian pop^n of these parts: they swim amazingly in money!

Give my love to the children.   Yrs. affctly,

---

[1] "Une Partie de Cricket," LXXXV (January, 1917), 117-126.

[1] "Clair de Lune."

[2] John Lane published the collection, *On Heaven and Poems Written on Active Service*, in April, 1918.

To Lucy Masterman

Dear Lucy:
Redcar, [Yorkshire]
15. 10. 17

I am touched that you shd. bother to write about my poems. But my reasons for suppressing them are so much more personal than a question of inclusions or exclusions. I know quite well what I shd. put into the volume for its own sake. But I really care nothing about it. Publication means very little to me—& the publication of poems, less than any other form. However, I am so hard-worked here that I hardly have any time to consider these matters. I spend all day wrestling with the wild beast of Ephesus & just tumble into bed, worn out, at night.

You don't say much about C. F. G. or I don't gather whether he prospers or not. I hope he does—& you & all! I am personally pretty fit—fit enough not to bother about how I am & generally rather prosperous in a military sense, tho' certainly not in any other.

Give my love to the children.
Yrs.

To James B. Pinker

Dear Pinker,
Headquarters, 3rd Battalion
The Welch Regiment, Redcar
6. 1. 18

Hurray: keep the old flag flying.

But won't you have a shot at something new?

I attach a long poem I have just completed.[1] It expresses the spirit of the poor old Infantry & of the Bn in which I have the honour to serve in a way that no other poet johnny [*sic*] has even attempted. Possibly a daily paper would publish it—or possibly the Fortnightly or the English Review. It might be worth £20 or £30. I know it isn't normally worth yr. while to handle poetry but this is a special occasion. Have a shot. I daresay Donald of the Chronicle would publish it. After all few poets—and *no* man of letters of my standing—[have] been twice out to France, actually on service & in the trenches, without wangling any sort of job on

---

[1] He called it "Footsloggers," and dedicated it to C. F. G. Masterman. Its first appearance was in *On Heaven and Poems Written on Active Service* (London, 1918).

the Staff, but just sticking it in the Infantry for the love of the job.

I wish by the bye you wd. advance me my share of what Nelson are to pay on pub^n. I am more than usually hard up as a Lt's pay is, to say the least, exiguous.   Yrs,

P.S. If you want to handle the poem, send the ms., will you, to Violet [Hunt] please.

P. P. S. Could you get me a commission for a novel—either about fighting or not about fighting. I have two ideas. I shall be going out again next month—& one has plenty of time to write in France; but I can't be bothered, & it takes too long, to negotiate with publishers from out there. I wrote about half a novel in the Salient, but got tired of it when I cracked up. That one was not about fighting—but I could do a very good one about trench warfare, too.

To Lucy Masterman

3rd Battalion,
The Welch Regiment
13. I. 18

Dear Lucy:

Thank you very much for the poems: I like them because they remind me of you—& you know I always think of you with affection, from the beginning of the year to the end, even if I do not often communicate the fact.

Yes, the volume with Lane is coming; it has got some pretty good stuff in it. I have just finished a patriotic poem that I fancy is rather beautiful—with nothing about "Britannia" & the Lion & so on, in it.

I have just put in an application to be attached to a Labour Bn in France. I have a desire to be out there which is almost nostalgia. The Col. of the XIV Bn applied for me—but York would not let me go because of my job so I asked to be allowed to resign that job, and the doctors won't pass me G. S., confound them. It is annoying because a Labour Bn is just as dangerous & uncomfortable as a Service one, yet the credit is less. However, I don't mind that. I am going to ask for leave for a week from Tuesday next. I wonder if you know of any cheap lodgings I cd. take, in yr. neighborhood. South Lodge[1] does not seem to be available. I

---

[1] Violet Hunt's London residence.

wd. not worry you, but you are the only people I care to see in London now, so does the world of men of goodwill shrink & shrink!

I hope the children flourish: it probably isn't so bitter in town as it is here where it is really as cold as France was last year.

All good wishes to C. F. G. & God bless you, my dear.

Yrs. affctly,

To Iris Barry[1]

Dear Miss Barry:

HQ
Ripon B. C.
4. 7. 18

I have been reading yr. poems & the adventures of Bridget with a great deal of attention—& pleasure. Of course I like them—& admire them. There is a certain—I was going to say ferocity—but let us say determination of attack on visible objects that I have always tried to get at myself—without much success—but that you seem to get in your stride. I have always been preaching to people not to write "about" things but to write *things*—& you really do it—so I like to flatter myself that you are an indirect product of my preachings—a child of my poor old age. Now that I am an extinct volcano you shall continue eruptions—*opera sub Tiburuo* etc— Of course you will say, with the proud assurance of youth, that you have never read any of my work. . . . But that is not necessary.

As for the poems I don't see why you shd. not publish them as they stand—tho' I wd. leave out the Apologia, wh. is too much Ezra [Pound]. I don't feel that they are the real right thing—the best of you—But it wd. probably do you good to see them in print. I will read them again &, if you like, I will do my best to force them upon [John] Lane. If I can express what I mean—in them you seem to be frigid towards words. I don't mean to say that you can't use them but you don't seem to use them with the sort of joy in words as such that is the province of the authentic poet. You seem to be looking at the reader and saying: "See what I can do with seven silver balls!" Forget yourself, mon amie—forget

[1] English poet and critic, author of *Splashing into Society* (London, 1923) and *The Last Enemy* (Indianapolis, 1929).

yourself & the admiring reader. At least—that is how I feel it. A poem—a volume of poems—isn't a set of cubes for mosaics exhibited in the black velvet of museum cases. It is a quiet monologue during a summer walk in which one seeks to render oneself beloved to someone one loves. It is a revelation of a personality that wants sympathy from men of goodwill—not a bludgeoning of Times Literary Supplements or a display of dexterity. That is what, for the time being, is wrong with yr Imagiste & Cubist Associates. They are too much "out" for the purpose of expressing scorn, & try to be loveable in original media—too little. Of course that is a phase that will pass with youth—which eventually sees that clubbing one's grandfathers is only a means to an end. One wd. have done more if one had perceived that truth earlier.

As for Bridget—that is another pair of shoes altogether. You get, I mean, the same effect of hard mosaic in words—but they are joined together & form a wall. . . .

However I am in bed with neuritis at this moment and not fit to write more—so I will write to you again about the rest of it when I am more fit—unless, indeed, it bores you. Still, you needn't read it.

Yrs,

To Martin Secker

3rd Bn, The Welch Regt.
Redcar, Yorks.

Dear Secker:

18. 8. 18

I have been thinking seriously about your request for a novel from me.[1] I do not think I should care to write a single novel for any publisher again, because I consider that my position has suffered considerably in the past from one publisher and another having persuaded an agent to give various books of mine here and there.

What I want to do is to consolidate. Do you think you would care to try a collected edition of my novels? It wd. suit me quite well if you began with a cheap edition of "The Good Soldier," "Ladies Whose Bright Eyes," "Mr. Apollo," & "The Fifth Queen"

[1] Martin Secker had published Ford's critical monograph *Henry James* (London, 1914).

—to see how they would go &, if they proved successful enough to make it worth while, to go on with the others.

In that case I would write you a new one called "G. C. M." to fill in the corner, & wd. continue to publish with you.[2]

Just consider the idea, will you?, & let me know what you think.

I don't want, you understand, large advances, but I so want to get my books under one roof & I am quite certain it wd. pay a publisher to get them in that way.

Yours truly,

[2] Probably "General Court Martial." This could be the first time Ford discussed a war novel with a publisher, but the title is not mentioned again in his letters. *Some Do Not*, the first of the Tietjens novels about the war, did not appear until 1924.

1919 · 1928

SUSSEX, PARIS, NEW YORK

To James B. Pinker

Private

Authors' Club
2, Whitehall Court, S.W.

Dear Pinker,

5. 6. 19

Here is that agreement duly witnessed.

Would you kindly observe the following facts:

Yesterday I changed my name by deed poll from Hueffer to Ford, partly to oblige a relative & partly because a Teutonic name is in these days disagreeable & though my native stubbornness would not let me do it while the war was on, I do not see why I shd. go on being subjected to the attacks of blackmailers indefinitely. Of course I shall retain the other name as a pen name; but will you be so kind as to address letters to F. M. Ford in future.

Also will you address them to

> F. M. Ford
> Red Ford Cottage
> Hurston
> Pulborough
> Sussex

& will you please not let the address go to anyone outside your office—I mean to *anyone whatever*. I suppose I can rely on you for this; it is absolutely necessary for me to have a place where I can write undisturbed if I am ever to write again.

Yrs. truly,

To James B. Pinker

Red Ford Cottage
Hurston, Pulborough

Dear Pinker:

25. 6. 19

Ref. the payment for the "Romance" cinema rights wh. from what you said I imagine to be obtainable now, would you be so good as to put £400 into War Loan & retain the certificates—or, if you prefer it, retain the money itself & would you, with the remainder—wh. I suppose to be a little over £50, tho' I don't know about the rate of exchange—open an account for me at the Pulborough branch of the London & County Bank—for Capt.

F. M. Ford, that is. I am buying a house[1] in that neighbourhood & shall not draw on the £400 until I want to complete the purchase wh. may not be for some time. I shd. be glad if you wd. open the acct. at Pulboro by return as at present I send cheques up to town & get them cashed wh. is troublesome.

Ref. Cinema Rights of the "Panel" I suppose you will be collecting the money for this soon. I shan't be actually wanting it till October, but I suppose we may as well have the interest on the money for the time.

I am occupying a period of invalidishness with writing some stuff about the country—gardening & birds & the like. Sometime ago someone connected with the *Saturday Review* wrote to a chap called [Clifford] Bax, who is a friend of mine, & said the Editor wanted my help. I don't know why, as I don't know who the Editor is & I didn't bother to answer. Has the *Saturday* got any money & if so wd. you care to drop in on the Editor & ask him if he wd. care to have this stuff as a weekly article? I call it "English Country" & it will in time make a book that you can sell to Duckworth if you will. I am not well enough yet to attend to business myself. What about the novels for Lane, by the bye?

Yrs.,

To C. F. G. Masterman

Authors' Club
2 Whitehall Court, SW

Dear C. F. G.,   28. 6. 19

The guns are going—so thank God it's over.[1] I am pretty well satisfied with the results: for me they have not gone far enough in splitting up L'Infame. Still it's like a fairy world. I daresay they go too far for you—still it can't be unsatisfactory to you.

I should like to say one thing, for what I am worth & that is that I believe after long consideration & some knowledge of the war that the greatest credit of all is due to the Asquithian Liberals; that the winning of the war was altogether due to you people & that the behaviour of the country at the last election was a piece

---

[1] The cottage called Coopers, in Bedham, Sussex. Ford and Stella Bowen, an Australian artist, did not move there until late summer, 1920.

[1] The signing of the Treaty of Versailles.

of dastardly ingratitude. I don't suppose either my pen or my voice are much good—but if you care to make use of either they wd. be as wholeheartedly at your disposal on these lines as they were at the disposal of the country during the war. I will speak for you anywhere you like & write for you anywhere you like & at any time. I don't suppose the offer is worth very much, but it is very sincerely made. So do command me if I can do anything in the way of "propaganda" either for yourself or for any other member of the original cabinet that carried on the war.

Turning to other matters.

I have left South Lodge for good & set up a house of my own in the country. At the time I did this, in April, I was fairly penniless & lived for some months as a jobbing gardener, but lately I have made a good deal—indeed, a great deal—of money, quite unexpectedly, by the sale of various cinema rights[2] in the U. S. A. & in other ways. I don't want to bother you, with my reasons for doing this, further than by saying that, at the beginning of the year, I gave Violet the choice between my leaving South Lodge or her giving up the acquaintanceship of certain people whom I regarded as my enemies. I found that she had been entertaining at Selsey the various gentlemen whose chief claim to patriotic activities, as you know, had been the denouncing of myself to the police as a German agent; & I also found that various gentlemen were stating, on her authority, various other untruths to my disadvantage. This simply meant my absolute ruin. Violet refused either to give up her Selsey friends or to disacknowledge the others &, altho' I am entirely indifferent to what anyone says about me, Violet's course seemed to me to be so radical a disloyalty to any form of joint life that I saw no other way open than to retire from the scene.

I accordingly took a labourer's cottage in the country where I am still. Today I have changed my name by deed-poll to "Ford." I would not do this, out of obstinacy, while the war was still on but I see now no longer any reason to continue to put up with the inconvenience that a Teutonic patronymic causes in the rather humble sphere of life that I now adorn. I have made a rather

[2] Probably to *Romance* (the collaboration with Joseph Conrad) and to *The Panel*.

beautiful garden with the work of my own unaided hands, & subsist rather largely on its products. I am also writing some rather pretty stuff. So *me violà planté* and so I hope to continue. I shan't appear again in London except that, in order to spare Violet the mortification of the appearance of an official abandonment, I shall figure at her larger parties from time to time—as, for instance, on Monday next. I don't like doing it, but I take it to be a duty.

I shd. prefer you to keep these various items of information to yourself—& of course Lucy—but I don't impose any vow of secrecy. As you may have observed I dislike talking about my feelings or affairs & I only do so to you because I am really grateful to you for all your backing in the past four years so that I think I owe it to you to keep you posted as to my motives & movements. If it is a nuisance to you, forgive it for that reason.

Anyhow do believe in my gratitude & in my extreme desire to be of service to you if I can in the way I have suggested. It is not much to offer—but it is all that is in my power.

I hope that Lucy & the children flourish. Do give them my love.

Always yours,

To James B. Pinker

Red Ford Cottage
Hurston, Pulborough
Dear Pinker,
24. 7. 19

All right ref. *Romance.*

I shd. be glad of the *Panel* money shortly to make up the purchase price of a cottage I am buying, but there is no vast hurry.

The Sat. Review affair is as follows:

A. I have been largely writing some stuff about Gardening wh. I proposed that you shd. offer to the Sat. in circ[umstance]s that will appear in para. B. The New Statesman however asked me for something the other day, so I piled it into them &, as serial, it is therefore na poo.[1] Remains the book: a chap called Cobden Sanderson wrote to me the other day saying he wanted a book of mine, was starting in the Autumn & so on. He is said to have plenty of money. Now cd. you plant the book on him? It is called "English Country," is like the "Soul of London" in tone, will make

[1] The English soldier's reduction of *il n'y en a plus.*

about 40,000 words or 40-50,000.[2] If it goes to him I want money for it, & on receipt of ms. & so on. I wd. rather it went to Duckworth who has all my books of the same sort in his Readers' Library. Cd. you, do you think, arrange that Sanderson had all the rights except the 2/6 ones, those reverting to Duckworth after a term of years?

B. *Sat. Review*: Attached please find a letter to one Clifford Bax. The said Bax offered me the editorship of the Sat.—wh. I cdn't take being in the Army. That was in July 1918 or so. In April of this year Bax sent me this letter wh. I did not bother to answer at the time, not being well enough. What I asked you about six weeks ago was this: cd. you call on the Sat. & see what they really want of me? I cd. write them a weekly article on sound Tory politics or Gardening, or the Army, or Books of the Week —but I cannot take the trouble to negotiate these things myself. If you cd. fix up a weekly article such as I used to do with success & general profit, for the *Outlook*, it might be worth both our whiles.

If it *isn't* worth your while cd. you hand it on to someone starting in business? I daresay you know of someone who wd. do it & not cross yr. path. I used to be worth a good deal to a paper as a Book of the Week Critic because publishers advrt[s] always followed my articles—but an Agent is better able to say these things to a paper than I am.

Let me have a reply anyhow.

Yrs.,

To Herbert Read

Red Ford Cottage
Hurston, Pulborough
2. 9. 19

Dear Read:

I have been an "unconscionable time" acknowledging your *Naked Warriors*, not for want of sympathy or interest but because of Preoccupations, Sicknesses, Visitors, Work, Housebuilding, Agricultural Operations & the general abstractions that go to the setting up of new establishments & environments. I daresay

---

[2] Ford published no book with this title, but a series of essays called "English Country" (*The New Statesman*, August 23–September 6, 1919) was later incorporated into the autobiographical fiction called *No Enemy* (New York, 1929).

I shd., however, have written in spite of all these, but for a sort of shyness & difficulty in writing phrases about Literature such as shd. be calculated to keep my end up in a too High Brow World. I can however still talk. Wd. you, on that account, care to Week End with me here? I have at the moment a rather ramshackle cottage, zealous but not well trained domestics, cats, dogs, chickens, ducks, goats, sweet corn, cabbages, tomatoes, French beans, plenty to eat but no liquor—prior to moving to a small property wh. I have just bought but out of wh. I can't get the tenants. If, in face of that, you wd. care to adventure either next Week End as ever is or next but one, a train leaves Victoria at 3:40 p.m. (1540 hrs) on Fridays wh. wd. be met at Pulboro' by the smallest groom in the world with the largest grin in, again, the smallest pony cart. I shd. personally prefer Next Week End, both because it wd. the earlier give me the pleasure of yr. society & because I have to fit in the visit of an Engaged Couple & other people—of less amourous but more High Brow characteristics. Also I rather want to put you in touch with some new periodical & publishing ventures that may help you if you are still inclined for a (part) literary career—& the sooner you get in the better, because, though these look like being lasting concerns One Never Knows.

In that case—or in any case—wd. you kindly note as follows: (A) I have by deed poll on the 28.6.19 changed my surname to "Ford" to please a relative from whom I have expectations; & in order to escape from the attentions of the Society of the neighbourhood wh., ranging from Monds to Meynells, is excellent but not to me congenial. I do not much want my whereabouts to be known before I move to my new place where my next door neighbours will be Sir Edward Elgar, Sir [illegible] Cole & Sir Bysshe Shelley. They may or may not be more congenial—but I don't know them & tho' Next Door they will be several miles away. You will therefore be so good as to address me as Ford Madox Ford, & to consider that the address at the head of this letter is for your private use.

(B) My Establishment (including of course, H. Q. Staff, Maltese Cart for use of M. O., cats, dogs, ducks, etc) includes a Mrs. Ford[1]

---

[1] Stella Bowen.

whom you don't know but who, besides ministering to my, really, declining years, paints portraits of—generally ugly—people.

Both A & B are intended for your private information: but I have no particular claim to impose confidences on you. I want, I mean, to pass some years without the attentions of people who are not my sort & in a selected society. (You will observe that there is a compliment here)—but I am not avoiding creditors, the Police, the King's Proctor—or indeed anyone except Monds, Meynells, and Writers for the Times Literary Supplement. So that, if you shd. prefer not to retain A. & B. in your inner soul, it wd. not ruin but only bother me, & I am not very well, the doctors having been cutting little bits out of me pretty continuously since last April, wh. makes one rather chary of being bothered. This is a rather long letter full of nonsense—but I feel I owe you a long letter & I can only write nonsense nowadays.

Yrs,

P.S. If you contemplate coming on Friday—or indeed if you *don't*—wd. you mind sending a wire? The posts here are atrocious.

To Harold Monro[1]

Dear Monro:

Red Ford Cottage
Hurston, Pulborough
30. 5. 20.

Of course I am a Poet: only, as I once wrote in a poem I never published:

> "When other Bards sing mortal loud, like swearing,
> Like poor Dan Robin, thankful for your crumb,
> If the wind lulls I try to get a hearing."

You write in rather a fortunate moment: imprimis, I am in a good temper, which is not always the case: sec. the Muse has lately visited me. I have just written two poems & feel a third bubbling near the surface—which has not happened for three years!

You might have had one of the first two (but others have snapped them up) if you had replied to a handsome offer I made you this time last year—but you did not, so I thought a cloud had

[1] Proprietor of The Poetry Bookshop, London, and publisher of *The Chapbook* (*A Monthly Miscellany*).

come over our relations. There is something curious—& rather rude, you know, about your office. I don't know if you are aware that I offered you the *Heaven* volume for nothing in '17 & was just checked off as if I had been a literary beginner. So it went to J[ohn] L[ane].

However, this morning, as I said, I am in a good temper, recognise your services to literature, admire your taste & discernment & will undertake to send you something for your July number if you will let me know the date by which you must have the m. s.; & I will take what you like to pay. I only put on the screw last year because I was still smarting under your office's treatment of *Heaven*.

I am afraid I can't get to your party, though I will have a shot. I am learning the difficult Art of Small Holding as I am unlikely ever to be able to live in the Great Metropolis again &, what with chickens coming out & draughts & the like, it is difficult for me to get away. Will you please ask your Firm to observe that my address will be as above until August when I hope to move to a small (*d--n* small!) Property I have lately bought? If you wd. care for a rustic weekend with some hardships I cd. give you one & lecture you on Poetry whilst feeding beasts.

I resume: i. If you want a poem please answer this giving date as above. ii. Please note address. iii. General Amnesty for all offences.

Yrs,

You are right about yr. selection of the early poems: but I shd. like to put in a plea for Perseverance d'Amour[2] as far as I remember it. You see, mon cher, there are plenty of other people—plenty—with the temperament of poets—but there is only One who knows how to use the English language, as it lives & as we speak it.

---

[2] A little play in three scenes and an epilogue, first published in *The Face of the Night* (London, 1904).

To Harold Monro

Red Ford
Hurston, Pulborough
9/6/20

Dear Monro:

I think you are misinformed. When you were away somewhere, I wrote to your people and offered them the "Heaven" volume. The answer was that, if I would send the manuscript it would receive consideration in due course. As I just hated to be written to like that I took it to Lane. You see, you yourself had asked me for the "Heaven" several times, and had printed much of the other matter, so I did not like, much, to be written to as if I had never been heard of in your establishment. However, I did not write a rude letter in reply and you too refrained; so we are both gentlemen and all is well.

So now to business. I have just finished typing out a long poem —between 7, and 800 lines of a Fairy Tale type.[1] Beautiful! A sort of (relatively) Jazz Patmore, Angel in the House Affair. I suppose that would be too long for your next number. Then, too I begin to be wishful of being taken seriously as a Poet. Why shouldn't I be? So I should rather *prefer* if you could "see your way" to publish it in a sort of pamphlet form for the Christmas season. (It might have that sort of appeal). I shall probably have done fiddling with it and may send it to you tomorrow. In that case you could do as you like about it—either print it in your July number or the other. If however it is in any case too long, drop me a line by return—*really*!!! by return—to say you want something shorter for the 18/6/20.

You see, I have begun two immense Novels that look like being seven million words long each, and I am sick and tired of writing immense novels and, anyhow, I don't seem to get well enough to write much. So I am rather thinking of going for the laurels of de la Mare or Masefield. (No respect wanting to either of them or both.) But I think that at my time of life it is time I turned my attention to becoming really Tol-Loll, enveloping myself in clouds of mystery and the like. Now, I have a contract with Lane to give him all my Novels which bore me to tears, and another with Duckworth to give him all my Serious books—which bore

[1] *A House* (*Modern Morality Play*), published in *The Chapbook* in March, 1921.

everyone else to tears. So what do you say to fixing up some sort
of contract for my poetic futures? I Love both Lane and Duckworth sincerely, but I can't help feeling that they aren't Poets.
Think about it, will you? I like contracts myself. They are grave
and useful domestic articles to have about the house—like patent
Fire extinguishers. They are no use: but you can go and look at
them and twiddle the taps from time to time. And with two
creatures like myself and your Office. . . . Well, possibly, a Fire
Extinguisher. . . .

To recapitulate: If, in the nature of things, 700 lines is too long
for your July number,—& I shd. prefer it to come later—get the
gentleman who sends out slips to send me another slip with the
code-word "Bumph!" on it and I will take it to mean that you
want something less than 150 lines and you shall have that by
the 18/6/20. See? I have got something else in my head, but I like
a month or so to fiddle away at things and make them look really
careless. Nevertheless, by the 18/6/20, it will have reached the
stage of looking really Tol-loll, with the five word sparklers of
old Time not taken out, and balanced, singularly blank verse &
you can have it. Tout comme les poemes de M. notre confrere. . . .
But that would be invidious.

Excuse these misplaced flippancies: I have just got a new typewriter and it carries me away . . . but it does not seem to possess
any accents)) at least, I have not found them yet"/@_£&'( )
¼⅛⅞:!%?. No, they aren't there.   Yours

To Herbert Read

Red Ford
Hurston, Pulborough
11/6/20

Captain Herbert Read, D. S. O., M. C.

Sir;

You appear to labour under a misapprehension. I can neither
recall your identity nor imagine what motive can have prompted
you to address to me your obscene and even blasphemous volume,
"Eclogues"! I should have thought that mere consideration for
the great Shades of Milton, Mr. Rudyard Kipling, Sir Henry
Newbolt, Author of "Admirals All," not to mention Major Beith

the admirable portrayer of the "First" (and subsequent) "Hundred Thousand" would have induced you to stay your hand. Not to mention, again, the sword, or rather swords, that it was our privilege to wear on ceremonial parades or when Orderly Officers!

But, on reconsidering the matter, a vague recollection—a vague recollection of an individual who, stating that he came from Middlesborough, had yet more the appearance of one originally of Southbank, and who, last year, forced himself into my establishment and, though behaving otherwise in an inoffensive manner, caused great perturbation by displaying so little knowledge of Elementary Map-Reading—surely, surely, a branch of Military Education.

In other words, "Come Off It!"

It is unnecessary to address me as if I were an obliviscent Panjandrum with head a mile above all clouds. Of course I should be pleased to hear from you and to get your volume. I like Childhood, Etude and Promenade Solenelle the best of them. I remember the second periodical and having quite an insulting time with a fierce young poetess of the Aesthetic type who said it made her gorge rise. Go on making them rise; I think you are on the right road.

Penny, (not Pound) the goat, the sweet corn, Mrs. Ford and the hole in the roof are still, here, going strong. The frost of the 7th inst. touched my special potatoes, annihilated the marrows and the haricots, upset the tomato plants but spared, curiously enough, the maize. Our tenant in Bedham paid the debt of nature in March, so we are in possession but shall not go into occupation till Michaelmas. The garden blazes with flowers; we have an old mare; also this machine which I thought would spare my eyes and get round my writer's cramp. It does the latter—not the former and is rather exasperating—as you can see between the lines. These are the short and simple annals of Red Ford. I haven't written another word to that Nuvvle and precious little of owt [sic] else.

No, not a bit have I grown tired of talk about books—and youth is a golden thing. Education Sentimentale is Stonehenge; but then What Maisie Knew is certainly Stratford on Avon (Though God forbid that the Old Man should hear me say so!) Le Rouge et le Noir is the perfect thing upon which to model one's style, if one does not model it on Coeur Simple—which is worth a wilderness of apes, monkeys, Times Literary Supplement Reviewers and almost every other thing in the world. . . . But the Real Thing is nearly as good. Only Henry [James] was just a *little* provincial-pharisaic, whereas Flaubert was so huge, untidy, generous—and such a worker! Still, as someone or other said, L'un et L'autre se disent and if you aren't in the mood for Stonehenge the Birthplace is a very good substitute—and Henri Beyle, perhaps, a better still.

I rejoice in your felicity; it is good to be happy and keep bees—good for others as well as yourself. And a Novel! I am really glad to hear of that. Why not come here and read it or talk it over. It gives one a lift, sometimes, to talk of one's stuff. We have coming down here for a fortnight a daughter of George Lansbury with no inside—cut out, I mean, last week (Shades of the Rev. North; the Treasury; the Morning Post and me a TORY. But these are Stella's friends, not MINE!!!), but the weekend after that is not booked, though, from that on, we are fairly; and we should be delighted to have you both, if Mrs. Read could stand the perforated ceiling and the other hindrances.

Give old [F. S.] Flint my love when you see him, will you and tell him I should like to have de ses nouvelles. I fancy I have lacerated him, I don't know how; but I don't gather that he bears malice. [Wyndham] Lewis, on the other hand wants, I believe, to cut my throat, because he wouldn't pay me his rent or something. However, give him my love too, if you lunch with him.

All sorts of good wishes,

Yrs.,

P. S. By the bye: Are you a cricketer? I have been invited to do a week's country house cricket in August with Snaith and Drinkwater and other Literary County Cricketers. I don't want to go—or rather I do, but shall be busy at Bedham, just then. Would you care for me to suggest you? Most Yorkshiremen are good between the sticks—not, of course, anywhere near Kent—but still. . . .

To F. S. Flint

Red Ford Cottage
Hurston, Pulborough
23/6/20

Dear Old Flint;

I am so glad to see your writing again,—though it seems unfeeling to write of gladness when your news is so distressing. You know I sympathise very deeply; for you must know that I have always been very fond of you so that anything that affects you must affect me. Do tell me something about your domestic circumstances: I mean the little things such as who looks after your children—and indeed, how many you have. It is so long since we met and my memory has so gone that I don't even know. And you will please remember, in all your calculations of the future, that here is a green nook where you will always be welcomed, and where life is extraordinarily simple and quiet. I mean, just exactly, that the holiday season is approaching and that if you would come down here with, say, a couple of children (provided they could go into one bed at night) this would be exactly the spot for them and you. For I know you would find it a sympathetic household and the place would be perfection for children. And there are many things we might talk about.

I have not yet read your preface or your poems,[1] because I am in a hurry to write you at once; but of course I have looked at the uncut volume. And I think we—you and I—ought to work out a formula together so as not to cut across each other in critical writing. You know the formula of another sort: A plus B squared equals A square plus 2AB plus B square—the 2AB being to the good! That has always been my rule of life. Supposing you came down here alone for next week-end and took a look around—and then, if you liked the look of things, embarked on a Holiday here! I know you are shy—so am I, though I have not the appearance of it—but get over it in this instance! I am really thinking about your views on Rhyme—which one should discuss. Because you rule me out in a phrase of your preface! and I don't think you can really rule me out![2] So come down on Saturday—Friday

---

[1] The Poetry Bookshop published Flint's *Otherworld: Cadences,* a collection of thirty-nine poems dedicated to Herbert Read. In the preface to the volume, Flint discusses prosody, criticism, and the state of English poetry.

[2] Flint wrote: "We have no critics [today], I have said. There is certainly Mr.

would be better still—and you will be met by an aged mare in an old cart. 3:30 p.m. from Victoria is a good train—to Pulborough. And I will cook you the most amazing French dishes with my own hands. That I take to be settled! George Lansbury's daughter is here too as a guest, but I suppose you are not afraid of Bolshevists. . . .

As for Grievances. . . . Someone told me, a long time ago, that you desired my head on a charger. . . . I had addressed to you from France the m. s. of my volume³ which you had said you would see through the Press; and you acknowledged neither the m. s. nor two letters that I subsequently sent you. I daresay it was only the b----y War—but when someone or other subsequently told me that you had a down on me I accepted the statement. But I gather now that that was only gratuitous mischief making. Let it all pass, pray, along with Early Morning Parades, Mametz Wood, and all the other finenesses and villainies! . . . There were too many of the former—and so unavailing; and too many of the latter; and they were too successful. As for me I am not done in and am gradually recovering physical fitness; and mental, too, I hope. The only thing that seems to have 'gone is my memory—and even that comes back slowly! You see, when I was in Corbie C. C. S. in July 1916, my memory went altogether. For thirty-six hours I did not even know my own name. It is, as I have said, coming slowly back; in patches it comes quite vividly. But when I consider that I wrote the whole of the Fifth Queen series without a single note more than went on the back of one visiting card—and that those were only dates!

That rather accounts for the English Review article⁴—which

Ford Madox Hueffer; but I could name off-hand half a dozen Frenchmen who, like Mr. Hueffer, are both critics and poets too. Perhaps the only real critic is the poet; perhaps criticism is poetry, as Oscar Wilde seems to have held; and perhaps this age is not rich in poets."

³ Probably *On Heaven and Poems Written on Active Service* (London, 1918).

⁴ "Henri Gaudier: the Story of a Low Tea Shop," *The English Review*, xxvi (October, 1919), 297-304. Ford describes Gaudier-Brzeska at a dinner in London "financed by a disagreeably obese Neutral whom I much disliked." It was an *Imagiste* dinner at the Dieudonné Restaurant on July 17, 1914, and the biographer S. Foster Damon calls Ford's account of it "probably the most violent attack on Amy Lowell in print." Flint, Pound, the Aldingtons, and Violet Hunt were among the guests. Ford was clearly confused and Flint justifiably offended.

I was not really fit to write at the time. Do you know, I had not the slightest idea that the giver of that particular dinner was Miss Lowell? Indeed, I hardly still believe that it was. I thought, at the time I wrote, that it was some sort of monstrous Dago, a friend of Perez Triana. You remember that both Perez and his wife were monstrous and they were always surrounded by Spanish and South American Portugese millionaires who financed reviews. Perez had two immense ones that he was always asking me to write for. And I only remembered at the time an immense creature who could not talk rationally because a motor car was held up at Southampton or somewhere and a most distressing dinner at which a number of young people were trying to do the Review Confidence trick on a Millionaire. There was, you will remember, a great deal of that sort of thing at that date and it was pretty loathsome. As for Miss Lowell I hardly knew her. I only met her once, or at most twice. I fancy she was very fat, but I don't really remember. So I suppose you will acquit me of attacking the lady. Why should I? All I knew about her was that she wrote some very exquisite verse in one or other of the Anthologies. But I daresay to you she is a vivid personality and I am really sorry if I caused you pain. It does not otherwise seem to matter very much. I suppose that if Miss Lowell came across it she might be hurt—but I don't see why she should; the poor old E[nglish] R[eview] is obscure enough. And, anyhow, she must know perfectly well that I could have no possible motive for attacking her. Indeed, I take slight umbrage at you for imagining that I was the sort of person to do it—even if I had any "down" at all on her. But how could I have had. As for any gentleman, other than yourself, I am perfectly ready and able to cut his throat on that point—the one, I mean, that supposes me capable of making physical fun of any unfortunate and sick lady—or for the matter of that, of not knowing that the Americans were our Allies, not Neutrals.

My dear Flint: will you take this as the settled basis for our future intercourse. I, Ford Madox Ford, being of sound mind depose that: I believe there are two exquisite poets in England, yourself and Hilda [Doolittle]. I believe that there is one exquisite poet in the U. S. A.—Miss Lowell. I believe that there are two

other poets in this country, myself and Ezra who are vital because
of a certain large carelessness, generosity—and scrupulous attention to words as means of intercommunication between man and
man. . . . All the others are just wearinesses on the make . . .
et j'en ai soupé. So surely have you! That being so don't let nasty
little people hypnotise you into believing that I would attack Miss
Lowell. I am used to that sort of baseness being used to undermine
me with my friends. It is why I have my fière idée de l'homme.
And did you ever in your long knowledge of myself ever hear
me say one bitter word of a fellow poet who was a real poet—
or of anyone else really! But this world is a place of potins!

It is true I am a great writer . . . probably the very greatest!
And you just wait, my dear! Give me three years to get all the
bits and poison out of my poor old carcase and lungs. . . .

Anyhow, come down next week-end and let us really talk
things out. Put anyone else off. It is a cock you owe to Aesculapius
—because of the sentence in your preface that wipes me out!

                                Yours anyhow always,

Remember: Flint
            H. D.
            Amy Lowell
            Ezra and Self
            And France!

You know me well enough to know that I would go to the stake for
anyone of those if I say I will. And I do say I will—solemnly! But
then, you may want my blood for coupling you with Hilda; or
for mentioning Ezra! I suppose you will spare myself and France!
(The country, not Anatole!) Or possibly even not!
   [Herbert] Read is a good boy!
Excuse machine: my poor old eyes suffer so if I write!

To Herbert Read   Red Ford
                                        Hurston, Pulborough
Dear Read: 30/6/20

   The advent of Flint—for putting whom on to me you have
earned my thanks—reminds me that I have not answered your

"psychic" letter. I don't understand your ps. state; you complex people are so—well, complex! Simple, bovine persons, like self and partner just carry on. (I see the word used is "psychological," but it does not seem to make any difference, except I suppose that we all have psychologies.) No; tell Mrs. Read that Stella and I are not aesthetes. At the present moment she is cutting ham sandwiches to take on the river for the day—just like anybody else! ! ! ! !

Ah, further on in your letter, I perceive the word "psychic"—well, we will gird up our loins and assume intense expressions against your arrivals! Putting the matter in other language: If you are coming here, the sooner it happens the better it will convenience us, because, after middle of July we shall be more or less in the throes of moving. That leaves next and the subsequent week-end at your disposal; so if your ps. condition seems to offer prospects of ameliorating itself by either period pray come along. . . . If you want to talk about and scheme out a novel it is—so I have found by long, long, long experience—better to begin it early. If you talk with a bloke to whose judgment you feel inclined to pay some deference the less you have actually written the better; because, if there is a lot put down it is apt to make one obstinate in its defence; the natural law of laziness comes in. Whereas if one talks of a project one sees it crystallise in various shapes as the conference proceeds and one has a more open choice. . . . I mean to say: there is the whole open question of Impersonalism to discuss. And then: the house is open to you: You can come and talk about it at practically every stage, if you want to—except that, during August, we shall be plastering and papering at Cooper's; during September, moving in and during October and November resting from our labours in one Metropolis or other, supposing us to have the car-hire left to go away. . . .

So speaking from the Cher Maître elevation—if that's the game you want to play; and it's quite a good one!—I should say YOUNG MAN, ahem! Come down next Friday or the one after and discuss your plan, dans le vide. Then piochez like H-ll till about Xmas when around the great Fire we will debate over the results. See?

Anyhow, that's my offer. Answer as nearly by return as you

can, will you? All our compliments to Madame; or, more simply
to express it: Yech y dach y!¹   Yours always,

To the Editor of *The Athenaeum*¹

Sir,—   [July, 1920]

In your last issue the whole subject of Vers Libre is dismissed
in a third part of an unsigned review.² But such a matter cannot
be so dismissed—so light-heartedly, summarily and flippantly.
Neither can the poems of the most consummately exquisite and
gentle master of the form that in England we have be so dismissed, and you hope to escape protest.

Not even THE ATHENAEUM, with the prestige of all its great
obscurantist dead trailing behind it, can so dictatorially put back
the clock. It is as if, once more from your columns, we heard the
voices of our dear old friend Norman Maccoll or our dear old
preceptor Theodore Watts-Dunton snuffling, as they and their
contributors used to snuffle, when they were confronted by anything that had not the support of their close corporation; that
was beautiful, sincere and unguarded. You are probably less acquainted than am I—who for twenty-five years lived as it were
in the *bas fonds* of those formidable shadows—with the Great
Traditions of your journal! So you will not remember the Great
Number in which you, dismissing Walt Whitman with two
semi-obscene words (Swinburne), stated that the sonnets of a
Mrs. Augusta Webster were "superior to anything that had been
written" since the days of the "Swan of Avon," and surpassed

¹ Ford claimed that in Welsh the phrase is equivalent to "may the devil be
on your side or no one else will."

¹ See no. 4707 (July 16, 1920), pp. 93-94.

² In a review of F. S. Flint's *Otherworld: Cadences*, Edith Sitwell's *The Wooden
Pegasus*, and Iris Tree's *Poems*, the *Athenaeum* critic brought strong objections
to Flint's view of free verse. "Poetic intensity comes with fever," he wrote. "Poets have, from time immemorial, expressed the strange, almost delirious sensa-
tions induced by that emotional fever in forms of speech that are not the forms
of their normal speech. . . . Almost never do we feel in reading Mr. Flint's poetry
that thrill of excitement and surprise which we feel in reading the lyrical utterance of the true poet."

indeed the similar metrical efforts of that Bard (W. M. Rossetti). And in the same Great Number you stated that the orchestration of the then Queen's Master of the Music, Sir Somebody Somebody—he had supplied two lost parts for instruments in Hummel's Quintette—wiped out for ever all the orchestral works of the composer of "Tristan" (Joseph Knight). When I was still *le jeune homme modeste* and very, very innocuous, an odious old gentleman, having damned in your columns my infant works, addressed to me the galling exhortation *Patrem et avum habes*; *eos exorna*! . . . May I now return those your words to your address?

Returning, then, to the present century, let me put it in this way: Your Reviewer must be a man with some of the knowledges and experiences of a man. He *knows* that when human beings are undergoing fears, joys, passions or emotions they do not really retire to studies and compose in words jigsaw puzzles: they relieve their minds by rhythmical utterances. These, if rendered by an artist, make up the utterances of passion that are endurable or overwhelming. He must have read some of the Authorized Version and be acquainted with the Book of Job; the Lament for Absalom; the Psalms of David; or the idyllic utterances of Ruth to her mother-in-law. Perhaps your Reviewer may never have come across really simple persons, peasants and the like at moments of great losses, great joys, great upheavals. In that case he will be surprised to hear that such elementals do not express themselves in rhyme. They do not. They come very near to the Vers Libre of the Translators. I have heard them say:

1. By God! We're alive: I never thought we should be./ 2. After tonight./ 3. Give it a name, Old Bird. It's a damn fine thing to taste hooch./ 4. After a strafe like last night./ 5. Evans copped it; so did Dai Morgan./ 6. Swallow it down, have another of the same./ 7. Cor! I am all of a tremble.
Or they say: sometimes with tears, sometimes not:

> That was my eldest son,
> Muss 'Uffer!
> He lay with his head twid my breastesses
> Six hundred mornings and more

Before it was properly light;
Counting the flies on the ceiling,
And me never to see him no more!

That may not be poetry; but it is vers libre and it is the expression of emotion. Nevertheless it does not rhyme "Greenwich" with "spinach," or get entangled in "ation" rhymes as the young do. (Heaven knows I do not wish to run down the young ladies your Reviewer so likes: Good luck to them, now and hereafter! His quotations are probably unfair to them, and they are no doubt emotional enough in other places. It is hard on them that he should have used their verses as sticks with which to beat his dog.)

And then . . . one does not like to see dog eat dog. One understood that *Normanno mortuo*—THE ATHENAEUM was to become the organ of the Morning Star; the New Day; the Young . . . Entreat, sir, your Reviewer to look up your files for the great number of Whitman *v.* Augusta Webster and Sir William Blank *v.* Richard Wagner, and then let him re-read his review of Mr. Flint and the two young ladies. . . .

Or at any rate let me say in your columns, you have trailed on the ground your august mantle-of-Elijah-tail, that for certain temperaments—*hominibus bonae voluntatis*—the poems in Mr. Flint's "Otherworlds" are exquisite, and extract from the life that we to-day live all the poetry and all the emotion of a non-blatant kind that can be got out of the poor old thing by those not suited for skipping about in meadows and exclaiming:

Ring a ring of roses!
Pocket full of posies!

Though that too is a lovely occupation.

And Mr. Flint's prose introduction is so quietly and beautifully written; so gentle in its cadences that are like those of Mr. [W. H.] Hudson; it expresses so modestly and so completely what the whole great world outside these fortunate islands is expressing, feeling, or discovering as to the art of poetry, which is the pursuit of intimate expression between poor lonely man and poor lonely man. . . . Well, your Reviewer might surely have let it alone if you were unable to place at his disposal space in which seriously to consider, or worthily to condemn, that manifesto.

I have the honour to be, Sir, Your obedient servant,

To Harold Monro

Red Ford Cottage
Hurston, Pulborough
5/7/20

Dear Monro;

Handy Aids to Memory Ref. Correspondence are the following:
(A) On Retiring:
    1. Knot Right Leg of trousers.
    2. Smear handle of walking stick or umbrella (a) with treacle; (b) with quicklime; (c) *very efficacious* with cow-itch.
(B) On Going Out to Dinner.
    1. Remove staircase.
    2. Instruct Housekeeper to open 1 tin Nestle's milk and pour contents between employer's sheets.
    3. Disconnect light switches and liberate 1 doz. toads, previously painted pink with phosphorescent preparation in bathroom, on landings, sleeping apartments etc, before going out.

I wired what seemed to be indispensable corrections to you this morning; I trust you understood the wire. If not, leave out corrections and carry on. It will look all right. Your letter dated 2/7/20 did not reach here till the 4/7/20 too late for post.

I am glad Flint liked being here; he needs filling up with food and looking after. If you think of coming, make it during the next fortnight, will you, as we are going away for August and shall then be moving. You had better come as you will never write an answer to that letter.

Yours

To Herbert Read

Red Ford
24/7/20

Dear Read;

Thanks for your letter, with its items of interest. I am glad Flint was pleased; the communication to the A[thenaeum] read very well and I am much obliged to you for taking it in. It is useful to have the Ed. unmask his little battery and declare himself Daimas, or Damas—for no-one knows which was the unrepentant thief, short of St. Peter. And may that Saint soon. . . . But stay, it is not permitted to the Faithful to pray for the death of any one save the Pope—who of course goes straight to celestial joys.

I am glad of the martial alignment of the Sweet Corn. It needs, by the way, a hell of a lot of watering, particularly after flowering.

And glad, too, that you have begun your novel. That's it really, get your formula and then pioche away with your head beneath the blanket. Then look up in a couple of months and take stock of results. If your formula is all right you will then begin to see, as it were, the split-loching of a Form and the rest will be straightforward spade work.

And there is one very great material advantage in having the line really planned out: it means one can sit down after interruptions—which in your case are diurnal—and just carry straight on because the work has been done in one's head. Whereas, if one has neither formula nor Form, when one comes to the Pen one spends immeasurable time in the effort to catch on or to invent.

I continue to spend unadventurous days like those you have sampled. My own novel—not the one you have seen the beginnings of—but another—is going slowly towards completion.[1] I have rather got hold of it at last which I had not for quite a long time. Stella is in Town, shopping, so I am in a great silence.

All sorts of good wishes to Madame. Would you tell her that if I didn't seem highly sympathetic to her desire that you should conspuer H. M.'s Treasury it was not that I was unsympathetic to the idea as such—for I sympathise deeply. But I know the ground so little. It might be the making of you—but then again it mightn't. At any rate you are living even if in tomb-like buildings and I fancy a year or two of that, after the War, which was too much, specifically like, the Simple Life, will probably do more to help you towards literary maturity than contact with the Good Brown Earth of the late W. E. Henley. . . . But, as for

[1] *The Marsden Case* (London, 1923) was the first novel Ford published after the war.

Health, Happiness and the rest—that is quite another matter. The Country is good when one has discovered for oneself various hollownesses—those of the plaster Pillars of the State and the papier maché hearts of men. But I think it is good to get one's disillusionment for oneself; if one obtains it vicariously one is rather apt to want another shy at the Aunt Sally of a thing, and so a later unsettlement comes on. That, at least, has been my own personal experience. But do not ever listen to me! I have always been too careless about the part of life that needs a Career to support it to be any sort of councillor, even by suggestion to others who may need Ambitions, Prosperities and Pomps to get the various bests out of themselves. Anyhow, good luck!

To Harold Monro

Red Ford
Hurston, Pulborough
26/7/20

Dear Monro:

Your letter and, particularly, the IMPRINT, put me in a very disagreeble quandary. I do not wish to be ungracious or petulant; I am conscious that you have done great service to the Art of poetry and that you wish to do something for me. But you propose to produce a poem of mine on which I have spent a great deal of care and attention so as to bring it into competition with the Daisy Ashford books and this causes me, I can assure you, more perturbation than you can well believe. The poem is a poem: if you publish it with these rather self-conscious naiveries of little girls of thirteen and fourteen there is no poem. One section of readers will buy it for the pictures and say: "How Ducky!"; another section will say "More children's stuff", and have nothing to do with it. . . .

You know as well as I do that a poem is written for its "look" on the page and if you kill that "look" you kill the poetry. That is why I loathe inset decorations, however truly decorative. Why can you not get it done by Lovat Fraser? Or I should prefer Lewis. Or, really, what you ought to get are the woodcuts of Bewick which you will find in old editions of Mavor's spelling books. These have the exact, non-self conscious, queer drawing that is wanted and would not stick out of the page. I suppose you would find them easily enough in the B[ritish] M[useum].

Of course there is the publishing side of the matter which I know cannot be ignored. That is a matter entirely for you and in it I do not presume to interfere. On that basis I am ready to say: Do exactly what you like as long as I never see the finished product. It is an attitude which all my life I have had to adopt and I am perfectly ready to adopt it now. So just let the matter go at that. I mean: do what you like and do not consult me any more about it. I have said what I want and do not want; it is for you to consider your own wishes and knowledge of what is expedient.

I am sorry "Recorder" thinks me boorish. I don't know who he is: but it's a funny word to use even to a Victorian Great Figure such as—Recorder hints—I am. I mean boorishness is an active, youthful quality; whereas the V.G.F. must be gaga! But of course I am much obliged to the gentleman, anyhow: that may not have got through to his mind.

I don't understand your political allusions; but in so far as they are pessimistic I agree with them. Indeed I go further than any possible or imaginable pessimist.

                                                                    Yours

To Alec Waugh

Authors' Club
2 Whitehall Court
26/7/20

Dear Waugh:

I am glad to hear you are becoming a publisher—for good, nice publishers are more rare and much more beneficent (I never shall know how to spell that word!) than the best of authors. However, I feel sure that, under the gentle sway of your father, to whom commend me, you will find time to cultivate your own Muse—which also is a thing you should do.

As for "Thus to Revisit," I had not thought to turn it into a book[1]—if you look at the last few pages of the proofs enclosed, you will see that they are rather occasional and more written with

---

[1] Ford's reminiscences, under this title, began to appear in *The English Review* in July, 1920, and continued there intermittently as well as in *The Dial* until April, 1921.

a purpose—to boost you young things!—than with the repose that a book should have. . . . However, I could easily turn it into a book[2] and would gladly do it for you—write into it, I mean, and add on to it and make it, possibly, a little more serene—and possibly a little more malicious, or at least teasing—to the self-important. It would make a sort of continuation of my "Ancient Lights," which your firm published and it might sell better as being concerned rather with today than yesterday. What is your idea about length?

As for the business side of it—supposing the idea appeals to you—I should have to put that through Pinker. I always get into mysterious rows and misunderstandings with publishers if I deal with them direct.

Yours sincerely,

To Ezra Pound

Red Ford
27/7/20

Dear Ezra,

Your heart is golden: so are your words. But the latter are normally—even when they can be read—incomprehensible. Remember that you deal with hempen homespun wits. Does "for a minute" = "at present" ? or that you wouldn't think for a minute of knowing our establishment? If the former: we abandon this place—hoping to let it furnished—for a month on the 4th prox, or six weeks: then we return to pack up and move. In Nov. we shall be in town for a short time—or if you intend coming it must be next weekend. I find by using this pen of Stella's I can write just like you! but refrain!

Thanks very much for the Mercures. All literature will be received very gratefully by

Yrs,

I am going to write some stuff about Vers Libre for the Dial, immediately.

[2] In 1921, Chapman and Hall published the expanded and revised version of these articles as *Thus to Revisit*. Ford had, however, used the same title as early as 1919 for a series of articles in the short-lived *Piccadilly Review*. That series is not part of the book.

To Ezra Pound
Red Ford
Hurston, Pulborough

Dear Ezra,   29/7/20

Het es al een seer invermaagliike vorstellung! Dichteren en eht solkliik verruckten man siin net te verstahn! Nackni Vlamsk. . . .

In other words we go on Tuesday to

> Scammell's Farm
> Bedham
> Fittleworth
> Sussex

where a few books would be most earnestly welcomed and where I shall be up to the eyes in painting, papering, plastering and bricklaying until at least the incidence of the autumnal equinox. And I am afraid we could not by any possibility put you up there, but I do want to see you. Could you by any means come down to the pub—a very gorgeous and replete one, for a night. An enthusiastic publisher has just commissioned me to turn the Dial-English Review articles into a book which I shall do as soon as I have got rid of my novel[1]—I hope before Tuesday. I think it important that we should agree on a formula for vers libre, non-representationalism and other things before I go any further. We want some manifestoes. I mean, I might tread on some of your or X or Y or Z's corns without in the least doing it intentionally unless as you would say you or someone puts me right. You forget that it is six years since I poured oil on these eaux puantes and I don't so hell of a well remember who were Imagists and what it was all about. I can't afford, either for time or money, to come up to Town before November, when I shall have to, whereas you are young, mobile, affluent, fortunate—and interested in getting the right thing said, almost more than I.

Anyhow: that is that.

As for writers . . . what do I know of them? There was André Gide—but perhaps you have consumed him years ago. . . . I used to like the prose of a man named [Henry] Tomlinson but I do not know what has become of him. Herbert Read also, I like.

---

[1] Probably *The Marsden Case* (London, 1923).

I miss from your list Cunny G; and Hudson;[2] but I suppose these are obstacles of age and the like. Wilfred Blunt also. I also much admire George Stephenson—but rather for matter and temperament than for manner. There is also Iris Barry who should certainly be supported. . . . Certainly. And of course Mary Butts.

So you see, I am not much good. . . . Why should I be? . . . I have done too much propaganda for too many years; I have rather to attend to my own Art, in these my—you would say—Indian Summer months. . . . Nux gar erchetai!

I suppose the Dial would not like to serialize my novel for twopence or three pence? It is turning into an Immensity—a sort of Literary Via Dolorosa. . . . I viewed it with suspicion at first; but it comes on. God bless you.

To H. G. Wells

Authors' Club
2 Whitehall Court
Dear H. G.;   1/8/20

There is one point in your letter in the English Review as to which I do not wish to preserve silence.[1] It grieves me a good deal—but rather because you seem to be hurt or possibly apprehensive. You may remember—or you may not remember—a number of years ago you took me to the zoo. Afterwards you walked with me round and round the Inner Circle of Regents Park. You told me your life; you said that that was your official biography

---

[2] R. B. Cunninghame Graham and W. H. Hudson.

[1] In the first installment of *Thus to Revisit* in the July, 1920 issue of *The English Review,* Ford wrote: "I remember, for instance, listening respectfully to Mr. H. G. Wells whilst he lectured me on how to write. But, as far as I could see, his only technical rule was this: *Never introduce your hero and heroine together in the first chapter.* I don't know why this should be so. For the sake of economy, I daresay." Wells countered with a sharp letter in the August issue. "This childish falsehood," he wrote, "about my lecturing him, or anyone, on how to write a novel is particularly incredible. 'How to do it' was the one topic upon which I never offered a contribution to my Kentish and Sussex neighbours." Yet Wells, in this same letter, "instructs" Ford on why he should not have collaborated with Conrad, what is wrong with Henry James' fiction, and why "these endless chatterings . . . about the New Form of the Novel, about who was 'greater' than who, about the possibilities of forming a 'Group' or starting a 'Movement' are things to be avoided at any cost."

and requested me to repeat it exactly whenever certain matters connected with your life were mentioned in my presence. I thought at the time that it was a good deal—and a dangerous service—to ask of anyone. It has proved dangerous. I can only assure you that, since that date, whenever that seemed necessary in your interest, I have repeated exactly what you asked me to say and no more and no less. In commenting on it, if I did comment, I have backed you through thick and thin—indeed with a violence that has made me several lasting enemies. I could, if it were necessary, prove this —but I see no necessity to prove it.

The fact that I have thus rehearsed your biography may have got round to you again: I can only say that you asked me to do so. If anything derogatory to you has got round to your ears as uttered by me I can only say that that is due to the—possibly ingenuous—misinterpretation set on my words by the hearers. You know as well as I do that heard words are easily misinterpreted and still more easily wrenched round in their context. And it is a pity to think evil.

I am sorry if you dislike the word "lectured"—but I should say you had always lectured me. You speak always with conviction which I seldom feel. I should say that, on that occasion at the zoo, for instance, you "lectured" me on the protective colouring of small birds—at any rate I remember very well what you said on that subject: as it were a dissertation on what is called camouflage nowadays.

On the occasion to which I referred in the English Review— & to wh. you also refer in your letter, you began by warning me that my association with Conrad might damage my career. You went on to say that all this talk about Literary technique was deleterious or nonsensical or something of the sort, and you ended up with the exact words: "There is only one rule for the writing of a novel: Never introduce etc." This struck me so much that I then made the remark about the Sonata Form. It was the first remark I had uttered. You speak much faster than I do; I daresay you think much faster than I do. Many people do; so that I frequently find it impossible to get a word in until three quarters of the way through what would be called a conversation. . . . When that happens I think I am being lectured. . . . Afterwards you said that the most important thing about a novel was the subject—whether it offered openings for strong emotions, or cast light on social conditions and so on.

This letter is getting rather long—but the matter is important, really. I have said against you frequently that I thought it a great misfortune that you wasted your immense talent on social aspects. I think that: I have frequently tried to convey to you that I thought so. . . . I have said over and over again that I thought you a genius who wasted too much of his time on journalism—by journalism I mean social speculations. Social conditions seem to me to be temporary matters which change and then what is written of them dies.

I am perfectly certain that that is the only thing that I have ever said against you: that is why I mention it. I do not see that you can object to it. If you said of me: "H. is a great poet. It is a pity he does not try to help in the reformation of social conditions," I should feel flattered by your calling me a great poet and should let the other slide.

Really you ought to believe this—if only for your own peace of mind. . . . For you can hardly wish to think of myself as going about denigrating yourself. Please consider too that there are probably several persons who would wish to make bad blood between yourself and myself and a great many more who will do it for sport or the love of God. . . . You must remember, too, that you guyed me in Boon and that might seem to give me a certain prescriptive right to poke a little fun back at you. There are other, less important matters in your letter that may as well go by the board. Perhaps in the light of this you may one day see fit to correct them; if not it does not much matter.

I am perfectly and absolutely sure that I have never to any living soul reported—or even hinted—that I had worsted you in conversation. That is altogether out of the picture! On the contrary, I have again and again talked of your quickness in repartee and sudden characterisation. I remember particularly that once you said that Mene, mene tekel upharsin was the first example of the Movies and I contrasted it with Labouchere's impromptu about Me Commissioner Tucker—which I happened to hear—I should say, to your advantage. I couldn't, you know, think of myself as getting the better of you in repartee!

I will ask you not to reply to this. Either you believe—and I ask seriously that you shall believe for good and all—the one point that matters: that I have never abused you: or you do not. If you do not, you will continue your abuse in the press and I shall continue to back you up in private. I realise that the pressure of mischief makers is too considerable to be really, ever, put right. I shall not make any public reply. But pray do believe that I do not wish —and never have wished—anything but well to the pen you hold. That is perfectly sincere!

Yours,

P.S. The present instalment in the English Review was written months ago and I have not since touched it. Had Harrison² advised me of your letter I should have modified it in certain points which may look as if they were gibes at private matters. I assure you that they are not.

To Ezra Pound

Scammells Farm
Bedham, Sussex
30/8/20

Dear Ezra:

Ref. Proust. It wd. amuse me to do *Chez S[wann]*—& I would do it if publishers wd. give me *plenty* of time, so that I cd. do a bit now & then when not in the mood for other work. If they wanted a complete Proust I wd. edit it: i. e., go through anyone else's translation to see that it was all right, & write an introduction: but I couldn't translate the whole: it wd. bore me to tears. If as I say, they gave me lots of time I shd. not be exigent as to price: but I shd. leave that to Pinker—to get the best he cd. for me. That is that.

I am getting along with the Dial articles—with interruptions from Violet [Hunt] who has planted herself in the neighbourhood & runs about interrupting my workmen and generally making things lively. I fancy she had you followed by a detective when you came down & so got the address. But I may be wrong about that. However, we flourish as the Abbey Theatre itself never did.

Yrs,

² Austin Harrison, editor of *The English Review*.

To Ezra Pound

Scammells Farm
Bedham, Sussex

Dear Ezra:

[September, 1920]

Your letter overwhelms me in a dismantled dwelling, on the point of moving; I can't answer it therefore, and what I do answer does not feel as if it would come coherent. I don't feel that I am the best person to try any of the writers you mention. I will however have a shot—if you like. Nor do I feel that [John] Lane is much good—Pinker at any rate, between ourselves, is violently trying to get me to go elsewhere and, as he will probably get up a quarrel over my body with L, I probably shall. But how would Chapman & Hall suit you? They are just now beseeching me to do things for them and, if you approve, I will try them. But let me know just what you want—an English imprint only, or more capital, or reprinting here. Chapman would probably be better than Lane as they have a much larger organisation—connection with booksellers and so on, that being really half the battle. . . . But I don't want at all to influence you against Lane if you think him all right.

You will see H. G. & Ethel Mayne dancing over my corpse in the English Review.[1] It leaves me only a little annoyed—but still annoyed! I will communicate my feelings as to Vers Libre and your letter's manifesto about it when I get into more tranquil surroundings. I think I rather—at first sight—dislike the "music" idea in the connection; but no doubt we mean different things by the word.

Do you see your Athenaeum's "Henri de Regnier writes well"! And the incredible Shelley stuff.[2] . . . It is the Hidden Hand of Professor Wirklichler Geheimrath Putz coming back via the Cocoa Press!

[1] In addition to Wells' letter (see note, page 119), *The English Review* printed in the August, 1920 issue a letter from Ethel Colburn Mayne in which she said that "all the reference in Mr. Hueffer's article to my 'influence' in the *Yellow Book* is simply *persiflage*. Mr. Hueffer knows as well as I know that I was the lowest of the angels."

[2] Probably the review of Regnier's *La Pécheresse: Histoire d'Amour* (September 3, pp. 317-318) and the column "A Hundred Years Ago" (September 10, p. 335).

By the bye: Why say in the Little Review[3] that I am gaga! Is it the voice of South Lodge[4] whispering across your great Atlantic to reverberate here? Or what is the game? In a very few years, mon vieux, you too shall be toothless, myopic, and resemble Maclise's drawing of Talleyrand. . . . But I suppose you have never seen it. So continue to dance in your beflowered meads au son des fifres de crotale.

I quite see the point of non-serialisement in the Dial; don't suggest it to them. I just thought it would give them cheap copy—but it would take four years to put through, anyhow!

Let us know when you will be able to tear yourself from the great metropolis and we will find you a room. Stella has been drawing vivid caricatures of you inspecting the pigs.

Yours,

To Ezra Pound

Bedham
nr. Fittleworth, Sussex
Dear Ezra;   19/9/20

I have been too much cluttered up what with getting a novel corrected for the typist and the continuing activities & incursions of Violet and her agents—which are really bad for Stella—to write about Instigations[1] which I will do in a full dress letter. Perhaps now if no one comes down the chimney!

Firstly; It is a very good piece of work; full of good definitions and makings clear. The JAMES I still think is the best of it; I don't know whether it would gain or lose by being more carefully ar-

---

[3] In "Hudson: Poet Strayed into Science," VII (May-June, 1920), 17, Ezra Pound writes: "F. M. Hueffer must not be forgotten; there is his 'Heart of the Country,' and passages in other of his books to maintain the level; and Hueffer is perhaps at his best when he approaches most closely to [W. H.] Hudson's subject matter; when he is least clever, when he is most sober in his recording of country life.

"This is not however an arranging of hierarchies and an awarding of medals for merit. Hudson touches Hueffer when dealing with England and Cunninghame Graham in dealing with La Plata. And it is very foolish to wail over the decadence of English letters merely because some of the best work of these three men is possibly ten years old."

[4] In other words, Violet Hunt.

[1] A volume of critical essays (New York, 1920).

ranged; perhaps it would lose in impressionistic value. . . . There are one or two points: In your appraisement of Henry's individual works you are too American (I daresay I am too European). If you look them through again you will notice that you cease to be interested in them as soon as the Transatlanticism goes out of them & only take notice again with the American Scene—after Antaeus had actually touched Western Earth again. You are in fact bored with civilisation here—very properly: and so you get bored with the *rendering* of that civilisation. It is not a good frame of mind to get into—this preoccupation with Subject rather than with rendering; it amounts really to your barring out of artistic treatment everything and everyone with whom you have not had personal—and agreeable—contacts. There is the same tendency in your desire for the STRONG STORY and in your objection to renderings of the mania for FURNITURE. You don't, as a cadenced verse writer, like prose at all and want to be helped to read prose by being given stories written à coups de hache; and, having no taste for bric a brac you hate to have to read about this passion. . . . But it is one of the main passions of humanity. . . . Stephen Crane used to say that he was not giving fancy prices for corner lots and battlefields—but he gave them all the time. . . . You might really, just as legitimately, object to renderings of the passion of LOVE, with which indeed the FURNITURE passion is strangely bound up. . . . Still, these are only notes; but I think you might think about them—because you *might* harden into the Puritanism of the Plymouth Rock variety—which would be a disaster. . . . Anyhow it is a very valuable piece of work and I am very glad you have done it; some passages give me real pleasure in the reading, I mean pleasure in the language, which is a rare thing. . . .

Having got that nuvvle off my hands I will go through the DIAL article at once & send it off, probably on Tuesday. . . . It occurred to me, ref. Bradley, that I really ought to have left the questions of terms to Pinker. I wish I had; but I suppose it is now too late?

I hope Dorothy flourishes.

Yours,

Anyhow I'm a damn better typist than you! What do I owe you for those copies—and the Gourmont subscription?

To Herbert Read

Coopers,
Bedham, Sussex
19/9/20

My dear Read;

I have been busy finishing up my own novel to go to the typist, or I should have written before. So now, firstly as to your searchings of heart:

I don't know that I am the most sympathetic person to come to for one inclined to desert the practice of novel writing for the indulgence of metaphysics. For, firstly, I never knew what metaphysics were, and, secondly, I have for years and years held that the only occupation to which a serious man could seriously put himself was the writing of novels—if only because, in all the varied domains to which the very limited human intelligence applies itself this is the only one that is practically unexplored—the only one in which it is possible to find a New Form. And it is only the finding of a New Form that is a worthy occupation.

So at least I see it—and the immense advantage that the Novel has over the frivolous apparition called the Serious Book—is that, if you are really serious enough you can say what you like. . . . I mean that you can ram all the metaphysics in the world into it and it can still be a fine work of art. . . . Or all the Strategy, Biology, Bibliography and Philately that count.

I don't see what Yorkshire has to do with it[1]—except that all Yorkshire people, as I have known them, are singularly lazy and singularly self-sufficient (Present Company, of course, always excepted!) My friend Marwood,[2] as you say, was a case in point: he had the clear intelligence of a poet, but, rather than trespass on his own shyness and shamefacedness, he would spend days making corrections out of his head on the Margins of the Encyclopaedia Britannica. He just—peace to his ashes—wanted to bolster up his self-conceit to himself (He didn't boast of his achievement to any other soul), and, of course, to remain très grand seigneur, Marwood of Busby, and so on. . . . That is at the bottom of most Yorkshire dislike of the Arts—a sort of shyness and love of ease! Your county folk see a Poet performing coram populo! They say to

[1] Herbert Read wanted to retreat to Yorkshire and become a regional novelist.
[2] Arthur Marwood, Yorkshire squire and one of the founders of *The English Review*.

themselves: We dare not appear in public: they say aloud: That is a contemptible fellow! And gradually their public utterance becomes themselves and they end as sidesmen at the local Bethel! And conceal the Venus of Milo, as she used to be concealed in Leeds Art Gallery, behind aspidistras!

Don't let yourself undergo that hardening process; it is a very stupid one; try to forget that you come from the Sheeres at all. ... Whitechapel is really a better lieu de naissance. ...

Of course I see you aiming at becoming another Henri Beyle: But it is a miserable ambition. ... Learn of Stendhal all you can —and there is, if you do not happen to be Middleton Murry— an immense deal to learn in an artistic sense. ... But don't model yourself on him. ... I can imagine no more terrible being to himself, than a Yorkshireman, true to type, and modelling himself on Mr. Beyle!—The end would be the most horribly costive neurastheniac you can imagine, with incredible sex obsessions sedulously concealed, swaddled up to the ears in red flannel for fear of draughts, and with more hypochondrias and phobias than are to be found in all Freud, Jung, and the late Marie Bashkirtseff put together. ... And with a yellow, furred tongue, and a morgue britannique beyond belief. ...

No, try not to become that. ... You may not like novel writing but it would be a good thing to stick to it so as to avoid turning your soul into a squirrel in a revolving cage. ... Still, it is not for me to interfere with the destiny of others and, if you will you will.

You are unjust, rather, to Conrad. ... He is a Pole, and, being a Pole is Elizabethan. He has done an immense deal for the Nuvvle in England—not so much as I, no doubt, but then that was not his job, and he is of the generation before mine. I learned all I know of Literature from Conrad—and England has learned all it knows of Literature from me. ... I do not mean to say that Conrad did not learn a great deal from me when we got going; I daresay he learned more actual stuff of me than I of him. ... But, but for him, I should have been a continuation of DANTE GABRIEL ROSSETTI —and think of the loss that would have been to you young things. ... And think what English literature would be without Conrad and James. ... There would be nothing!

You may say that Conrad's prose is always a Ceremonial Parade of words, with a General Salute and a March Past twice in every chapter. . . . "And her mute glance conveyed to me the silence of an ineffable love; the glory of pain which is without end; a profound and inalterable. . . ." and so on. . . . And Trench Boots (See A. Ci. I. 99946781, 1897!) must not be worn on ceremonial parades! That is true. . . . But you *must* have gallant and splendid shots at Prose with a Panache. . . . Yorkshire needs them more than anything else in the world! More than anything! Because we can always do the "A-Oh!," reticence stunt! Nothing, nothing is easier. . . . And then we call it selection. . . . But Conrad is Rennaissance, because Poland is a 16th century nation—and we want all the Rennaissance stuff we can get in these islands. . . . A great Master! (There is only one "n")

I liked your Beyle-Byron projection. . . . Have a shot at more of it! But why publish in the Cocoa-Pacifist-Stamp Collector's Weekly?[3] You have your reward in this week's number. . . . Yes, do some more of that; it certainly left an impression and is creative, too. Read Landor, by the bye, if you have not. . . .

Compliments to Madame; I hope she does not think I am corrupting your Northern Lights. . . . Stella is flourishing; we have got the water laid on and four goats; the hens are laying again; we have pulled this house to pieces a good deal and successfully —et patati et patata!

                                                  Yours always,

To Ezra Pound

                                                  Bedham
Dear Ezra,   11 October 1920

Here is that second article. You may differ from it in places: but I will right your wrongs—and those of Waller, Suckling, Lawes, Purcell and Arnaut Daniel when I come to section PHONETIC SYZYGY.

It occurs to me that I wrote rather ungraciously, yesterday, when I uttered no thanks about your appreciation of A HOUSE— and Dorothy's.[1] The fact is that, writing after lunch and beer, I

---

[3] *The Athenaeum*, then edited by Middleton Murry. Herbert Read's article, "Beyle and Byron, 1816" (August 13, 1920), was followed by an angry correspondence.

[1] Dorothy (Shakespear) Pound, Ezra's wife.

was a man of but one purpose—to assure you that I did not care about the DIAL contretemps. . . . But of course I like your liking A HOUSE: I daresay, one day, I shall appear as a better Patmore— Quien sabe? . . . A Patmore crossed with Grimm, Heine and— disons!—Gautier. For I begin to think we have let ce pauvre Théo be too much overshadowed by the others of the Soirées de Medan. And now it looks as if the whole lot were about to disappear before the moonrise of Henri Beyle—of whom I wrote impassionedly somewhere in 1894! And then it will be the turn of the Goncourts —or me—or you! God bless you both!

To F. S. Flint

Coopers
Bedham, Sussex
11/10/20

Dear Flint;

Stella asks me to say that if you and Miss Ianthe Flint and Master Flint would care to spend Xtmas here, it will give her great pleasure. It will give me great pleasure too and there will be a sucking pig, a goose, a Xtmas Tree, a Yule Log, several other children, retainers, snapdragon and the other material adjuncts of the season. Think of it with attention before refusing and then let us know how long you can stay; I suppose you get some days off at that time, so dedicate them to us and the Muses!

I hope Inthe (with an a accidentally dropped) flourishes after the operation.

Yours always

To F. S. Flint

Coopers
Bedham, nr Fittleworth
20/10/20

My dear Flint;

Let me begin a tardy answer with warm felicitations. We were quite sure that you needed looking after and it is a great satisfaction to think that now, surely, you will get it. May you both have ever so much happiness for ever so long and no cares—not even enough to keep you healthy. And you know you have no well-wishers more cordial than those in this small house.

I should have written before, but we have been trying to find, somewhere within reasonable distance from here, a room in which we could have put up you and Mrs. Flint. Alas: it seems as if that would be impossible. The cottages about here seem all to expect to be full up at Christmas. We could have managed you and the children because they could have slept in the considerable-sized maid's room, and the Poet would have been accommodated with a bed in the Studio which is really a glorified landing. . . . But for anything more formal I fear we must wait till in a little time we have got the new rooms built; unless strikes and things and beggary stop these projects. However, I hope we shall meet in Town before then and all be happy there for at least the short space that Town happinesses endure.

I am dreadfully sorry: but you know, alas, that one can't make silken chambers out of a poor old sow's purse, like this dilapidated mansion. . . . I am hoping to finish a novel[1] today—the first for how many years. . . .

Then I shall take a fortnight's wood-cutting to get in the winter's fuel. . . .

With all and every sort of good wishes from us both to you both,

Yours always

To Herbert Read

Coopers
Bedham, Fittleworth
3/5/21

My dear Read;

Many thanks for the TYRO. It is good but there is not enough of it to strike its note. With that immense page you might have got more letter press in. Still, one is thankful for small quantities of good stuff. You ought to have got more instances than that one review—there are plenty. . . . And then your full marching, review order would appear more justified. You seem to break a cigale under a steam-roller, solemnly.

I am annoyed with you for getting yourself tied up in that coccoon way: you ought to have days to pass down here. I don't believe you are the chilly intellectual—or is it metaphysician?—that you think yourself: you are a temporarily unthawed emotionalist. And a day will come. Anyhow, drop in when you can.

Kind regards to Mrs. Read.

Yours always,

[1] Perhaps *The Marsden Case.*

To F. S. Flint

Coopers
Bedham, Fittleworth
12/5/21

Dear Flint:

Very pleased with yr. letter & delighted you are coming. I know nothing at all about trains, but suppose you will wire & we will meet you. If by any mischance you should not wire or the wire not come, I have an account at the Railway Hotel, Pulboro' so just tell their man at the station to run you up here in a car.

Bring an old dinner jacket with you if it's not too much of a bore. I go about in filth all day & put on a cricket shirt & very old dress things at night—not for swank but because I have only one other respectable suit which I have to save for the metropolis.

I don't know why people talk about my writing well:—that sort of stuff I just write. Still, it's pleasant to be told that one wields a pen of gold (Ballad metre, accidental).

But of all these things we will discourse at just length between feeding the pigs.

Kind regards to Mrs. Flint.

Yrs,

The postmistress was bitten by Bo [the pig] whilst delivering yr. wire—wh. is why it is possible yr. next may not be delivered.

To James B. Pinker

Coopers
Bedham, Fittleworth
17/5/21

Dear Pinker,

My friend Mr. Daniel Chaucer whose work Mr. John Lane is so anxious to get hold of writes me that he is just as anxious to get out of the clutches of Mr. Lane.[1] He suggests that you should offer him the refusal of a m.s. that you have in your drawer, called the WHEELS OF THE PLOUGH,[2] as against so considerable an advance of royalty that either Mr. Lane pays it—which would be agreeable to Mr. Chaucer—or Mr. Lane refuses. I understand that Mr.

[1] Ford never tired of playing the pseudonym game with his agent. John Lane had published not only the two Daniel Chaucer novels but also *The Good Soldier* (1915) and *On Heaven and Poems Written on Active Service* (1918).

[2] This novel appears in Ford's correspondence under several titles. By 1928 it had become *That Same Poor Man,* later *Mr. Croyd.* It was never published.

Chaucer's agreement with Mr. Lane stipulates that Mr. Chaucer should let Mr. Lane have the refusal of three novels. Of these Mr. Lane has already published two—THE SIMPLE LIFE, LTD. and the NEW HUMPTY-DUMPTY which sold very well in their day.

If you agree to this perhaps you would send me the m. s. of the WHEELS OF THE PLOUGH so that Mr. Chaucer could make some alterations in it and return it to you for forwarding to Mr. Lane —you acting of course as Mr. Chaucer's agent in the matter.

As for me, I am as usual short of money. Could you get hold of the American royalties for THUS TO REVISIT and send me them? My famous pedigree pigs ANNA and ANITA, 344702 and 344704 in the herd book of the Large Black Pig Society cost a deuce of a lot to keep; but when, as they certainly will, they take prizes at the Lincoln Show I will stand you a champagne dinner. I could supply you with February hatched ducks at 96/- the dozen. You never seem to reply with any enthusiasm to my offers of farm produce? Why is this?

What has become of the Cinema rights of the PANEL?

Yours,

To Harold Monro

Coopers
Bedham, Fittleworth
Dear Monro;   16/6/21

I am really sorry that you should imagine my intentions to have been wounding or offensive: they were merely explanatory of my situation. I had bought a number of pigs for fattening on the 4th of June and a quantity of food, for which I have to pay on the nail, at the same time, you having announced that you would send me a cheque at the end of May. Otherwise I should not have bought the pigs and the feed would not have had to be paid for.

You see, I did not know—and don't rightly now—what is your position vis à vis the Poetry Book Shop. It is naturally no affair of mine—and all I meant to say was that, for the future and if the P.B.S. was yourself H.M., not a Company, I would willingly, your services to Literature being so splendid, contribute work for nothing to keep the good work going. I hope there is nothing insulting about that way of putting it.

I am truly concerned to hear such depressing reports as to the business of poetry selling: I suppose the coal strike and the fine weather together are too much for the devotees of the muses. Perhaps we shall have industrial peace and prolonged wet soon. I cut my hay yesterday so I do not want it to rain before Saturday but after that it may rain black cats.

I have just given a letter of introduction to you to a professor of literature of Berkeley University, Cal. He is on the purchasing-advisory committee of that fane and they buy an immense number of new publications so, from that point of view, he is worth talking to—and he is a nice modest soul too. Introduce him to Miss Mew and Hodgson and others and he will write them up for the Boston papers.

Anyhow, pray do believe that I had no idea of insulting you; I really had not. Come down here when you like.

Yours,

To Herbert Read

My dear Read: Coopers
                                                  25/6/21

Curse you! Just as in H. M. Army you mopped up that staff job over my head, so you have mopped up the New Age Lit. Page. Orage[1] asked me to write it about the 1/1/21 & I did not reply, accepting, until the 1/6/21 or thereabouts, when he replied that he had just commissioned a young man etc. etc.! Thus do the ungodly grow fat on the too early worms of the righteous. But come down & talk about it—*soon*, & *d—n* the Treasury.

My good chap: Thus to Revisit *isn't* a good & inspiring book. How *could* you? It is a bad, wicked, unXtian pitchfork stuck into the behinds of certain snobs. If you, Les Jeunes du Mont Blanc,[2] were capable of being inspired it wd., true, be an inspiring book— but as 66 1/3% of you are engaged in cutting my throat a tergo, it is not too effective. Anyhow God bless you. Come down here SOON. IT IS THE SEASON OF DUCKLINGS & GREEN P--S.   Yrs.,

[1] A. R. Orage, editor of *The New Age*.
[2] The young writers who gathered at the Mont Blanc Restaurant in Soho.

To Edgar Jepson

Coopers
Bedham, Fittleworth

Dear Jepson;   9/7/21

The holiday season approaches—or is here. Would any of your household care to spend a little time here? Yes, I know it is useless to invite—but our accommodation being one spare bedroom with two beds, we could put up: either Mrs. Jepson and a daughter: or two daughters or a son, this month being our free month. And it would give us great pleasure.

We are, but for the drought which is ruinous for my agricultural pursuits, remarkably flourishing, for us in our humble scale —at least, I am enjoying a mild boom-kin in the U. S. A. and thus the New World redresses. . . .

Of course, if you yourself would come it would be delightful and I could give you plenty of poker of which I have been playing a good deal with U. S. A. pilgrims to this shrine. They come in small shoals to talk highbrow; and we set them to feed the pigs—of which I have a number—or to carry the hay of which we have successfully harvested a nice little stack. And in the evenings I take their money at poker—and we have sweet corn and punkins growing, so they feel homesick. But really piquette is the better game—the only game, really.

There is only one danger here—if Stella thinks you—or anyone —sufficiently unattractive she gently but firmly makes them sit. This spring she did a portrait of the Mayoress of Edgbaston so successfully that the Mayor fainted.

Esther Julia[1] is all that she should be, but feels the heat. With good wishes to your caravan.

Yours,

To James B. Pinker

Coopers
Bedham, Fittleworth

Dear Pinker,   15/7/21

Would you mind telling me your movements—I mean when you go on holidays. For although I should like to sleuth you and remove from you the immense bags of gold which nightly you

---

[1] Their daughter, born in November, 1920.

transport to your treasure house I do not see my way immediately to embark on that enterprise.

But Macmillans of New York have just written to me: "We have never published for you, I believe, but it would be a pleasure to consider doing this" and asking me to correspond with them as to their becoming my publishers. I should like to talk to you about this—but not soon as I want to think the matter over carefully first—and besides I am very rushed with my agricultural matters just now. Will you be in Town, say, during the week after next? And if so, would you give me a date?

My hay crop is singularly well harvested. I could supply your stables at extremely low prices considering the quality of the article: I could let you have store pigs as per photo enclosed at 50 (fifty) guineas per half dozen; March hatched cockerels 30/- a brace; ditto pullets 1 guinea each, pure bred light Sussex.

Yrs.,

To Herbert Read

Dear Read:

Coopers
5/10/21

I was pleased to hear from you after all this long time. I don't get press-cuttings &, tho' I do get the *Morning Post*, seldom read it —so but for your *envoi* I should have missed the salutation of my "genius." Do these boomings of me in the M. P. & the *Spectator*[1] (did you see *that*!) mean that in the eyes of Les Jeunes ci-devant du Mont Blanc (where I lunched last Monday in solitude) I ought to sing Nunc dimittis, De; or "Onward Xtian Soldiers!"?

Anyhow we are mildly flourishing. I have got an immense contract from New York which shd. last me all my life: *Thus to Revisit* is going into editions & I get cheques in excess of advance of royalty which never happened to me before: οἱ πολλοί not Les Hauts du Front—& indeed in spite of them!—are reading me. It is all very funny & as it should be, and we pass our time speculating on whether it is to be a Rolls Royce or an Overland. . . .

Stella, by the bye, is in Town at the Coles: if you cared to ring her up she'd no doubt be flattered. (She returns on Friday).

[1] Flattering reviews of *Thus to Revisit*.

E[sther] J[ulia] is a flourishing monster & wastes so much of my time.

(I wish you wd. chuck writing about that b----y fellow St--d-hl! What's Pallas Athene to us or we to P---- A----?)

Did I hear you say: "Metaphysician? . . ." or was it only "N. Riding"?

The drought has simply made me give up Agriculture: nothing will grow: but we live on our own chicken & bacon, drink our own cyder & reel hoglike to bed. None of yr. cultivating the Muses on a little thin oatmeal.

All sorts of good wishes to Madame.   Yrs,

To Harriet Monroe[1]

Dear Miss Monroe,   November 7, 1921

I am really extremely touched and pleased by the award of your prize[2]—I don't know whether more touched or more pleased. It is the first public—or "buckshee," to use an Army adjective—recognition that my writings have ever received, except from France. And of course it is all the more to be valued when the recognition comes from those who use one's own tongue. For, in the immortal dictum: "It is certain that my conviction gains immensely as soon as another soul can be found to share it."

Will you please assure the anonymous donor that if his or her purpose was to encourage poetry by giving a measure of new courage to one poet the kindly plan has been a complete success in this case? I thought at first of returning the cheque to you and asking you to bestow it upon someone younger. But then I said: "Hang it, No! My need of perpetuating pleasant memories is at least as great as can be that of any youngster who will probably besides have longer years in which to accumulate them. I will buy myself an Alsatian wolf hound such as I have desired to possess for a great number of years and it shall be a reminder of the

---

[1] Editor, from 1912, of *Poetry: A Magazine of Verse.*

[2] In October, 1921, Miss Monroe announced in *Poetry* that a prize of $100 had been awarded to Ford for *A House.*

kindness from Chicago." And so I will, as soon as I can find one good enough to serve as a memorial.

Thanking you again for all you have done for poetry—and for me—these many years, I'm

Yours very sincerely,

To Edgar Jepson

Coopers
Bedham, Fittleworth
8/11/21

Dear Jepson:

The Yale *Review* wants me to write an article on the second flight of English Novelists—they mentioning Lawrence, Walpole, & N. Douglas as specimens.[1] (Walpole I shouldn't touch.) Who else is there? I really don't know. Are Brett Young & [Frank] Swinnerton any good? And to whom else should one give a friendly lift—not first bookers? The Yale I believe carries a good deal of weight in the U. S. A. where markets are valuable. If you had any of their books and cd. lend me some—second flighters —I'd be much obliged—or for suggestions.

How are all your brood? I see the young hero's novel being favourably noticed here & there. If he'd send me a copy I'd probably give it a lift in the N. Y. Evening Post or somewhere.

Mrs. B——— & child & maid are still with us, so we're barred rather to other society: otherwise we're cheerful. *Poetry* of Chic[ago,] Ill. has awarded me 100 dols prize for the best world poem of the year—for *A House*. It pleases me as the first public recognition I ever received—except from the Institut de France & that hadn't any $ attached.[2]

All sorts of luck
Yrs,

To Edgar Jepson

Coopers
Bedham, Fittleworth
12/2/22

Dear Jepson;

I am ever so touched by the gift of your novel,[1] being the first with which you ever honoured me. I have glanced at it and find

[1] See note, page 140.

[2] Probably for *Between St. Denis and St. George*. See letter to C. F. G. Masterman, 29 November 1916.

[1] *The Whiskered Footman* (London, 1922).

it to be obviously a play; but Stella has torn it away from me and so I have gathered no more. May it and the play bring you fortunes and fortunes. And then more fortunes.

It's extremely kind too of you to think of having Stella and Esther Julia; but at the moment E. J. is going through such a peevish stage with her teeth that to have her in the house would be no pleasure at all to you and it would, mothers being in these matters self-conscious, be tortuous to Stella. But when this stage is past they will, if you ask them again, come with rapture.

I am worried out of my mind myself by the death of Pinker which happened in New York without any warning at all just as he was—or was supposed to be—fixing up my contract with Macmillans that was to have kept me in clover for the rest of my life. I believe he has a son who will carry on but know nothing of him and I do not even know whether I am tied to the firm or whether, Pinker being dead, I could go elsewhere, which I should be rather inclined to do. I suppose you do not happen to be a member of the Authors Society so as to tell one whether they are any good as advisers? I have just caught a publisher out, doing me in the eye flagrantly over concealed profits and don't just know how to deal with him. I want to get hold of someone fitted to investigate publishers' books. Pinker was to have done it but, he being dead, I am at a loss—and even at that he did not much rejoice being given the task of rendering publishers hostile.

However I don't see that I should worry you about these things except that you have so businesslike and truculent an aspect.

I have just finished my novel for Macmillans:[2] a long way the best piece of work I ever did. I am sure of that: not quite such a good subject as the *Good Soldier* (Thanks for kind mention!) but a better popular subject and a good deal better machined and written. Anyhow may the Whiskered footman bear in butter in a lordly dish!   Yours always,

P.S. This has now lain three days unposted and I have now read the *Whiskered Footman*. He is a fine creature full of ingeniosity

2 Possibly *The Marsden Case* (London, 1923), but the Macmillan Company never published it.

and entertainment. But I thought there were to be three Dukes!
Or are they still to come?

To Anthony Bertram[1]

Coopers
Bedham, Fittleworth
16/6/22

My dear Bertram,

I was just about to write and remind you that you had promised
to send me some of your work—and [Dyneley] Hussey too—and
that you must not let any diffidence interfere with that, when your
stories arrived; had they arrived ten minutes later they would
have crossed my letter in the post.

Of course I will write you some remarks on them; but I do so
hate writing. Are you doing anything this Saturday to Monday?
If you aren't—and Hussey—just pop into a train and come down
on receipt of this. I am at this moment editing a New York
quarterly—the British section of it, that is—and, although what
you have sent isn't what I want, I daresay I might some day do
something with something of yours.

We couldn't put you up for more than Saturday to Monday as
someone has just gone and someone else comes on Monday; but
if you feel like it there are the beds and cup and welcome.

You might send a wire on starting, if you start. Take a car from
the Railway Hotel, Pulboro', and tell them to put it down to me.

Yours,

P.S. I don't think the Good Soldier is out of print. Where did you
try; if it was not Lane's you might go there and kick up a row to
oblige me?

To Anthony Bertram

Coopers
Bedham, Fittleworth
23/6/22

Dear Bertram,

Would the underlined portion of enclosed letter interest you at
all? I know nothing at all about the matter except that the young

[1] Novelist, short-story writer, art critic for *The Spectator* and *The Saturday
Review*, and lecturer at the National Portrait Gallery.

woman who addresses me states that she played with me as a child, a fact which I forget but which surely throws a baleful light upon her age. That sort of thing sometimes leads to other sorts of things (I don't mean childhood's playtimes but unpaid secretaryships!)—but sometimes it does not.

Return the letter, will you? with any comments that you may have to make, and then if you think you can get amusement out of it I will put the lady onto you.

I have also written to Herbert Read to ask him to let you know where their Monday lunches take place—but as your joint connections with the Spectator, the Outlook, particularly, and the Times, may make you appear antagonistic to the real Jeunes, you may have to fight for it. Still a scrap is always a good thing.

Yours. . . . Your letter has just been handed to me. Yes, send along anything you like: I hope you'll have a good time in the New Forest! Yrs,

By the bye, if you resent the apostolic suggestion in Miss DeFries' letter console yourself with the thought that in a year or two you will be sitting on my head!

By the bye: on the 28/6/19—or whatever was the date of the signature of the peace treaty—I changed my name by royal licence from Hueffer to Ford for testamentary reasons, refusing to do so whilst a state of War existed out of a comprehensible obstinacy. So that if you persist in addressing me as H. you are breaking the law: not that it matters enormously!

To Edgar Jepson

Coopers
Bedham, Fittleworth
1/7/22

Dear Jepson:

I am forwarding you under separate cover a copy of the *Yale Review,* you having helped me with what it contains.[1] I had in-

---

[1] "A Haughty and Proud Generation," *Yale Review,* XI (July, 1922), 703-717. At the top of the "second flight" or younger novelists, Ford puts James Joyce and then, in no special order, D. H. Lawrence, Dorothy Richardson, Norman Douglas, Wyndham Lewis, Katherine Mansfield, Frank Swinnerton, and Clemence Dane.

serted a compliment to you and skilled insults to several *un-*whiskered footmen but the editor seems to have cut both out after proof. That may have been wise but it's damned annoying.

Have you any wicked stuff that wd. do for an American mag. of advanced tendencies that I am supposed to be editing from this side? I am making inquiries but can't find out much of its financial status. Do you know anything of a New York publisher named Roth?

Compliments to the family. Stella had rather a bad bicycle accident the other day and has had to be X-rayed and massaged. But she is getting better. Otherwise we are fairly all right.

Yrs,

To Anthony Bertram

Coopers
Bedham, Fittleworth
14/8/22

My dear Bertram;

I have been a brute to you—and certainly I have been still more of a brute to [Dyneley] Hussey. But I have—a change for me!—been writing desperately and doggedly about books for over six weeks, and the house is full, full, full of babies, nurses and mothers and I haven't seen an opening to invite you both down. If you would care to come one by one you could sleep in the hut where I write or if you would prefer to wait till the second week in September, come both.

I *can't* write much about your stories now, for I am sick and tired of writing about writing, having suddenly determined to get a real move on with my History of British Literature. But certainly you, Bertram, have in this last batch improved a great deal on what you showed me down here: the haunted house one is quite another matter (from what it then was!) and, with an illuminative phrase here and there, you might make something *quite* good of it.

Felicity Chimney is a much more ambitious matter: the only thing that is wrong with it is that it is too written. You try—literally!—talking as you write for a month or so and, after that, try writing as you find you talk. I believe you would then find words have quite another savour. Reading French—the best

French—is nearly as good if you try here and there to translate as you go along. Nearly as good but not quite, though it does not make you so personally unpopular as if you try to talk like a book to your intimates. Best of all is to combine the two processes. I am really quite serious in writing that.

What is wrong with your style is that you combine two vocabularies, our spoken language with the English-literary jargon and the introduction of one type of word into a passage of the other type *blurs* the effect tremendously. And if you intend to go on writing stories with, for basis, metaphysical ideas, you cannot afford a blur anywhere. You may be as chary, as delicate, as you like in the amount of matter you vouchsafe, but what you do give must be extravagantly clear. And that clearness dies the moment there is in the reader's mind the least hesitation about a word. For, remember! If a narrator is telling a story—and particularly if the story be a narrative of personal adventure—the words he uses will be enormously powerful sidelights thrown onto his character. They can be used to illuminate a man's history, his tastes, his sensitiveness to his surroundings—innumerable things. Supposing a man of whom you knew nothing and who knew nothing of you said to you suddenly, at a tea-fight: "This room is more like a J[unior] C[ommon] R[oom] than a lady's drawing room!" You might work out a great deal about his character, tastes, and past. Of course the Reader is not a detective all through; but he is that instinctively and unwittingly, to the measure of his knowledges, as soon as he takes up a Short Story. So that, my dear Watson. . . .

However we will talk about these things one day.

Ref. what probably interests you more: American publication: If I can get together a sufficient batch of the work of British youth to make an impressive collection I will stick *Felicity Corner* [*sic*] into it and send it to the American Magazine in which I am interested; but I have not got enough yet to make a start. Do you happen to know—or know of—[A. E.] Coppard? He seems to me to be pretty good; I'd like to get to know him.

Yrs.,

By the bye: Have you got a copy of Mrs. Williams Ellis' book on

POtry? She very kindly asked me to get it and read it! If you could lend it me it would save me 7/6. If you haven't it would you ask your bookseller to send it me with acct. which shall be promptly settled? I have no bookseller of my own.

To Edgar Jepson

My dear Jepson;

Coopers
Bedham, Sussex
15/8/22

We're both much concerned to hear of the illness of your daughter. Which daughter is it and what is the illness? Do let us know. And would convalescence be at all likely to be helped by her coming down here: because if it would that is really what this house exists for. I needn't assure you that I take the liveliest interest in the healths and achievements of all your children whom I must have known all, since they were about two or less.

Other matters: *Ulysses* we shall no doubt differ about till the end of the chapter; personally I'm quite content to leave to Joyce the leading novelist-ship of this country, think he deserves the position, and hope it will profit him.

Ref. *My own publication in this country*. My quite firm resolution is to have nothing to do with any publisher who will not take up my work for good. America seems ready to provide that, Great Britain does not so I see no prospect of publishing any more in Great Britain since there is not in these islands any periodical at all that would publish me or in which I could contemplate with equanimity being published. In America there are ten or a dozen. Obviously, one does not stick to one's even firmest resolutions and if any English publisher approached me on bended knee and asked for the privilege of publishing the novel[1] which I have in my drawer beneath this machine, and offered a large lump sum down for that privilege I should probably succumb to the temptation. But I see little likelihood of that occurrence. You see, I have written four or three—I am not sure which—books that ought to be "classics" and from which I ought to draw a comfortable if small provision for my approaching old age. They are all out of print and unlikely to be re-published. I *want* to

[1] Probably *The Marsden Case*.

force the hand of some publisher to the extent of getting him to
republish those books and to keep them on the market—and to
go on publishing whatever I write, on equitable terms which are
not difficult of working out. I probably shan't succeed in so forcing
the hand of any publisher: if I can't I can't help it and I seem
to be able to make just enough out of America to scrape along.
If I've any admirers in this country—of which I discover no
trace whatever!—they can go to the trouble of procuring copies
of my new books from the U. S. A. If they can't they are hardly
worth counting as my admirers. That naturally does not apply
to yourself who may rely on being the sole recipient of certain
Presentation Copies.

Forgive this elaborate self-revelation: you rather asked for it,
you know.

Ref. *South Lodge*. I am afraid that what you suggest is impossible. If you will look at the last—not the current—Saturday
Review you will see one quite sufficient reason why you should
not even have suggested it. For it is really too much to expect
the very mildest of men to aid in sharpening a pen whose sole
occupation is the describing of himself as, let us say, maquereau.
There is such a thing as trying a horse too high.[2]

There are of course many other reasons, now, against any such
course and those I leave to your perspicacity to divine for I am
finally determined—and from *this* determination I don't think I
shall draw back—never to speak a word on these subjects. One's
friends must accept one's actions and divine the justifications for
those actions—or one must do without friends.

Again: forgive this rather full-dressed style for, again, you
ask for it: I really do try to avoid mentioning these subjects to
anyone.

Do let us know about the daughter!

Esther Julia flourishes, the centre of a perfect cloud of other
babies whom she flaxenly dominates, like a monstrous Germania
amongst the Nations. At the moment the sun shines.

All sorts of compliments to the Family.   Yours,

[2] Violet Hunt published in *The Saturday Review*, cxxiv (August 5, 1922), 222-
223, a sketch called "Read, Mark . . ." which was designed to ridicule both
Elsie Hueffer and Ford under the thinnest of disguises.

To Anthony Bertram

Coopers
Bedham, Sussex
22/8/22

My dear Bertram,

A note to say that we shall expect you, Hussey, and, if possible, Coppard for the weekend Friday the 8/9/22 to Monday the 11th; one of you must sleep in this hut, the scene of great labours.

Thanks very much for Mrs. Williams Ellis' book which I will return to you in a fortnight or so unless you want it before. It is amiable, fanciful, and inaccurate, all of which, no doubt, it set out to be. It suffers from lack of standards and indignations. People think that you can write criticisms without these, but you can't really—or only English Criticism, which blows hot-and-cold, or rather tepid-and-lukewarm, all the time. Still it isn't so bad!

I hope I haven't demolished Hussey with my—quite foreignly! —heated denunciation of his style; but I don't think I have because I see him in the *Saturday* [*Review*]. That is an amazing journal! Present company always excepted, it seems to be written by lunatics in their sleep. . . . *Britain awake, bared for battle, blows*! But maybe you missed that. The only answer seems to be: Cheerio!

Yours,

To Anthony Bertram

Coopers
24/10/22

Dear Bertram,

Do be an angel and order those bulbs from Telkamps: I would not worry you, if it were not just across the way from you. 200 Darwin tulips. I cannot still remember the number or I would write myself—it must have been either 37-8 or 57-8.

Your [essay on] Boxing in the Spectator is quite good; it might have been a bit longer, but I daresay you were tired of the subject!

Would you, by the bye, care to have the loan of this machine for the period of your stay in France? I am rather afraid of the damp here for it, and it struck me that you might be convenienced by having two machines in your literarily teeming house. Besides, one can write a good deal faster on a large instrument.

I am still writing at that immense poem: you will have to send a lorry down for the ms!

Yrs.,

We sold Anna [a prize pig] last Thursday to T. Dallyn, son-in-law of Mrs. Meynell! So she remains in a literary family!

To Edgar Jepson

Hotel de Blois
Paris VI
25/11/22

My dear Jepson:

I'd be glad if you'd let me have a line here just to say how you all are. Someone—a young fellow I met at your house, but I don't know his name—told me the other day that your daughter was quite well again. I needn't say how much I hope that's true or how much satisfaction it would give us if it were!

We have been here about a week; shall be stopping till the middle of next month & are then going to the Riviera near Nice, till mid-spring. The lowness of the franc makes this just possible even to persons of our exiguous means!

I signed just yesterday a contract with Duckworth to take over all my work, future, present & past as the copyrights revert to me. This is what I have been waiting for all these years, so I am rather pleased—& you will yet see my next book in an English frock. I have also just finished an immense Poem[1]—3,000 lines or more!—wh. is to be serialised in [Harold] Monro's *Chapbook*! & afterwards to be published with illustrations by Paul Nash.[2] It will, I fancy, annoy quite a number of people.

Do you suppose by the bye that Mr. Dark[3] would like a lightish article or two about French literary life? If you happened to see him you might suggest it—tho' perhaps you don't see him? I suffer

[1] *Mister Bosphorus and the Muses.*

[2] Serialization was begun in *The Chapbook* in May, 1923, but Monro's miscellany expired with the next issue. Six months later Duckworth published a handsome edition with Paul Nash's illustrations under the title *Mister Bosphorus and the Muses, or a Short History of Poetry in Britain: Variety Entertainment in Four Acts.*

[3] Sidney Dark, editor of *John O'London's Weekly.*

from a constitutional disability to write letters to editors suggesting articles or I wouldn't even think of bothering you.

Paris I find, personally, rather fatiguing: but the rest of my small caravan trots around to Museums, parks, parties & so on with great enthusiasm & vigour, Esther Julia having developed such a passion for motor cars that, if one draws up on the sidewalk near her, she bolts into it before the occupants can get out.

Ezra [Pound] is here, going very strong; [James] Joyce going rather weak; my brother Oliver enormously fat & prosperous; but there is very little French stuff of much value coming out, & Proust's death has cast an extraordinary gloom on literary parties— tho he was pretty generally disliked personally. I just missed seeing him & had to content myself with solemnly attending his funeral, which was a tremendous affair, Stella being the only person in the church who did not shake hands with the next of kin. But her shyness made her bolt out of a back door whereat the venerable Suisse nearly wept.

All sorts of good wishes to your household.
Yours,

To Anthony Bertram

Villa des Oliviers
St. Jean Cap Ferrat
20/1/23

My dear Bertram,

How are you all? Suppose you write me a nice gossipy letter recounting the fate of all les Jeunes from Allan Porter to anyone else!

I hope all your fortunes are greatly on the rise; if not, the best thing to do would be to come & live somewhere in this neighbourhood where you can live well for about two pence a week— say 15/—(not just here which *is* rather expensive—but a mile or so back in the mountains).

This is a comic place: we have the Duke of Connaught on one side of us, & the Rothschilds next door & the Louis Mountbattens with all the wealth of Cassell just above us & all the divorcing duchesses, Westminsters & Marlboroughs in rows along the water's edge below; & white marble & palm trees & Ricketts' blue sea & Monte Carlo & its vices & splendours ten minutes away & Claire de Pratz—the lady about whom your Mr. Armson was groaning—

comes in & cooks omelettes for us & Stella is painting pictures for all the world like the posters of the P[aris]-L[yons]-M[éditerrannée Railway] & I can't write at all.

Anyhow God bless you & Hussey to whom present my respects: I hope both the N[ational] G[allery] & the N[ational] P[ortrait] G[allery] are going strong.

Yrs.,

To Harold Monro

St. Jean Cap Ferrat
Feast of St. Veronica
[March, 1923]

Dear Monro:

What an admirable number of the *Chapbook*.[1] I really must congratulate you: I believe it's the best number of any periodical I've ever seen. You're gradually getting together a [illegible] that ought to have a real effect on Literature—with the largest of L's. At any rate in this number there isn't anything that's not interesting. And there's a sort of homogeneity of tone!

I wish you'd tell S[acheverell] Sitwell how much I admire his *Bolsover Castle*. It's the Real Impressionism applied to history: a truly beautiful thing. I think it ought not to have been printed without capitals at the beginnings of lines. I know what is aimed at. But Prose is too strong to make that sort of attack upon it. The sentence is the sentence & the paragraph the paragraph. Verse would make a mistake if it abandoned the constructional licence that capitals give it & tried to get Prose effects, at least as I see it. We ought really to have a Congress to settle points of printing like that. It is quite right for Mr. Aldington to throw his handful of shrapnel-substantives at people's faces. It's quite a good dodge in that case—but Sitwell's is too good poetry to be risked in experiments. However, perhaps this bores you.

On the 20th of last month I wrote to you with several queries & also a cheque. I hope you get them. You might answer the queries. I have got the garden here quite tidy & spic & span by now & have tried several experiments with manures. I shan't put anything in until I hear whether you are coming.

[1] See no. 35, March, 1923. It includes, in addition to Sacheverell Sitwell's poetry, work by Thomas Hardy, Robert Graves, Richard Aldington, Iris Barry, and others.

The proper time for planting here is *August*. I will fix up a scheme for this before we leave & will submit it to you. If you approve I will tell the gardener what to do. He's quite a decent fellow really. The great difficulty here is manure, the cost of the carriage being so high. But manure you must have, the soil being so very poor.

I have thought out this scheme with the aid of local dignitaries:

The bottom of yr. garden is only a very few feet above the road. Now you have a statutory right with access to the road over the next door field & Cremonini Aldo says he could make you a gate & path down to the road for a very few francs—he said 25 frs! Shall I get him to send you an estimate for this? It wd. make a tremendous difference to the "property"—for one ruins oneself in pourboires getting the mere necessities of life brought up here by the path.

You might answer these questions.

Yrs,

Not having heard from you to the contrary we propose to stop at any rate till April 20th. Stella has gone to Italy & won't be back till after the 20th March. I *think* we'd be ready to take this over from you from next November or so if that wd. suit you: but she really arranges these things.

By the bye: I gave that sovereign [?] to Leonini [?] as being your representative.

To Edgar Jepson

Hotel Terminus
Tarascon
8/5/23

Dear Jepson:

I'm sending you a copy of the *Marsden Case*.[1] I hope you'll like it. I believe that, as 'treatment,' it's the best thing I've done—but the subject is not a very good one, though it's one that has haunted me certainly ever since I was eighteen on and off. It's the story of [W. R. S.] Ralston, the first translator of Turgenev—a man I liked very much. At any rate, that suggested it to me.

Drop me a line, if you can, by return to say how you all are—to above address. It's too tropically hot here to stop for more than

[1] Dedicated to Edgar Jepson.

a day or two. I don't quite know where we are going next. Stella is in Paris having some lessons (the cover is by her) & seeing the Salons for a day or two—then we shall probably meet in one of the foothills of the Alps which are quite close to here & where I have heard of a cheapish pension. Living is really so relatively cheap in France & I find I can work so well—& Stella too—that I shouldn't wonder if we settled down here for good. Besides, the French make much of me—which at my age is inspiriting.

Take a look at my serial in this Chapbook:[2] it gets quite amusing later on & should annoy a number of people, if they can understand it.

I hope all your family flourish. Give them my love!

Yrs. always,

Excuse grease on this paper. E[sther] J[ulia] has been wiping the butter knife on my blotter.

Oh: wd. you make a note (ref. accuracies) that I am quite aware the orthodox Psychotherapeutics don't believe in Remorse Complexes? Some Reviewer might drop on that. I *mean* my Novelist "I" to be inaccurate now & then—as in that case or as when he represents the Common Sergeant as charging the Grand Jury at the Old Bailey.

If you don't write by return, address to

Hotel de Blois
50 Rue Vavin
Paris VIe

& Stella will forward.

E. J. is growing like a giraffe, but learns no French at all.

To Anthony Bertram

Grand Hotel Poste
St. Agrève, Ardèche
4/7/23

Dear Bertram:

Glad to hear from you again. I thought you must have eloped with la belle au bois dormant or have come to some other romantic end. I should have written myself except that I thought I had lost

---

[2] Act I, Scene 1 of *Mister Bosphorus and the Muses.*

your XXI address. However, in going to put yr. latest in the address book I found I had duly, in my methodical way, already inscribed your penultimate one!

We shall be in Paris in October & delighted to see you there. I daresay you know all about Paris cheapnesses & if you don't Stella is an expert in the inexpensive & will take you under her wing. It's a pity you can't come here for romanticisms in Pubs—every house without exception in Agrève being a cafe, as well as bonnet-maker, clockmaker, mid-wife, & the rest. Still Paris too has its estaminets. . . .

This however is only a note. I can't consider "subjects" quickly & write about 'em—wh. is what you probably want—because I am in the middle of "subjects" of my own wh. exhaust all the small brain I've got. But—règle générale—I think it's more practical to begin with an action or incident & spin your subject round it than to begin with a "subject" and work architectonics out of it. Every incident—anecdote—has of necessity subject, atmosphere, & the inevitabilities of character behind it. I believe that is really the sound way to elaborate a novel; think of an anecdote: double it: halve it: add three . . . & so on as we used to set problems at school. But there's no universal formula: only that's the least *boring* way, for oneself!

I will write to Duckworth *tomorrow*: so on the day after you get this go & ask for him. He's quite accessible; if he's not in ask for Millsted who's a good fellow. But have your scheme—size, no. of pages, price all out and dried before you go & some prints as well. I daresay they will find it attractive. If you play your cards well, hinting ingenuously, Duckworth will probably give you some of my books for nothing. He publishes several.

Oh: I hear that Bertram Higgins is wandering over France exclaiming faintly, "Ford! Ford!" in the effort to find me & getting shown into garages—for there is a Ford more famous! Drop him a post card, will you—I don't know his address—& tell him I'd be delighted to see him here. It is very cheap, working out at less than 4/- a day all told. The junction to aim for is St. Etienne on the P. L. M., dept of Haute Loire: after that there's a sort of train. It's on the roof of the Cevennes about the same height as the top of Snowden.

You don't say what you are doing beyond "subjects." I suppose still at the N. P. G. & *Spectator*? When does yr. *Nash* book come out? Yes; I like his woodcuts ever so well. All sorts of good wishes from us both.

Yrs.,

To A. E. Coppard

65, Boulevard Arago
Paris XIII

My dear Coppard;

28/9/23

Have you a short story—or two, or three—that you could let me have for a Review that I myself am going to edit from this city & to publish in New York & London;[1] so there won't be any doubt as to publication or payment, the latter fairly miserable to begin with, though getting better if the Review paid? So that the real advantage to you—as to others of a struggling world—is simply that here is going to be a periodical in which you can print work that the more popular periodicals won't print & mop up a very little money that you otherwise wouldn't get.

It isn't an exaggeration to say that I've started this review with you in mind as I started the *English Review* to publish stuff of Hardy's that other periodicals wouldn't publish. I've a great admiration for your work & though I hope you can serialise all you write I imagine, this sad world being what it is, that you may have some that you can't.

I may say that I *prefer* not to have sexually esoteric, psychoanalytic, mystic or officially ethical matter but don't bar any of them obstinately—& if you hadn't short stories available I'd be just as glad of "essays" or any other form.

Let me have an answer at your early convenience & believe that I'm always

Yrs. very cordially,

Later in haste: the flat rate of pay proposed by my proprietors,

---

[1] The first issue of *The Transatlantic Review* appeared in January, 1924, with Pound, Conrad, Ford, and E. E. Cummings among the contributors. Ernest Hemingway acted for a time as associate editor. Before the magazine expired in December, 1924, it had printed a portion of Gertrude Stein's *The Making of Americans*, Hemingway's "The Doctor and the Doctor's Wife," and work by Paul Valéry, James Joyce, Tristan Tzara, William Carlos Williams, John Dos Passos, and Djuna Barnes.

the Société Anonyme de Publications Etrangeres is 30 frs per page = 100 frs per 1000 (rather aver 25/- at present rates but the franc may rise). If you wrote & advised me I cd. probably squeeze a little more. The trouble is that you can get almost *any* French contribution at above rates & I am going to publish both French & English.

To Edgar Jepson

65 Boulevard Arago
Paris XIII
October 14th, 1923

My dear Jepson:—

I am starting a Review here with the above title which will be published also in London and New York and, as you were one of the regular contributors to the old English Review, I should very much like to inscribe your name on the list of those who are going to write for me now.

I hope that you are well.

Yours very truly,

P.S. We have had, as is always the case, to change our name at the last moment. Hence the heading.[1]

I'll write a proper letter in a day or two. I'm just rushed out of existence. All sorts of good wishes.

This is only a circular, tho' it tries very hard not to look like one; so you see I'm at it again—but thank goodness with no financial responsibility of my own. If you'd send me something rude about literary London I'd love it. I hope you're ever so well. For once in a way we're flourishing. I have fixed up a contract in U. S. A. for all my work as in England—and though I shan't make a penny out of this thing & work myself to death on top of it—it pleases me. Stella also has three pictures in the Salon d'Automne and plenty of commissions for portraits and that pleases me more than anything else.

[1] "The Paris Review" is crossed out and "The Transatlantic Review" inserted.

14 October 1923

To H. G. Wells

65 Boulevard Arago
Paris XIII
14/10/23

Dear Wells,

I am much touched by your letter.

Thank you: I am as happy as it is decent to be: very fit and with all the success that anyone as unambitious as I could want. I've got all the work for the rest of my life commissioned and though this Review gives me plenty to do and no pay, thank Goodness I've this time no financial responsibility.

We shall probably sell our small place in Sussex and with the proceeds buy a small house here and one almost smaller in Provence. It is egotistic to write in this strain but after many years of great anxiety and strain things have rather suddenly gone all right together. I've got over the nerve tangle of the war and feel able at last really to write again—which I never thought I should do. Also Mrs. Ford—whom you met at dinner—has got all her pictures hung in the Salon d'Automne and has more commissions for portraits than she has time for; (She hasn't *much* time). This really pleases me as I've backed her gift for a long time against more than sufficient opposition. I ought to write unberufen—but it is pleasant for once in a way to let out a yawp of satisfaction on a Sunday night. . . . Let me reciprocate your wishes for happiness —those for success I needn't. I suppose you are the most famous writer in the world. I daresay, all in all, the most famous man. And believe me nothing gives me greater pleasure than the thought. So there we are; in the most striking lines of a poem[1] I am just publishing—which will annoy more people than anything I've yet written:

> The Gods to each ascribe a diff'ring lot:
> Some rest on snowy bosoms—some do not.

Yrs,

[1] *Mister Bosphorus and the Muses.*

To A. E. Coppard

65 Boulevard Arago
Paris XIII
15/X/23

My dear Coppard:

Thanks for your kind letter. (By the bye, if you continue to call me Capt. I shall, since I can't hit you from this distance, certainly ill-wish you). You'd help me, between ourselves, if you'd write me a much more violent letter for exhibition to my proprietors, on the question of the three copyrights and pay in general. In addressing that you may use Captain. They are obtuse people. And—again between ourselves—I can in special cases, of which yours is one, squeeze about fifteen pounds, more or less, according to the state of the franc out of them for a short story, however short, or however long, or in violently special cases—of which yours again would be one—it might run to 1500 francs, which at the moment is twenty guineas, but in that case it would have to be a very violent letter you wrote me. And of course I want your vers libre: the sooner you send it the better.

As for Martin Armstrong: I have by me a story of his that I don't like *much*. I *might* print it—but it is extremely over-written and, although in the case of quite young men I am ready to accept any extravagance, the extravagance I least like is over-writing. Ask him to send me something else.

I am doing this beastly thing quite without pay myself in the hope of creating a better market for the sort of stuff one likes. Of course if the Review went the prices paid would go up and we should all be rich.

Why not come and stay a day or two with us. We should make you thoroughly uncomfortable—but Paris vaut bien une messe and we could have a good talk. Mrs. Ford asks to be remembered. Esther Julia on seeing a fig-leafed statue in the Luxembourg Gardens yesterday exclaimed: "Oh, the naughty man: he's stolen a pretty flower to keep his tummy warm." Yours always,

To Joseph Conrad
65 Boulevard Arago
Paris XIII
November 8th, 1923

Dear Conrad,

I have not properly answered your last letter, principally because I have been laid up for some little time—like everyone else in Paris—with an attack of something resembling influenza, which has put everything with which I am concerned back a fortnight or so and with normal printers' delays in this city to boot—will mean that I shan't get my first number out till the beginning of next month. This seems to be usual here, but it is still annoying.

In the meantime Dent's branch here[1] have approached the review with a proposal that I do not think is very workable with reference to your collected edition. But what follows seems to be more possible. They are, that is to say, anxious, as my first number is going to be very widely distributed in Europe & America, that I should include in it a sort of Conrad supplement of appreciations and the like. I haven't got these and I could not get them in time from anyone worth mentioning. But it occurs to me that what would please me very much would be this: You remember that, shortly before the *English Review* was started we wrote in collaboration a short story called the *Story of a Crime*. This you gave over to me and it was published in the first number of the *English Review* under a pseudonym principally because as we were both writing in that number it would have seemed as it were tautological to publish a collaboration.[2] I have looked at it again and it seems to me a pretty good piece of work. I had forgotten about it till the other day when Dents asked me if I could not print a page or two of ROMANCE with indications of which passages were your and which were my writing. They say they have received thousands of requests for this. I could do this as I have still a good deal of the original m. s. and all the proofs with corrections, but I could not reasonably print more than a page or so and I do not know how you would like the idea. But I think

---

[1] J. M. Dent & Sons of London published the collected Conrad.

[2] Under the pseudonym Baron Ignatz von Aschendrof, "The Nature of a Crime" appeared in the fifth and sixth numbers of *The English Review*. It was reprinted in the first two issues of *The Transatlantic Review* and then in boards by Duckworth and Company (London, 1924).

that to reprint the *Story of a Crime* as a collaboration with a note
to the effect that it is old & was published under a pseudonym
would have a certain literary and sentimental interest and I should
very much like to do it. In that case I'd propose to pay ourselves
fifty pounds for it and to hand over twenty-five to you, and I
would add about three pages of ROMANCE analysis in my *chroniques*
in which it would quite legitimately appear. Of course I'd submit it to you before publication. The copyrights of all the original
matter that appeared in the *English Review* are mine by agreement
with the present company so there would be no difficulty about
that. I hope you will agree, for it would give me real pleasure:
in that case my original proposal would stand over till you can
write something at your easy convenience. Indeed, if it would
amuse you, a little later I would come over to a near-by pub &
see if we couldn't again evolve something like the original passage of the *Mirror [of the Sea]*.[3]

I am telling Duckworth to send you a copy of my new book:
it might amuse you.[4] One has always a temptation to write a Dun-
ciad once in one's life and for once I've yielded to the temptation,
though I don't suppose the intention will be obvious to the general
reader.

I'm typing this myself from a table across my bed, so its typographical errors are not attributable to my admirable staff.

Yours,

To H. G. Wells

Dear Wells,

65 Boulevard Arago (13ᵉᵐᵉ)
15th November 1923

I am rather in a predicament as to an item of my first number
of the TRANSATLANTIC REVIEW which ought to be out but has been
hung up by impossible printers.

Conrad, Thomas Hardy and T. S. Eliot have all written notes of
a sort of commendation of the REVIEW as an enterprise and I don't

[3] In *Joseph Conrad: A Personal Remembrance*, Ford writes: "Indeed a great
part of his *Mirror of the Sea* was just his talk which [I] took down in a shorthand of [my] own extemporising, recalling to Conrad who was then in a state
of great depression, various passages of his own relating."
[4] *Mister Bosphorus and the Muses.*

want either not to ask you to do something of the sort—or to put you to the trouble of being asked and either consenting or refusing. Naturally I'm most anxious to have a note from you—not eulogising me, but applauding the attempt to help youth—but on the other hand I hate to be a nuisance. So in that tentative way I leave it to you.

I never expected to be connected with a financial success but, by way of advertisements alone, this really looks like being one. We have more than paid for the first number by the Paris advertisements alone and if the New York and London advertisements are on anything like the same rate I ought to be able to buy the moon in the shape of contributions.

The first number will be pretty good anyhow—except for the fact that a serial of my own, for motives of economy, takes the place of TONO BUNGAY, it's better than the first number of the ENGLISH [REVIEW].

If you would write a note you might do it by return as near as you can.   Yours,

To Martin Armstrong[1]

Dear Mr. Armstrong:

65 Boulevard Arago
Paris XIII
November 29th, 1923

As far as the Spectator itself is concerned I have said all I am going to say about the collected edition of Conrad. They can deduct from my cheque the amount necessary for them to re-purchase the volumes they sent me and there the matter ends. They did not write to me for an article on Mr. Conrad but for an article on this edition and I do not even know which volumes they sent me as Messrs. Dent have also sent me a number of volumes for review in this organ.

But on the public aspect of this matter there is a good deal more to be said. Books are sent out by publishers with the consent of authors for review. It is understood by the author that the paper sends those books to reviewers who in order to add to their insufficient pay are at liberty to sell these copies to booksellers. To this, as an author, one has no objection. But if the books are to be

---

[1] Poet, novelist, and associate literary editor of *The Spectator*.

retained by the papers I for one should have the very strongest objection to my books being sent to certain papers at all. Why should I put money into the hands of capitalists who are nothing to me? Put it in this way:

Of my writing this year, the Spectator has had:

THE MARSDEN CASE	7/6
WOMEN & MEN	8/6
ROMANCE (1/2)	5/3
INHERITORS	5/3
	———
	26/6

They have received or will receive

MR. BOSPHORUS	10/6
	———
	37/

For all these I have received in the way of notices three, or possibly four, rather sniffy lines of review of the MARSDEN CASE. In the course of my life the Spectator has received upwards of thirty pounds worth of books of my writing and has never paid the least attention to any one of my books with the exception of THUS TO REVISIT. This is the business way of putting it. As I have said, I don't in the least object to this if a hard-up reviewer is to benefit; but I do object very strongly if the proprietors of a paper are to. It is not a matter which touches me personally. I do not imagine that I have ever reviewed more books than you could number on the fingers of your hand and then only to oblige some one or other —and I certainly never will review another book to oblige any one. As for your saying that my non-return of the books, when I am perfectly ready to have the price deducted from that paid for the article, will damage either you or [Allan] Porter I can only say that the threat is a monstrous one—since neither you nor Porter can possibly control my actions. I wrote the article to oblige Mrs. Williams Ellis because I promised her a long time ago that I would review something for the Spectator; and neither you nor Porter had anything to do with the matter.

On another point: I have a story of yours by me that interests me a good deal. I think I should very likely publish it when a

number comes along that it would fit into; but I believe you wrote
it some time ago and one changes towards one's work sometimes
with some rapidity. As a story it is attractive but it strikes me as
being too "written." You may reply that my own work is not
"written" enough; but I believe that in the end you will see that
the weight of writing makes toward simplicity. Shall I send it
back to you and let you look it over again? In the numbers that
I have so far planned it would probably be rather overshadowed,
so, if you cared to spend time over it you might. [. . . . .]

I have been trying to imply that I am not irritated with you personally, if that interests you, but I don't seem to have got it out.

Yours faithfully,

To A. E. Coppard

65 Boulevard Arago
Paris XIII
1/xii/23

My dear Coppard,

How delightful! But of course you will stop more than a day—
if you can put up with moderately primitive housing and a very
warm welcome. For Paris cannot be seen in a day. Neither can the
Fords.

I was just going to forward a cheque to you; but as it is in
francs and you would lose on the exchange in London I propose
to keep it till you arrive. I don't know if you have yet taken your
ticket, but I believe you save a great deal if you take it no further
than Paris and then from Paris to Italy; indeed, if you feel really
active enough it is even cheaper to take a ticket only to Calais and
then to Paris. There is of course rather a crowd by the South-going
trains at this time of year, but by going very early to the station
you can generally get a seat and we can help you in most of these
dodges.

If you let us know the route you are coming by and the time
of the train we will either meet you or have you met by Bunting[1]
—a dark youth with round spectacles, in a large Trilby hat and a
blue trench coat with belt who shall hold up a copy of the TRANS-

---

[1] Basil Bunting, a young poet, one of Ford's assistants at *The Transatlantic
Review*.

ATLANTIC REVIEW towards passengers arriving at the barrier and smile.

I take these precautions because one usually forgets them until just after the past proper moment, but of course I will come myself if I at all can.

Till then, Yrs. always,

To James Joyce

29, Quai d'Anjou
Paris
29/7/24

My dear Joyce,

I am afraid the news about [John] Quinn[1] is about as bad as can be. I saw him once in New York, on the day after my arrival, but after that he was steadily under morphia, and I was told that his state was very precarious indeed. I have since received a wire from Mrs. Foster to say that he was even worse than when I left New York . . . but of course miraculous recoveries do take place.

As far as I am personally concerned my trip to America was very successful indeed; as regards the affairs of the review Quinn's illness has naturally interfered a good deal and I am rather in doubt as to whether I shall continue it at all. The work connected with it is naturally very great and the expenses, though not enormous, fall entirely on myself, as they have for months past. Quinn in fact has really been incapable of attending to business at all since January when this thing struck him, which really explains why he answered neither your call nor my letters.

I am very glad you are through with your operation: it must be a long drag to have one hanging over the head. I feel quite confident that it will be successful—why I should be I don't know; but as these irrational convictions have some of the quality of what the Yankees call a hunch, I communicate it for what it is worth.

The Straters sent a great many good wishes to you and Mrs. Joyce, and I take the opportunity of including mine with them.

Yours,

[1] A New York lawyer and patron of the arts, one of the major backers of *The Transatlantic Review*.

To Gertrude Stein

Private.   29, Quai d'Anjou, Paris
Dear Miss Stein,   Sept. 18, 1924

I have just got your letter of the fifteenth. I am very sorry that you have had to wait for your cheque. The business management has passed, to my immense relief, out of my hands into those of a capitalist who is a little slow in parting with money but who *will* part immediately.[1] I have had immense trouble in re-starting the review and it is only just beginning to run smoothly again, but, at any rate it runs, looks as if eventually it might really pay. That at any rate makes your shares in it for the time safe. If it stopped I should of course buy those of you at par.[2]

As for the novel: Hemingway, when he first handed me your manuscript, gave me the impression that it was a long-short story that would run for about three numbers.[3] It was probably my fault that I had that impression. Had I known that it was to be a long novel I should have delayed publishing it until my own serial had run out and should then have offered you a lump sum as serials are not accounted so valuable as shorter matter. I do not get paid for my own serial at all, neither does Pound for his.

Hemingway now says that you have been offered what he calls real money by the *Criterion* for the rest of *The Making of Americans* so I really do not know how to deal with the situation. Apparently your book consists of three or four novels. In that case, if the *Criterion* really is offering you real money I suppose you could let them have the second novel and rook them all that you possibly can. I should be very sorry to lose you, but I was never the one to stand in a contributor's way: indeed I really exist as a sort of half-way house between nonpublishable youth and real money—a sort of green baize swing door that every one kicks both on entering and on leaving.

---

[1] Ford realized in April that the *Review* was having financial difficulties. When John Quinn died in July, disaster threatened until Ernest Hemingway persuaded Krebs Friend to invest.

[2] Gertrude Stein had been one of the original shareholders.

[3] *The Making of Americans* first appeared in the April issue and continued through the last, December, 1924.

You might let me know your private reflections on the above in a letter marked *private*. And would you, in any case, let me know the full length of your book and its respective parts? I will then stir up the capitalist to make an offer which you can compare with the *Criterion's*.

I would like you to understand that owing to Quinn's defection and then death I have had an immense amount of trouble with the review and have lost what is, for me, a good deal of money: over frs 100,000 in all. Otherwise I would just put my hand in my pocket and pay you whatever the *Criterion* offered. As it is, until I can get a book of my own finished, which with all these interruptions is a matter of some difficulty, I am simply not in a position to do so.

With kind regards, I'm yours

Very faithfully

To Monroe Wheeler[1]

Private & Confidential
Dear Mr. Wheeler,

The Transatlantic Review
29, Quai d'Anjou, Paris
24/11/24

Mr. Friend has handed to me a letter from Mr. Kitchell to him dated the 12th inst. Will you please—ref this—observe the following two points? Mr. Kitchell says he is convinced that Mr. Seltzer is an honest man and has made no money on the review. That is perfectly immaterial. The point is that Mr. Seltzer owes us money that he will not pay.[2] [. . . . .]

The second point is this: I will not continue to edit the review if Mr. Seltzer goes on publishing it. Absolutely not. Mr. Seltzer owes me money on my books which I see no chance of getting. I pay for the review out of the earnings of my books, the money paid by other people being a mere flea-bite compared with what I have spent on it. If then Mr. Seltzer does not pay for my books

[1] American art student and critic, co-founder in 1930 of Harrison of Paris.
[2] Krebs Friend had written from Paris to W. C. Kitchell in New York, directing him to collect the money Thomas Seltzer owed *The Transatlantic Review* for the 800 copies he distributed each month in the United States. Seltzer had published *Some Do Not* in October, 1924. The rest of the Tietjens tetralogy appeared in America under the imprint of Albert & Charles Boni.

and does not pay for the review, I cannot continue it. That should be self-evident. If Mr. Kitchell likes to continue the publication after the next (European *December*, U. S. A. *January*) number I should be pleased to let him do it supposing I decide to continue the review at all, but in no case shall Seltzer.

A third point is this: Mr. Kitchell's letter says: *Mrs. Putnam will certainly help substantially and we may all be able to interest people to advance more substantial amounts.* Will you please find out and cable me exactly the amount this means? We need exactly £1,000 to go on here for another six months. If your people can find two thirds of this I am ready to go on and find the other third. £1,000 equals 4,500 dollars, so that the sum wanted from your side is $3,000 which does not seem a considerable sum for the proud American continent to find. I have already found nearly frs 120,000 personally and as it has mostly gone to boosting American writers it is time your side took a hand. Anyhow, there it is.

I hope you flourish; I'm infinitely obliged to you.

                                                        In haste,

To Monroe Wheeler   16 Rue Denfert-Rochereau
                                                        Paris
My dear Wheeler,   1/1/25

Many thanks for your sympathetic letter of the 7th December; I am sorry you have had so much trouble for nothing. It cannot at the moment be helped.

I must for the moment take some time off to do some writing of my own as I cannot afford to go on paying for the *Transatlantic Review* and doing no work. All that talk of hundreds of thousands of dollars being needed to run a magazine is just swank. I have spent just £1200.00.00 on the review, Quinn about £300.00.00 and Mr. Friend a little less and it would have paid its way quite well [. . . . .] if I had [had] any sort of capable business assistance at the start. The costs of production here are so very small. In the meantime it did what it set out to do—give a leg up to a number of young writers. I shall re-start it as soon as I have finished the novel I am writing, but I suppose I shall have to come to New York to make arrangements about publishing before I do—or else drop the American branch altogether. Mr. Friend's friend, Mr. Killick, is it?, seems quite to have misunderstood Mr. Seltzer's accounts. Mr. Seltzer according to the agreement was entitled to charge us nothing but binding. Of course if Mr. Seltzer charges us for his female-typist's permanent Marcel waving and his own shaves, we owe him money. . . . But that seems an extravagant theory. However, I will come to New York and attend to Mr. Seltzer myself quite shortly.

You say you will be coming to Paris in February. Let me know the exact dates so that we need not cross on the broad Atlantic and in the meantime thanks for liking my books. It helps one to be liked by the right people and I hope to do some more before I die.

Tell [Glenway] Wescott that I admire the *Apple of the Eye* quite a lot. I have lent it to someone, or someone has stolen it from my shelves, or I would write to him about some passages that I marked in it. However, perhaps he too will be coming to Europe and we can have a talk. [. . . . .]

Yours always,

Mrs. Ford asks to be remembered to you.

To R. A. Scott-James

GUERMANTES près Lagny
Seine et Marne, France
3d Feb 1925

My dear Scott-James,

Your letter dated 4th Sep and announcing your intention of visiting Paris on the 6th of that month has only just reached me so I could not answer it in time to say that we should have been delighted to offer you hospitality—as we should have been.

I should have been inclined to attribute the delay to the eccentric nature of the address which was

16 rue Denfert-Rochereau
GUERMANTES. . . .

However I enclose the envelope which had been thrown away but has been recaptured for your edification. The rue D-R is a street in Paris where we have a flat; this village contains eight cottages of which I have one. Here I write my novels and here I am now desperately writing away at the next, for I cannot write in Paris.

But the delay does not seem to have been caused by the address for, as you will notice, the London postmark bears the date Jan 29th 7:15 p.m. So I suppose that you or someone to whom you confided the task, more likely, simply forgot to post the letter. Indeed, it looks as if you had handed it in to Duckworth's, for the writing of the name is yours, and that of the address obviously some clerk's. It is a great pity, for I should have liked to have seen you. However perhaps you will be coming over again soon. I have not myself been to London since last May and see no prospect of ever going there again.

Thanks for what you say about *Some do not*.[1] It seems to have been pretty well received, but as I do not get reviews and indeed nearly never get an English paper I do not really know. It has done well in America which is much more to the point. It was about time that I cut my notch in that country. Otherwise I am rapidly becoming a French writer.

Anyhow, I am glad to hear from you. I hope you are prospering. Except for grippe and a houseful of people I manage to get a good deal of work done which is at the moment my main preoccupation. If you come over in the spring you must come down here. It is pleasant country of an insignificant sort, not far from Paris and just this side of the devastated zone. Next winter we shall buy a little house in Provence for the winter climate of Paris is too much for my chest and there is no sense in being so far north if one cannot be in Paris itself.

It's not too late to wish you a splendid 1925.   Yours,

To W. H. Thompson*[1]

Dear Mr. Thompson,   5/2/26

I am rather bothered by a matter as to which I should be glad of your advice:

I wrote in collaboration with Conrad two books called *Romance*

---

[1] The first of the Tietjens novels, published by Duckworth in April, 1924. It was highly praised in *The Saturday Review, The Manchester Guardian*, and *The English Review*, but condemned elsewhere.

[1] Ford's solicitor.

and the *Inheritors*. These appeared originally in 1901 and 1903 respectively[2] as collaborated works. At some date which I have been unable to discover, the late Mr. J. B. Pinker (whose son carries on his business under the name of J. B. Pinker and Son) who had been my agent but had ceased so to be, made, without consulting me, an agreement with Messrs Dent and Co of London and Messrs Doubleday Page of New York to publish the two collaborated books in a collected edition of Conrad's works and subsequently in a number of de luxe and other editions. The subsequent editions have perhaps been arranged by the son—at any rate the editions must have been arranged for by J. B. Pinker & Son.

I was not informed of these arrangements and only heard of them through third parties and the press in cuttings after the publication had taken place. It then appeared that these two books had been published without my name as part author on the back and sides of covers, wrappers, and the catalogues of the various editions, the catalogues being very widely circulated. I saw Mr. Eric Pinker, the son, about this and also Conrad himself on the 9th and 10th of May 1924 and they both promised to see that this was remedied, so I then let the matter alone.

To my astonishment I was offered in December last in a Paris bookshop copies of an edition purporting to be the "Gresham Edition" of the collected works of Conrad but which was obviously only a rebinding of Messrs Dent's edition. In this too my name as joint author was omitted from the covers, wrappers, and catalogues of the two books named.

For various reasons which I need not go into I am anxious that this should be stopped. The Gresham Publishing Co refuse any information as to the matter to my Paris agent[3] whom I got to write to them and Messrs Pinker refused any information as to what editions of these books they have made arrangements for; so do Messrs. Dent, as you will see.

I wish to obtain from Messrs Pinker a complete list of all editions of these two books for which they have arranged and specimens of the volumes as well as copies of all agreements they have

[2] Should read "1903 and 1901 respectively."
[3] William A. Bradley became Ford's agent after he left Eric Pinker.

made with the respective publishers and then, if practicable, from the respective publishers accounts of all payments made to Messrs. Pinker on account of these works.

I wish also to have from Messrs Dent and the Gresham Publishing Co an understanding that they will suppress and call in all copies of these works which do not bear my name wherever the author's name is exhibited, the same applying to catalogues and circulars relating to these volumes. I do not wish to, but I am quite prepared to, resort to litigation to ensure these points and, in addition, I wish to receive from Messrs Dent and the Gresham Publishing Co letters of apology for the omission, the said letters to be at my disposal to publish in the Times Literary Supplement and such other English and foreign journals as I shall select.

I should be much obliged if you would give the matter your attention at your convenience. I am asking my Paris Agent, Mr. W. A. Bradley to forward you the correspondence that has passed on the matter since December last.

We have been here about a month and expect to remain here some time longer. Mrs. Ford asks to be reminded to you.

To Gerald Duckworth*

My dear Duckworth,

Toulon, France
9/3/26

Yours of the 23d ult. Ref German Translation of NO MORE PARADES.[1]

I've thought about this a good deal and indeed I've been approached about a German translation before. I don't much like the idea of presenting to the (late) Huns a work that might have the aspect of discrediting England—I mean the political parts of the book. On the other hand, I suppose they can translate fragments without permission if that is what they want. So, after thinking as I have said, a good deal, I have decided to let them have N. M. P. if they will undertake to publish a translation of the one I am doing now—which is rather nasty to the said H's, redressing the balance.[2] So I have told Bradley to write to you

---

[1] The second of the Tietjens novels, published by Duckworth in 1925.
[2] *A Man Could Stand Up*, the third volume of the tetralogy.

about it on those lines; (Bradley handles all my stuff, so I can't not.)

I enclose some American literature that may amuse you. I really do seem to be booming: last Thursday a deputation of American citizens from a liner came over from Nice to shake me by the hand and thank me for existence. I mean my existence, not theirs: yesterday by the same post I had two contracts from Lecture Agencies asking me to lecture—and so on. I suppose I probably shall next winter—and that will kill me. A ten weeks' tour of not less than fifty lectures a month, tour not to extend further than Nebraska!

I suppose all this will re-act favourably on England: or doesn't it make any difference? I suppose not: I suppose nothing ever does.

Why don't you come to Toulon? It's delightful here now and wonderfully gay with the Navy—and cheap because the Navy has not got any money. However, in a week or so we shall move on to Tarascon and go to the bull-fights at Nimes. I am getting on pretty well with my novel. A month's good work will finish it.

Yours always,

To the Editor of The New York *World*[1]

Sir: [November 6, 1926]

In his account of yesterday's meeting of the Joseph Conrad Memorial of the Seamen's Church Institute,[2] your representative lamentably misreports my speech.—It was made before *not* after lunch, too!—He makes me say that Sir John Masefield wrote the first chapter of a work called *Romance*.

This is a terminological inexactitude. What I said—it *was* before lunch!—was that that admirable British poet now visiting these shores wrote the first review of *Romance*.

No one—not Sir John, not the Poet Laureate, not Sir Edmund Gosse, not Sir Herbert G. Wells—(The titles are perhaps only intelligent anticipations: I have been for so long absent from my

[1] See the issue of November 8, 1926, p. 12.
[2] "Masefield Spins Sea Yarn," November 4, 1926, p. 17.

native country.)—no one then of the great galaxy of writers that make England in truth a nest of singing birds: no one of them had any hand in the creation of *Romance*. It was written—where it is splendid—by Joseph Conrad: the rest of it was by,

> Sir, Yr. obedient servant,

To the Editor of The New York *Herald Tribune Books*[1]

51 West 16th Street
February 15, 1927

Dear Sir:

You will perhaps afford me the hospitality of your columns for the following statement:

It has just come to my knowledge that a Mr. [T. J.] Wise, who I understand, is a collector of autographs, is advertising in his catalogue the fact that he is in possession of private letters addressed to myself by the late Mr. Joseph Conrad. I desire to state that I never either sold or authorised the sale of any letter, presentation copy from, or anything in the nature of an autograph or personal memento of, the late Mr. Conrad. I should consider myself disgraced had I ever done so.

It has also just come to my knowledge—with regard to the late Mr. Conrad—that in Messrs. Doubleday Page's edition of a book called *The Nature of a Crime* written by the late Mr. Conrad and myself in collaboration, in an analysis of another book called *Romance* equally written in collaboration by Mr. Conrad and myself, there is a singularly unfortunate misprint. This analysis, which was composed by Mr. Conrad and myself and printed first in "The Transatlantic Review," ascribes certain sentences and fragments of sentences to Mr. Conrad and myself, respectively. This should read, and so reads in Mr. Duckworth's English edition and in "The Transatlantic Review," from the text of which Messrs. Doubleday's edition was reprinted: "Passages in Roman type by Joseph Conrad; passages in italics by F. M. Hueffer."

Messrs. Doubleday's edition states exactly the reverse.

The misprint is all the more singular in that both Mr. Conrad

[1] See the issue of February 20, 1927, p. 18.

and myself corrected the proofs of this work with particular attention, and it is all the more regrettable in that Mr. Conrad attached
particular importance to the additional editorial matter we added
to the book. He says in a letter to me of May 17, 1924:

". . . From the point of view of the book's future and also from
considerations of copyright in the United States, I think each of
us may contribute a few words of introduction over our separate
signatures. The inclosed is my contribution. I hope it will meet
with your approval (I mean as to its being suitable from the point
of view of the public), and that you will find time to say something in that or any other vein.

"If you are too full of work, or do not want the bother, from
any other reason, you may delete the last paragraph and move
my initials up accordingly.

"But I hope you will not. For your contribution of an introduction will not only be valuable *per se* but may influence the fortunes
of the book in a considerable way. After all, this is the last piece
of our joint work that is likely to appear and it seems to me
becoming that we should both be heard on this occasion."

For certain private reasons I thought it might be of advantage
to Conrad if he did not insist on emphasizing at that moment
the fact of his collaboration with myself, and I sent him a copy
of a preface I had written suggesting at the same time that I should
be perfectly willing for him to suppress not only it but the book
itself.

He answered on May 22, 1924, less than three months before his
death, in a letter that I received in New York—to which city it
has returned now a second time, since it lies before me as I write:

"I do not know what may be coming in the nature of (mentioning the expected vicissitudes of my own. F. M. F.) . . . but
I am totally unaffected by your kind warning. The Preface is
very nice and characteristic and, to tell you the truth, very much
something that I expected. I am not sure I did not mean "dis-
cussions" when I wrote "quarrels," but the last word was right,
since it provoked your friendly contradiction. As to the analysis—
if the two publishers consent (and I don't see why they shouldn't)
it will be, in my view, an interesting addition. This opinion of

mine will be conveyed to Duckworth and Doubleday without loss of time."

The Preface here referred to was the last piece of completed literary work that Conrad lived to execute; the correction of those proofs—of that preface and of the analysis of *Romance*—was his last completed literary action. The last words of that Preface run, after a request that I in turn would give an account of our joint struggles in collaboration:

"For it would be delightful to catch again the echo of the desperate and funny quarrels that enlivened those old days. The pity of it is that there comes a time when all the fun of one's life must be looked for in the past."

Had it not been that Conrad set so much store by this piece of work I should not venture to break my life-long rule of never writing to the press.

I have the honor to be, your obedient servant,

P.S. Since I have broken that rule, perhaps you would permit me space to correct another misapprehension. A monthly journal of wide circulation in this country prints in this month's issue in a review of various novelists' activities:

" 'You're forgetting Ford Madox Ford,' I interrupted (these singularities appear in the course of an interview), 'or do you include him with the Americans?'

" 'Frankly, I'm in doubt about his nationality. He is English by birth, but for a time he became a German citizen for purely legal reasons.' " . . .

I never became a German for legal or illegal reasons or for any reason. I should be flattered to be included among your countrymen, but I always was and shall always be a British subject.

To Ezra Pound

Toulon
Dear Ezra,   28th March 1927

I ought to have written to you before—but I have not, and that is that. I have such a tic against writing letters that I cannot do it—and yours are always so incomprehensible that it is as good as getting no answers.

I have not yet seen EXILE.[1] I did not want to send you those poems for they are not good enough to appear amongst the offerings of your roaring lions & besides, you will have a much better chance with it if you keep it severely American.

I spoke to Lee Keedick[2] with empressement of your lecturing in the U. S. A. I certainly think you ought to do so, now, or at any rate the autumn being the moment, for your star there is on the wax. I have hopes then that we might go there together—or at any rate togetherish as to boats—in September. I am finishing a book now,[3] and if you are to be still in Rapallo, Stella and I might run over for a day or so in mid-April. Answer this, if you would like it, in comprehensible phrases. We could then discuss American plans and if you still wanted me to write something for EXILE we could discuss that and I would do it.

In any case may the God of Villon, Hearst and Big Business in general prosper you and yours.

To Burton Rascoe*[1]

My dear Rascoe: November 9, 1927

I have read the Conrad story and reflected over it still more carefully and I don't think I can do what you want though it would amuse me to try it.[2] But, as a matter of politics, I think it would excite too much hostile comment. I remember pretty well the plot of the story and could quite easily furnish you with that and some comments on the writing which is extraordinarily interesting to me because it is so different from anything else that Conrad ever wrote. If that will suit you I am quite ready to do it but I am quite certain that I ought not to write a formal con-

---

[1] Ezra Pound's review. The first number, Spring, 1927, included Richard Aldington, Ernest Hemingway, and John Rodker among the contributors.

[2] Manager of a lecture agency.

[3] *New York Is Not America*, published in London in July, 1927.

[1] Editor of *The Bookman*.

[2] Conrad's unfinished story, "The Sisters," appeared in *The Bookman* in January, 1928, accompanied by Ford's article "Tiger, Tiger: Being a Commentary on Conrad's *The Sisters*." As Burton Rascoe tells it in *We Were Interrupted*, he wanted Ford to finish the story but settled for the commentary.

tinuation. I have several other things that, if you will permit it, I will suggest to you but, for the moment, I feel myself quite written out having finished a novel only a little time ago. This is called "The Last Post"; it is also the last of the Tietjens series and, D. V., will appear in January.

Yours very sincerely,

To W. A. Bradley

New York

November 28, 1927

My dear Bradley;

I have been very lazy about writing to you but I have been so worried and rushed until almost today that there seemed nothing definite to report whilst Brandt and Spingarn have, I believe, kept you posted about what is going on. Now however I seem definitely to have concluded a very advantageous arrangement with the Viking Press. The contract is not signed yet but all the details are agreed. You will, of course, have them duly from Brandt. So, from a business point of view my visit here has not been wasted. Socially, however, I have kept very quiet, hardly really seeing anybody except intimates or people on business. In revenge I have really done a great deal of work what with articles here and there and ten or eleven thousand words of my new novel up to yesterday.[1]

"New York Is Not America" does not appear to have been published yet—at any rate no review copy has reached the Herald.[2] "Last Post" is to appear early in January.[3] Ginsberg of the Guild and the Viking is very anxious that I should stop on until it does appear for the sake of publicity, but I hardly think that will keep me as I do want to be back for Christmas. But Colliers might if they wanted me to give them a larger chunk of serial before they start—and their money is too important to be ignored. It is rather harassing not knowing what one's movements are going to be, but I suppose one must get used to it.

I hope you are well and not too busy. I met quite alarmist re-

[1] Probably *A Little Less Than Gods* which Duckworth published in 1928.
[2] This collection of essays had appeared in England in July, but Albert and Charles Boni did not publish it in New York until December.
[3] The fourth and last of the Tietjens novels.

ports here as to your condition but was able to allay the general anxiety. I don't know that I have met any of our common friends except those who reside here—I mean, none of the floating population who ply between Paris and here. I am seeing Galantière practically the first time on Wednesday. Glenway Wescott was to have been at a party I was at last night but did not turn up. I have hardly seen Elinor and the Boyds not at all except at Mario's which resort her voice frequently makes cheerful.

I really think this is all my news—at any rate it is all that comes into my head and I am rather stupid with overwork. When I tell you that on Saturday I refused a ticket for the Army and Navy football match you will appreciate what my labours have been. Or perhaps you are not sufficiently a New Yorker.

Anyway all sorts of good luck. Please present my compliments to Mademoiselle and Madame. I hear that Julie now frequently enjoys playing with the former. A tantôt, then,

To Gerald Duckworth*

84 Rue Notre-Dame des Champs
Paris, France
13 Feb 1928

My dear Duckworth,

Your letter of the 10th distresses me very much. In the first place I hate to hear of people being in that state of health when they have to have all their teeth out. It is a distressing and lowering affair. However it frequently results in what Mrs Keary of Selsey used to call re-virgination. May that be so in your case! Have a lovely holiday in Algiers—and particularly visit Boussada [*sic*] before it is quite ruined.

The other question is this matter of income tax—that is to say a tax on what is not income at all, for royalties on books are as much payment for sales as if one sold a sack of potatoes and indeed much more so, since one is selling a portion of one's brain which is exhaustible whereas the land on which potatoes are grown is inexhaustible so that I have quite decided that I will give up publishing in England at all rather than submit to such a pettifogging injustice. And indeed, it would really pay me not to publish in England, for the English editions coming out before the American ones really do skim the cream off the American market, and extinguish the Paris one for the American editions on which my royalties are larger. And I suppose the four or five hundred enthusiasts in England who purchase me—for that is all it amounts to when the New York and Paris purchasers of the English editions are deducted—I suppose those four or five hundred could still obtain copies from New York or Paris, of the American edition.

Of course, as you probably know, the commercial side of it has never bothered me much and I should not let it bother me now but for this last straw. So I propose to write to your firm asking them to consent to the ending of our agreement and there will be an end of it.

I write to you first to explain why I am doing this which I do with a great deal of grief—I assure you with a great deal. We have always, as I have ventured to say over and over again, worked together with all possible cordiality and if you have not contrived to sell me in any large quantities I have always recognised at once the difficulties that stood in your way and the fact that I am not built to be an English popular author. But I think you will agree that the time has come to make an end of the whole business. I don't imagine that your house will much regret it for they cannot have very much profited by the transaction and the moment is appropriate as coming at the end of the Tietjens books.

Do contrive to come back over to Paris and let us look upon the largest possible quantity of wine when it is at its rosiest. I am being coerced into learning a number of new Charleston steps, so Mrs. Duckworth will know what to expect. Stella asks me to convey her love to you both and I'm   Yours as always,

To Isabel Paterson*[1]

My dear Isabel,

[New York, N. Y.]
March 5, 1928

You might like to mention in your notes—or at any rate I should be very glad if you will mention—that the translation of Francis

---

[1] Among Ford's New York admirers was Isabel Paterson, who wrote a column called "Turns with a Bookworm" for the New York *Herald Tribune Books*. The Dedicatory Letter to *The Last Post*, the end of the Tietjens series, is addressed to her.

Carco's *Perversity* which Mr. Pascal Covici of Chicago advertises as being by myself is not by me at all. I daresay Mr. Covici may be able to explain the mistake but in the meantime I wish to contradict the announcement as soon as possible.[2] The translation which in itself is admirable is by Miss Jean Rhys.[3] I could not have done it myself half so well if at all because translating is not one of my gifts and I do not know the particular Parisian *argot* that Mr. Carco employs.

I hear that you started in on my reputation the moment I left New York but I have not seen what you said so I reserve comments until I get back there. I suppose Irita [Van Doren] will have left by the time this reaches you. Anyhow more power to your elbow!

Yours always,

To Eric Pinker

84 Rue Notre Dame des Champs
Paris
Dear Pinker, 16 April 1928

I return herewith o HYMEN; I am sorry to have been so long about it but I could not for the life of me remember what the missing page contained!

I ought to tell you by the way that I have made up my differences with Duckworth and shall be going on with him at any rate for the next book or so. I am glad for I hate changes and D. have always treated me very well. Indeed, they have now gone to prices that I don't believe any other puglosher in London would remotely approach—"puglosher" is a misprint but I think it a rather nice one, so I leave it.

By the bye, I have just had a letter from [George T.] Keating, a passage from which runs as follows: "About the 1897 'Nigger'— ten or twelve copies of this book were issued at the time and most of them were given away by Conrad. Five or six copies

---

[2] Yet paperback reprints in 1950 and 1956 continued to ascribe the translation to Ford.

[3] Jean Rhys lived with the Fords in Paris for "many weeks," as Stella Bowen writes in *Drawn from Life*, "while we tried to set her on her feet. Ford gave her invaluable help with her writing." In 1927 he wrote a preface to Miss Rhys' collection, *The Left Bank and Other Stories*. Her novel *Postures* (London, 1928) is, in oblique respects, based on these years with the Fords.

have been preserved and located (One of them is mine. F.M.F.) and it would mean a good deal to me if I could obtain a copy in the original wrappers with an inscription in it or Conrad's signature. I would pay you five hundred pounds for your copy which is a record price for a Conrad book. However it means a good deal to me because it rounds out the collection with which you are so familiar. I would appreciate your cabling me because I have heard of another that may be available next month, although I understand this particular copy has been re-bound and is not as desirable to me as one in the original wrappers. Or if you hear of another perfect copy I would pay the same sum."[1]

I don't know if you have by any chance an office copy that you would care to sell, or if you know of any other. I believe K. would go to an even larger price.

I will not sell autographs or letters or things for any price, but you might know of somebody to whom the offer would be really useful and Keating is a good fellow so I would be glad to put him on the track.

Yours,

To W. A. Bradley

Hotel Bristol
Marseilles
13 August 1928

Dear Bradley,

I got your letter duly on the boat this morning but not the packet of forwarded letters of wh. you speak. As they were sent apparently before your letter—of the 9th—I suppose they must have gone astray. I daresay it does not much matter as I was expecting nothing of any importance, still it is vexing. But it is no good expecting anything of French steamship lines in the way of correspondence.

The voyage over was very pleasant—as smooth as a millpond from start to finish, and one visited the Azores, Lisbon, Palermo and Naples where Vesuvius was in eruption. So I have improved the knowledge of the world that I had. I daresay I should have improved it more if I had not written the whole time, having

---

[1] In 1929, Doubleday, Doran published *A Conrad Memorial Library: The Collection of George T. Keating*. The books and manuscripts are now in Yale University Library.

done half a book for Lippincotts.[1] I didn't quite see why I do it for I certainly get nothing out of it, finding myself here with no money at all—or rather with exactly frs. 312. Brandts swore they would cable me $200. to await my arrival, but naturally they have not done it although heaven knows they had collected more than that by yesterday for various things.

I don't know exactly what to do. If you could telegraph me frs. 1,000 here I should be obliged, but I dare say you are hard up too. But the point is that this place—the only one I could get into on account of the fêtes—is very expensive and I can't get away without paying the bill and can't pay the bill without money.

I enclose a cheque valued $200.00 on the Guaranty Trust in Paris dated the 16th. Brandt ought to have sent me some money there by that date and you might cash it and hold the money until I cable you where I am—but if you *could* wire me something to-morrow it would act as a calmative, for I am really sick with rage at the methods of payment obtaining in New York . . . though obtaining seems not to be the appropriate word! I suppose that if the money has not arrived in Paris by the 16th you could ask them to let you know when it has. I really think these continual annoyances will drive me to suicide in the end—that is to say I wish they would, but I probably lack that kind of courage. I have written over 100,000 words since I left for New York and have not had a day's holiday and several thousand dollars are owing to me and I am perpetually penniless.

Your fisherman's hostel sounds attractive, but, at the moment, très lointain. I am glad Marianne seems to flourish. I have, naturally, no word from Julie.

Yours,

To Gertrude Stein

Hotel Beau Rivage,
Carqueiranne, Var,
Sept. 8th [1928]

My dear Gertrude,

How nice to hear from you. I have been playing hermit and incidentally working rather hard here for a month or so past and am thus recovering from the strain of N.Y. which was rather

---

[1] Probably *The English Novel: From the Earliest Days to the Death of Joseph Conrad* (Philadelphia, 1929), a contribution to Lippincott's One Hour Series.

considerable in the heat. I bathe a great deal—and treasonable as it may sound to the Rhone, the sea does make swimming an easier affair. Apart from that I have seen nobody and heard nothing for a long time now. I wonder how long you are going to remain in your retreat. I rather meditate going up through the Jura from here towards the end of the month—to Strasbourg, and if you were still there might stop off and see you—if agreeable; but my plans are rendered rather vague because Duckworth clamours that I should come to London to attend on the birth of my next book and, since I do not know when that feat of the accoucheur is to take place—or indeed whether I can afford to go—I remain suspended.[1] . . .

However one day—extraordinarily pink!—I may look in on you.

I rather gather—out of what I *can* gather—from your letter, that you want me to send you something—in the way of an article, I think! If you will take a postcard and write in capital print letters what it is I will do my best to supply the need. There is, by the bye, a lot about you in an article by Muriel Draper in the August no. of HARPERS. Not really offensive!

In any case I hope God may bless you and forward the labours of your right—though to judge by the visual results it is perhaps your left—hand. My kindest regards to Miss Tocklas,[2] (I hope that is spelt right, for I never remember to have seen it written!)

Yours always

To W. A. Bradley

Dear Bradley,

Carqueiranne
Sat. 22 Sept. 1928

[. . . . .] Certainly Herlitschka can have his option if you think it all right but naturally I should prefer him to pay for it.[1] A short story of mine called, I think, THE MASCOT appeared in the ENGLISH MERCURY a little time ago—I should think you could get hold of that easier than the YALE—or perhaps the YALE could be

---

[1] Duckworth published *A Little Less Than Gods* in October, 1928.
[2] Alice B. Toklas, secretary to Gertrude Stein.

[1] Herberth E. Herlitschka of Vienna wanted to translate *Romance* and *A Call* into German.

got out of the American Library in Paris.[2] It was the last number but one. Another is to appear in September, called, I think, A MIRACLE.[3] They are neither very good. I also published one sometime ago—several years—in the English Review called RIESENBERG[4] that is said to be very good and would be, I should think, suited to German tastes. It is usually included in English short story anthologies and the like, but I cannot remember anything about it myself. I daresay the English Review people would look it up in their index and even get it typed out—or that could be done at the British Museum. I should be rather glad to have a copy. Some fellow forged my name to some short stories published in the SMART SET during the war—but they are not mine. The above three are all that I can remember.

Now I have got that novel[5] off my hands I am going to Corsica for a day or two for rest and change and then shall return here for a day or so, afterwards drifting up towards Paris. If there were anything you wanted to cable me about do it poste restante Ajaccio, will you? I expect to be there till Wed or Thursday, but letters or anything postal had better come here. Or anything really urgent before that you might telegraph me about at the Savoy Hotel, Monte Carlo, where I shall stop on Monday night before taking the boat from Nice. I don't *want* to do any work for a month or so except that I shall write a sort of epilogue to that novel, lazily [. . . . .].

Yrs,

To George Oppenheimer*[1]

32 rue Vaugirard

My dear Oppenheimer,
9th November 1928

I was very glad to get your letter with the specimen sheet of publicity.[2] For myself I should have preferred a little less of dwelling on Conrad and a little more as to the sterling romantic qualities

---

[2] "A Mascot" appeared in *The London Mercury* in December, 1927. It was reprinted as "The Romantic Detective" in *The Yale Review*, April, 1928.

[3] *The Yale Review* (Winter, 1928) printed "The Miracle."

[4] In the April, 1911 issue.   [5] Probably *A Little Less Than Gods.*

[1] Of The Viking Press.

[2] The Viking Press had just published *A Little Less Than Gods.*

of the book, for I am a little tired of being tacked on to C's coat-tails and I don't believe the public cares a damn about it. Still I'm sure you know best as to publicity and that I am probably wrong. Anyhow it is a very handsome display and makes my bosom swell with pride. I hope the book will do well for all our sakes, but I should think the election suspended the sales. Still, I suppose there is plenty of time before Christmas for them to pick up.

I am mortified to find that Bradley only seems to have got about half of THAT SAME POOR MAN[3] typed, for I had wanted to send it to you long before now. But, as I dare say you know, he lost his little daughter and afterwards was knocked down by a taxi-cab so he has been away for some time and work in his office has suffered. At any rate the book is finished and ready as soon as the typing out is done, and I am doing my best to hurry that on.

I am writing to Brandt by this mail or the next about my collected edition. As I suppose you know Bonis [*sic*] had begun this, but it stopped when our agreement—mine with them, I mean—stopped. I quite thought you had been spoken to about taking it over but was surprised to find when I left N. Y. that no one in the office had heard anything about it—but I suppose you know that it is quite in *my* mind to give you all my books for good, for I hate changing publishers; and indeed nothing is more unprofitable.

Anyhow may all good luck attend yourself and your partners in all your enterprises from now on until the sun shall set in the East.

Yours,

[3] A reworking of *The Wheels of the Plough*, the novel Ford started after the war but never published.

1929 · 1939

NEW YORK, TOULON, OLIVET

To Bernice Baumgarten[*][1]

Dear Miss Baumgarten,

[. . . . .] I have reflected carefully on yours of the 8th inst. and what seems best to do is this. Will you please not offer NOTTERDAM[2] further to anyone but proceed, if you will be so good, with the placing of the HISTORY OF OUR OWN TIME?[3] I do not like the idea of a novel of mine being hawked about from publisher to publisher. It never happened to me before in my life and I am too old to bear the experience with equanimity now. The Viking Press ordered the book and it is theirs to publish or not as they see fit. I am sorry if they do not like the book and I note your own strictures on it, for which I am obliged.

That is hardly a matter that I can discuss. I was trying in the book a technical experiment which seems to me to have been successful and you are, I suppose, aware that I have been a good deal praised for the technique of my fiction and that I have had a good deal of influence on the technique of the more modern novelists of today. It seems therefore more likely that I am right in the matter than a group of tradesmen who have no literary experience, whatever their skill or want of skill in marketing the literary products of others. But that is an agelong struggle and when you have lived as long as I have you will see that in such affairs the publisher is invariably wrong. They are not unnaturally afraid of innovations and the innovations almost invariably win out.

I am not, by the bye, referring to yourself in the above paragraph; there are ever so many non-literary reasons why you should not like the book. And anyhow in my eyes you are a privileged person. You read it by the bye in a very defective copy that I sent to Mr. Brandt who was proposing to offer chunks out of it to the BOOKMAN or THE FORUM which I imagine he did not do. However,

---

[1] One of Brandt and Brandt's most capable literary agents.

[2] The original title of the novel called *When the Wicked Man* which Liveright published in 1931.

[3] Planned for three volumes: 1880 to the death of Victoria; 1901 to the Armistice; 1918 to 1930. The manuscript was left unfinished and unpublished at the time of Ford's death.

I am not absolutely pigheaded. If you will send me the better copy to look through I will certainly make it as letter-perfect as I can before returning it to you but I do not imagine that I shall materially change it.

There remains the question of ENGLISH COUNTRY.[4] If you do not mind I should prefer to handle that myself—not because I doubt your management of the matter but because it is disagreeable in the extreme to wait for months on end without knowing what is being done. I propose to sell that book quite apart from any other transaction so that if you will continue with the HISTORY OF OUR OWN TIME and my collected edition there need be no clashing —and of course if I succeed in selling it the house of Brandt will have its usual commission.

I think I should be also glad if Miss Josephs would return to me any articles of mine that she has. It is so difficult to synchronise publications here and in England, and my English prices are so much higher than anything she has obtained for me here that I should much prefer to have the matter altogether in my own hands or to dispense with American publication altogether. Of course if you can arrange for the serialization of the HISTORY OF OUR OWN TIME I shall be delighted.

I should really be obliged if you would use the telephone in communicating with me about any matters that arise. As I have told you I am at the moment extremely unwell and the writing of letters about complicated matters is very fatiguing to me.

In the meantime, do pray believe me

Yours very cordially,

To Eric Pinker

32, Rue de Vaugirard
Paris VI
Sept. 11th 1929

Dear Pinker,

I had been waiting, so as not to burden you with letters, until the arrival of the proofs of my book that is coming out in New

[4] Probably Ford's working title for the autobiographical "fiction" which The Macaulay Company published in 1929 as *No Enemy*. It incorporates material from the series of essays called "English Country" which he published in *The New Statesman* (August 23–September 6, 1919).

York this fall. It is to be called there NO ENEMY which I do not think a good title, but I cannot think of a better. I hear from Macaulay that they are on the way now and when I get them I will forward them to you. Please deal with it as you think best. It was written, as to one chapter, in the front line, and as to the rest just after peace was declared. I thought at the time that it was too personal to publish at once and determined to keep it for ten years which have just elapsed. It won't appear in New York till November.

I am forwarding under another cover a great number of agreements that go over a lot of years. My agreements with Cape and Duckworth are in my apartment in New York. I will get my secretary to send them over unless I can get copies earlier.

As for Cape I have practically broken with him. I daresay he will have told you so. The real reason is, between ourselves, that he told my most intimate friend in New York in a moment of incaution such as comes over one on New York nights that he had only got me away from Duckworth in order to wipe Gerald's eye and that he did not believe anyone could sell me in England and did not expect to himself. I did not at first believe it—I don't mean that I didn't believe he had said it for I believe my friend implicitly—but that that was actually his motive. But when he continually put off publishing the book he had called NOTTERDAM and later turned down the book called NO ENEMY, as above, and said he did not want either my HISTORY OF OUR OWN TIME or my collected edition I decided that something of the sort must actually have been in his mind and told Howard before I saw you that I should prefer to take Notterdam which I consider my best book to any one else. Besides I don't like Cape and, if I have to have personal dealings with a publisher I don't like, I generally let him feel it before long and that is not good for trade or anything else. Of course if you think fit to re-open matters with him I am quite agreeable—or at least I should not mind much as long as I do not have to meet or correspond with him personally. But I'd prefer almost anybody else. In any case I leave you an absolutely free hand.

He has of course paid £250 on account of NOTTERDAM and that will have to be paid back. I have not got the money available at the moment but shall have it pretty soon, or if you could sell it for that same amount to another publisher, or something like it that would still be more gratifying.

I have, by the bye, another novel which I don't like and don't want to publish if I can help it though the Viking have bought it in the U. S. A. It is called THAT SAME POOR MAN[1] and the ms. is in the hands of either the Viking or Brandt. I don't want to do anything about it at present, but of course it would come in if I died or had apoplexy or anything of the sort. It isn't an ignoble book but I just do not like it. I daresay I shall rewrite a good deal of it one day and then it will be all right.

I am working pretty hard at the HISTORY OF OUR OWN TIME and will send you the first two parts before very long.

Yours,

To Isidor Schneider*[1]

32, Rue de Vaugirard
Paris VI
14th Sept 1929

My dear Schneider,

I see no reason in principle why I should not write for the PHILADELPHIA INQUIRER what you request, but I wish you could send me a specimen of what is wanted—because books can be useful from so many points of view. In my early days, for instance, I used to use the ENCYCLOPAEDIA BRITANNICA as a trouser-press and certainly the house that was without it was to be pitied. Books are very useful also for pulping; bibles and other works set over the heart will deflect bullets; works printed on thin india paper are admirable if you happen to run out of cigarette papers. Their use for that purpose is in fact forbidden in France where there is a tobacco monopoly. In fact, if you are ever without a book you are certain to want one in the end. For the matter of that, my grand aunt Eliza Coffin used to say: "Sooner than be idle, I'd take a book and read." According to her the other uses of books were (1) for the concealing of wills (2) for the ditto of proposals of marriage by letter; (3) for pressing flowers; (4) folios piled one on the other will aid you to reach the top row in the

[1] The Viking Press never published it.

[1] Editor of The Macaulay Company.

linen cupboard; (5) they have been used as missiles, as bedsteads when levelly piled, as wrappings for comestibles; (6) as soporifics, sudorifics, shaving paper etc.

I was once accused of using slices of bacon, at breakfast, to mark my place in a book. That is untrue.

It is alleged that the reading of books will improve intelligences capable of improvement. By keeping their eyes on the pages of books ladies may avoid the too ardent glances of admirers in public conveyances. The reading of books in small print is advised for friends of oculists, spectacle makers, and breeders of dogs sufficiently docile to lead their owners on strings. The purchase—the reading is optional—of books enables publishers to ride in Rolls-Royces. House-decorators find that books work into rooms with admirable effect. . . . This is all I can think of to say about books. . . . Oh, one wishes that one's enemy would write books. One could not wish him a worse fate.

Above must be 200 words.

As to photograph, I have asked Hoppe's of London to send Miss Kerr a photograph or two of myself in uniform of the Welch Regiment with dragon complete. I hope it will reach her in time to be useful. I enclose also one of myself as agriculturist as I was when I wrote NO ENEMY; also a photo of the house in which it was written, called COOPERS, BEDHAM, FITTLEWORTH, SUSSEX. You can use them if you like, but pray preserve them carefully and return to Miss Kerr. The photographs of myself that I like best were taken by Hutchinson in Chicago about three years ago. The latest were taken by a firm in Fifth Avenue; I forget the name. I did not like them nor the firm. They refused to give me free copies!

As for the title of NO ENEMY, wouldn't ON EARTH PEACE be better if it is not too late?

If it is too late and you prefer NO ENEMY, put on the T. P. as motto

Here shall he see no enemy,
But winter and rough weather.

The worst of it is, for me, that the galleys of NO ENEMY have not reached me. Where did you address them to? It is rather disastrous for me because my English publishers will not publish after New York and I have to send my agent trotting round to find another who will, with consequent derangements of dates and distractions. In all other matters I am yours to command.   Yrs,

By the bye, the beast in exhibit no II is not ANNA 2d my world-champion Black Sussex sow whose picture was in all the papers, but PENNY my champion Angora (male) goat. He was so-called because he facially resembled (but was not) POUND, Ezra.

To Hugh Walpole

32 Rue de Vaugirard
Paris VI
2 December 1929

My dear Walpole,

I have been touched by a note about myself by you in a copy of the N. Y. H. BOOKS that someone has sent me.[1] It is very kind of you. I don't however *feel* a blighted man, for I do quite as well as I want to in America which is all one man ought to want—and indeed I have almost forgotten that I am an English writer at all and have not even published my last three books in England. That is partly of course out of pique but also because as I have a large sale in Paris here it really pays me better because the Americans charge more for their books. Besides, as I have every reason to be grateful to them, I really like Americans and as they pay large prices for my first editions and prefer the first editions to be printed in America, I like to do what they like. Obviously if I had any sale in England I should publish there, but A MAN COULD STAND UP earned only $251.00 in England and as I have to pay out that special income tax on authors residing abroad, amounting to $50, agent's fees of $25, and ordinary income tax of $84 with again no rebate, because I reside abroad—and five per cent of the residue Federal Taxes and a small per centage for N. Y. State taxes because I am domiciled by U. S. law in New York where I principally live; and as according to French law I am domiciled in Paris and have to pay ten per cent for State and ten per cent for municipal taxes the amount I actually receive for a novel published in England is not more than $40 for a year's work. It seems

---

[1] "London Letter," New York *Herald Tribune Books* (November 24, 1929), p. 9. Walpole wrote: "There is no greater literary neglect of our time in England than the novels and poems of Ford."

insufficient for one who is the doyen—not of course of merit but by reason of priority of imprint—of all novelists in England or America—for I think my first novel pre-dated George Moore's, and the doyen but two of French ones. And I don't even get a gratis wooden spoon out of England whereas Chicago has awarded me a solid gold laurel wreath and my last French book sold a quarter of a million copies.

I don't believe that the fault lies with the reviewers. I am told —for I don't receive cuttings—that my books secure amazingly good presses. It is just that the public *will* not read me. Someone told me years ago that the Americans would never read me because they could not tell whether I was in earnest or not, whereas the English knew I was too damn in earnest to want to read me. The U. S. A. has got over that coyness but England has not and probably never will. The book I have just published in America which I wrote partly in the line and partly just after the Armistice and which is a perfect paean to the English countryside in the middle of war reminiscences—and which has sold very well there and sells out here every copy of the batches they send over within a day of its arrival, has not even found a publisher in England. I should not mind publishing it there because it is the best prose I ever wrote and because it is a tribute to the country and my comrades in arms. But Pinker says no one will touch it so you will never read it.[2]

I write at this length because I had an operation a day or so ago and am forbidden to work so I take it out in letters to fill in the long day.

By the bye, there is an English writer I saw a good deal of in N. Y. C. this summer, called Richard Hughes author of INNOCENT VOYAGE, or HIGH WIND IN JAMAICA who I think is really a fine writer and a keen intelligence—as good as any American *jeune* except Hemingway or Elizabeth Madox Roberts—though he is not a novelist per se. But I could tell you forty others who are of the same order in New York alone, let alone Chattanooga, Pike's Peak and Rockford, Ill. Not that by that I mean to deprecate Hughes. But how can one poor swallow make a summer all by itself?

[2] *No Enemy* has never been published in England, for no clear reasons.

I hope you flourish. Except for a troublesome form of blood-poisoning I am pretty well and in spirits. I shall leave for New York as soon as the holidays are over.

Yrs,

Excuse pencil; I am dictating on my back. Thank you!

To Susan Jenkins*[1]

Dear Miss Jenkins,   27 Feb 1930

As the lady exclaimed when her little boy said DAMN!: "It's worse than wicked. It's vulgar." So it's more than exasperating—but I can't think of a word. Though I *can*. . . .

You—I don't mean you personally but the House of Macaulay—sit on the ms of NOTTERDAM four months and more, at first saying that you are waiting for the return of Mr. Guinsberg from Europe and then without pretext at all and now it's too late for the Spring season and that will throw my HISTORY back till next year. Of course I am aware that you are busy and that mine are not the only mss you have to deal with but publishers get told so often that whilst the grass is growing the ass is starving that they might remember it now and then and even if you wanted to see how you handled NO ENEMY four months was enough for that and for all you knew I might have been lying on a straw pallet with my ribs sticking through my skin.[2]

It is good of Allen and Mr. Fisher to bother themselves about my work. I am glad that biographical details as to my career—save the mark—are difficult to obtain in N. Y. From the reports that reach me from that city I should have thought it *far* otherwise, quite far.

It looks to me as if it would be quite a long time before I shall reach New York again because I shan't until the house of Macaulay—or some other House—makes up its mind about these books and that will take years. If only you would instruct your

---

[1] Of The Macaulay Company.

[2] The Macaulay Company published *No Enemy* in November, 1929. *Notterdam* did not appear until 1931, under the title *When the Wicked Man*, published by Horace Liveright.

post-clerks how to address letters for Europe it would expedite matters a lot. Your letter, mailed on the 10th did not reach me till the 26th. It could have done so by the 16th if the words Per S. S. Bremen had been inscribed on it. Ask Allen Tate how it is done or get him to lecture your envelope-addresser on the subject.

In the meantime I hope you flourish—I mean you, Miss Jenkins, though I don't object to the House of Macaulay flourishing too.

To Hugh Walpole

Villa Paul
Toulon, Var
30th March 1930

My dear Walpole,

I ought to have written a long time ago to thank you for your good offices chez Gollancz. But I did not know until the other day that you were back from the Caribbean and since then have been bothered moving into the above villa which I hope one day will shelter you. It is however a very simple place where we live a life of a frugality which would astonish and for all I know appal you, but by dint of almost complete vegetarianism, a prohibition such as Gotham never knew, an immense view of the Mediterranean and agricultural labours that begin at dawn and end after sunset, I have recovered a good deal of the vitality that I thought had gone for ever with my heart attack last December. And indeed I have got back into complete writing form and have made immense strides with my book[1] so that even if another heart attack *did* carry me off Gollancz would have at least *a* book, for Reminiscences don't need either beginnings or ends. That firm is singularly dilatory. I wish they would let me have the agreement, for although I quite believe they mean to adhere to it, I have had such a lot of trouble with other publishers that I am, I suppose, unnecessarily fretful and this Australian repudiation on top of my American losses has hit me so hard that, if they did go back on their letter, the worry of finding another publisher would be devastating. But I suppose they won't.

I hope them islands were kind to you.—Do you know my story of 'I ought never to have left them islands'? One day when we sit beneath my orange trees and gaze on Corsica I will tell it you!

[1] Probably *Return to Yesterday*, which Victor Gollancz published in 1931.

And would you do me another favour? There is an English firm of seed merchants called I am almost sure Sutton but I have no idea of their address and don't know how to find out. Would you much mind giving the enclosed letter to them to your club porter and asking him to post it?

Oh, no—I needn't bother you. I have just remembered that the English consul here will be sure to have the address.

May Allah—one just sees Soheil [?] from here—further the desires of your heart.

Yours,

To Ernest Rhys*¹

My dear Rhys,   21st April 1930

I am indeed flattered and touched by your request. Alas, though modesty is foreign to my character I know that I cannot do certain things; the understanding of the Higher Mathematics is one; swimming far under water another. But great as is my incapacity in those sports it is as nothing to my inability to write a short story. Had I ever been able to I should today be a rich man. But I can't.

I have in my life, I think, published three—two in the Yale Review and one in the English Ditto.² I have also written one quite lately with which I am completely dissatisfied. If you would like to look at the one that appeared in the English Review and the one I lately finished I'd be delighted to send them to you, if only to prove my initial proposition. But you have only to say "Don't" and I won't. I daresay you are flooded, head and heels under, by offers.

I don't think the HISTORY is going to come off with Dent and Morrow for which I am naturally sorry—and which is indeed rather disastrous to me because I have been kept hanging about for a very long time, when in America at least I could have sold the book long ago. However there is no need to worry you about that, but I really marvel at the folly of publishers. There would

¹ A Welsh poet and anthologist, Rhys had been one of the founders of the Rhymers' Club of the Nineties. In 1930 he was editor of Everyman's Library.

² Ford's memory failed him. Between 1903 and 1930 he published at least nineteen short stories.

I am sure be a great market for such a book by anybody if it were competently done and I am fairly sure that I have done it competently and I know the market better than most publishers—for there must be at least fifty of those gentry in Europe and America who have at one time or another wrung their hands because they refused to publish my babies—by which I mean first books of young people I recommended. Four in England and two in America boggled at Hemingway! (I will by the bye write and ask him if he has anything for you.)

Do you know the story of the old lady who was being taken to die in the workhouse and seeing dimly some objects moving on the horizon asked their nature. The attendant replied that they were trees and she said: "Trees! Well, I'm tired of 'em!" . . . . I feel like that when I think of what used to be called Paternoster Row.[3]

But more luck to *your* elbow!

To Hugh Walpole

My dear Walpole,

32 Rue de Vaugirard
Paris VI
28th May 1930

I owe you an apology for dedicating that book to you without your permission, but I wanted to do it and you were in America at the time and I did not see that what I said could do you any harm. I will send you a copy as soon as I get one and should have done so before had I known that the book was out.[1]

It is good of you indeed to take an interest in a Collected—or rather it ought to be a Selected—Edition of my work, but I do not see much chance of its coming yet. I should certainly like to reprint six or seven of my books in a uniform edition but do not imagine any English publisher would interest himself in them and I have not had time to approach the matter in America. I spoke to Evans of Heinemann's about it some years ago and I thought he was interested in the matter but Duckworth or someone objected

[3] Adjoining St. Paul's Cathedral.

[1] Ford printed a seven-page letter to Walpole as the dedication ("author's apology," he calls it) to *The English Novel: From the Earliest Days to the Death of Joseph Conrad* (London, 1930).

and it dropped. But if you know any publisher sufficiently well to suggest such an enterprise with authority I should be very obliged if you would do so without giving yourself too much trouble.

There is one of my four or five books that have appeared in America and not in England that I should much like to see published there. That is NO ENEMY which I wrote during the Armistice mostly, though some of it was actually written in the line. Pinker declares that no English publisher that he has approached will touch it which rather astonishes me for it has had quite a remarkable reception in the United States where they say it is a monument of prose which it probably isn't but when you consider that it is the war-reminiscences of the only British novelist of anything like, say, my age who actually took part in hostilities as an infantry officer it seems singular that no-one should want to print it as a document. And I really believe it is rather a beautiful book and can almost afford to say so since it was written so long ago—part of it in 1916—and in such different circumstances that it really seems to be the work of another man.

But no, my dear Walpole, you will find it difficult to make me believe in the esteem of my English colleagues for myself. The heart, you know, knoweth its own bitterness and there are circumstances in my career of such an extraordinary nature that you would hardly believe them. But that only makes your own kindness doubly precious. Do believe that I am deeply sensible of that.

I hope you had a prosperous and agreeable stay in the United States. I wish I could get out there myself, but I am finishing a tiresome and laborious book that prolongs and prolongs itself.[2]

With reiterated thanks.   Yours very sincerely,

To Eric Pinker

32 Rue de Vaugirard
Paris 6

Dear Sirs: August 17, 1930

Yours of the 15th inst: ref. Tietjens Saga

I am quite in favor of this publication but wish to put the fol-

---

[2] Probably the rewriting of *Notterdam* (see letter dated 10 July 1929), completed in December, 1930. Horace Liveright published it in 1931 under the title *When the Wicked Man*.

lowing points to you as to which I should be glad if you would
let me have your reply at the earliest possible opportunity as I
am leaving for the United States on the 6th prox. and if the publication goes through I shall have to do a certain amount of work
on the books.

(a) I take it that publication of this edition will not interfere
with ordinary editions intended to figure in my collected works
at a later date. [. . . . .]

(c) I strongly wish to omit the *Last Post* from the edition. I
do not like the book and have never liked it and always intended
the series to end with *A Man Could Stand Up*. Please consult
Duckworths about this. I am ready to be guided by them but
should much prefer the above course.

(d) *Ref. title*. I do not like the title *Tietjens Saga*—because in
the first place "Tietjens" is a difficult name for purchasers to pro-
nounce and booksellers would almost inevitably persuade readers
that they mean the Forsyte Saga with great damage to my sales.
I recognize the value of Messrs Duckworth's publicity and see no
reason why they should not get the advantage of it by using those
words as a subtitle beneath another general title which I am inclined to suggest should be *Parades End* so that Messrs Duckworth
could advertise it as

PARADES END
[Tietjens' Saga]

(e) The copyright of these books in England is the property
of Mme. E. G. Bowen, having been conveyed for value received.
Will you please observe that that is the case in making any payments and this being the case, are payments made under such a
heading liable to special author's income tax? [. . . . .]

Yours faithfully,

To Hugh Walpole

32 Rue de Vaugirard
Paris VI
16 Dec 1930

My dear Walpole;

Fate seems to be against our meeting for I fear that when you
return from the West Indies I shall be again in New York. I

wanted to run over to London but have been kept by all sorts of little worrying things until now it is too late.

I don't believe I ever thanked you for the efforts you made in my behalf last Fall. The failure of the attempt must have shewed you—what I was perfectly aware of—that it would be impossible to find any three English people connected with books who would not automatically put a spoke in any wheel of mine that passed them by. But I am none the less sincerely obliged to you.

I wonder if you would further oblige me. I am engaged on writing my reminiscences—mostly literary, but a little political, social and military, of the last thirty-five years. They are of course placed in the United States—with Liveright and *Scribner's Magazine*.[1] But to whom should I offer them in England? Judging by the results of the efforts of Pinker who has had my work in hand for some time it is impossible to place me in that country so that there are actually three books[2] of mine at this moment that have no English edition though they do pretty well in New York. So I want to dispense with P., but know nothing about London publishers today. Thus a word of advice from you would be extremely opportune if you could find time to write it before your departure. I feel myself rather like Oliver Twist, but I daresay you won't mind.

In the meantime all sorts of good things be yours whether in Cokaigne [*sic*] or the Caribbean. If you should go to Antigua don't omit to call on Miss Branch who keeps school in that Island. She is a particular friend of mine and Mrs. Ford's[3] and, if you can get her to talk, will give you the raciest possible information as to the inhabitants, White, Black, and Carib.

I hear Hemingway has broken his arm whilst hunting exotic beasts in Montana, so the race is always a little precarious, even to the strong. But perhaps you don't know him. Yours,

[1] Horace Liveright published *Return to Yesterday* in 1932; *Scribner's* (October, 1931) printed only "Three Americans and a Pole," the second chapter of the book.
[2] *New Poems* (1927), *New York Essays* (1927), and *No Enemy* (1929).
[3] Janice Biala, Polish-born painter. Ford and Stella Bowen had separated in 1927.

To James Joyce

3 Quai du Parti
Toulon, Var
9th March 1931

My dear Joyce,

I have at last received Italo Svevo's books and have read some of them, finding them quite charming.

I do not quite gather what you want me to do about them. I fancy it is to write an introduction to a new volume of translations.[1] If so would you suggest to whoever is going to publish it that they had better let me have either proofs or a ms. copy of the volume with some indication of how long they want the introduction to be and when they will want it? I should certainly be glad to be of any service I can to Svevo's memory.

I hope you have given up white wine and prosper, though naturally I do hope you prosper whether or no. Still le premier devoir du vin est d'être rouge. I am sure the wine of Cana must have been. But alas! all the really drinkable wines about here—and there are one or two really lovely ones—are white. There is one in particular—Domaine de Cavalière—that is one of the best I have ever imagined. I wish I could send you some but it will not travel. So you will have to come and drink it *in situ* if you really want to know on this side of paradise what vinous bliss is. It is rather like the best Moselle.

Do you know the local story of Mr. Walker, Mayor of New York. He was given a dinner by the Winegrowers' Association of France at Marseilles. He put his lips to a *Château Mouton Rothschild* 1906, I think, spat it out and shouted: "Aw, Gee, give me a whiskey highball!"

Kind regards to Mrs. Joyce.

Yours,

To T. R. Smith*[1]

[Toulon]
March 14, 1931

My dear T. R. Smith:

What has happened to WHEN THE WICKED MAN? I am so amazed by the various cables that I don't know when to expect its publi-

---

[1] Svevo's widow had asked James Joyce to write a preface to the English translation of *Senilità*, but he refused and suggested Ford as an alternative. Putnam's, however, rejected Ford, compromising on a preface by Stanislaus Joyce.

[1] Of Horace Liveright, Inc.

cation. In the meantime I've had no letter from you so you may, for all I know, be expecting me to leave for New York today.

I am getting on like a house a-fire with the Reminiscences now and have reached the point when if I suddenly drop dead, you could just clap "Thus to Revisit" on to what is written and with a little editing have a very good book. So you may consider yourself safe. However, though you precious near did lose me in December my health is immensely improved by staying down here and I hope to finish the book, as I've said, in July and that it will be one of my best books. The only real trouble is that I have such an immense lot of matter to write about that I don't know what to select and what to leave out.

I have asked Miss [Ruth] Kerr to call on you and delicately to extract as much money as she can for me on account of WHEN THE WICKED MAN. The collapse of Australian Securities has hit me even worse than the collapse of your market and I have a lot of payments to make early in April. Please do what you can.

The more I think of WHEN THE WICKED MAN the more I feel that it is one of the considerable *moral* books of the world. If you can get your advertising people to take that line it might have an enormous sale as a problem book. If it is advertised merely as a phony or funny it will just go down with the ruck of novels until God in his good time sees to it that laurel wreaths are put around the marble brows of my statue in the Hall of Fame. But you and I will be dead by that time and others will enjoy the fruits. In the meantime you occupy the place of the Deity.

I am taking a villa down here and in all probability giving up my Paris apartment so when in search of youth and beauty—I mean of course the restoration of your own, little necessary as that may be—you come sailing to these shores, you will be able to find a bed and the goodly fruits of the earth such as my hands shall cause to grow, each in their due season and also if the villa I'm trying to get falls to me, one of the most beautiful views in the world. In the meantime more power to your elbow.

To Theodore Dreiser

My dear Dreiser: Toulon, France
18 April 1931

I have been meaning to drop you a line for sometime, but prevarication [*sic*] and moving and ills of the flesh have prevented it. However, I am now installed in a spot where I have wanted to be as long as I can remember, and am fairly at ease in sunlight that is only interrupted by the night.

I had a pretty bad winter, suddenly developing a weak heart which reduced me to about the half of a man but working hard in the garden has restored me to about ¾ of what I was. I hope to do better yet.

This is really a lovely place, looking over the Mediterranean & various islands. Come and see if it does not beat Mount Kisco for views. It couldn't for hospitality, though if you are passing by and wd. look in for a day or two—or as long as you like—we'd be delighted to see what we could do.

I have been working pretty hard but Mr. T. R. Smith has been playing the devil with my affairs which has annoyed me and put me out. How can he expect me to recommend other authors to go to him when he treats me more [illegible] than any other publisher I ever had to do with I don't know.

This by the bye isn't a grumble at you. I guess I shd. have gone to him whether you recommended it or not—& it does not affect me much except in the way of being annoyed at letting myself rely on people's representations. One never gets cured of that.

I hope you are well and working. I often think of you all and wish myself back in your neighbourhood. But with my heart still very irregular I am not allowed to go out at all alone so I can't say when I shall be up to crossing the Atlantic.

So do you try it and let us devise *de natura rerum* above the sea instead of the lake.

My kindest regards to Madame. Yours always,

To Ezra Pound

Toulon, Var
6th June 1931

Dear Ezra,

This is to authorize and empower you without let, hindrance, fee, honorarium, deodand, infangtheff, utfangtheff freely to translate or cause to be betrayed any work of mine save only my commentary on the Book of Genesis into any tongue or language save only the dialects of the Isle of Man and of the City of Philadelphia, Pa. in its pre-1909 variety or sameness.

We may shortly be passing through Genoa and would like you to lunch with us at any hostelry there designated by you.

I had yesterday the agreeable news that my latest novel[1] is a best seller in New York. As however the largest sale of any book in that city has not yet exceeded four hundred copies this year and since no publisher has more than $11 in his bank I do not—though they need it—propose to have the seats of my pants reinforced.

May God and your country pass you by in their judgments is the prayer of

To Victor Gollancz*

[Paris]
Nov 8th 1931

Dear Mr. Gollancz,

This is very annoying. Of course, as far as I am concerned, you may delete that paragraph in subsequent editions.[1] I certainly

---

[1] *When the Wicked Man*, published in May, 1931.

[1] Victor Gollancz published *Return to Yesterday* on November 2, 1931. *The Daily Herald* of that date printed what Gollancz called an "absurd headline" in his letter of November 6 to Ford: MONSTROUS STORY ABOUT THE KING: INDIGNANT DENIAL OF ANY PRE-WAR THREAT TO ABDICATE: COURT OFFICIAL SAYS IT IS NOT TRUE. Ford had written in the last pages of his reminiscence that C. F. G. Masterman told him King George had threatened to abdicate in June, 1914 over a proposed meeting of Irish party leaders at Buckingham Palace. *The Daily Herald* quoted David Lloyd George (Chancellor of the Exchequer in 1914) as saying he had never heard of such a threat by the King. Ford had never been one of Lloyd George's admirers, but what both Gollancz and Ford clearly wished to avoid was bad publicity for the new book.

had no idea of causing annoyance to the King and I hope I have not—though I do not see how I can have for the substantial accuracy of the pages devoted to that phase of the Irish question does not seem to be challenged either by Mr. George or by the 'High Court Official' who is no doubt the gentleman who blacks the shoes of the Second Silver Stick in Waiting and who, significantly, limits his denial by the words 'So far as I know.' Mr. George too limits his denial by saying that he 'never heard of such a thing.' It is in short the lamest piece of denial I have ever seen and if the objection to the paragraph came only from those two personages I should ask you to retain the passage. But I am quite literally and naively a subject of H.M. and entertain the greatest admiration for him as Head of the State. So pray act as requested by the Palace. After all it is doing a sovereign no disservice to emphasise the fact that he was sincerely and actively concerned to put an end to assassination, mutiny and chaos in a part of his dominions.

I hope you will do what you can to let the matter drop out of view as quietly as possible for I have a great horror of publicity from a side wind. I presume that all that is necessary is that you should inform the Press Agent that I am quite ready to agree to the suppression of the paragraph objected to and if you would add a word of apology on the above lines I should be obliged. I suppose it is naive of me—but I imagined that the Court had ways of its own of stopping the printing of anything that it objected to. Otherwise, I should have given the passage a different turn.

Yes, I can quite well wait till within ten days of Christmas and shall be glad to see you then.

Yours sincerely,

To Percival Hinton [1]

Dear Sir:

32 Rue de Vaugirard
Paris VI
27 Nov 1931

I am much obliged to you for your letter of the 21st inst. and its enquiries wh. I will answer as best I can.

[1] English free-lance journalist and bibliophile.

Yes, RETURN TO YESTERDAY must be the work announced as I SAW THRONES. At any rather there is not any other. R. T. Y. has appeared almost simultaneously in New York.

I don't think MR. FLEIGHT was ever completely published.[2] I understood from Byles that it was seized by the sheriff's officer immediately after copies had been sent out for review and the copies thus seized were sold to someone—Bell, I think—who used them for a colonial edition. I may of course be mistaken but I do not remember ever having seen a copy other than that of the colonial edition referred to. [. . . . .]

I think the GOOD SOLDIER is my best book technically unless you read the Tietjens books as one novel in which case the whole design appears. But I think the Tietjens books will probably 'date' a good deal whereas the other may—and need—not.

I am sorry not to have seen your review in the BIRMINGHAM POST but I do not get cuttings.

Thanking you again, I am

Yours sincerely,

To Victor Gollancz*

[Paris]

Dear Sir,   March 1st 1932

I am afraid I cannot wait any longer for your coming to Paris and do not see much chance of my getting to London before I go South. I see nothing for it therefore, much as I dislike writing long letters which are a nuisance to everybody, but to write my publishing plans to you.

I am forwarding you under a separate cover a copy of the American edition of one of my books which has not been published in England. NO ENEMY is in effect my reminiscences of active service under a thinly disguised veil of fiction. I have not wanted to publish it in England until now for fear of hurting various susceptibilities. It has, such as it is, a certain additional value because it was written during the war and the armistice by an actual ordinary combatant, part of it having been actually written in the line. So it seems to me to be of a certain documentary

---

[2] Howard Latimer published *Mr. Fleight* in April, 1913 in London. It had at least three impressions in less than two months.

weight. At any rate it is the last thing that I propose to publish about the war. It is, I believe, regarded as the best prose I have written, at any rate in America, and although it did not sell as well as my novels in that country it did pretty well and should, I imagine, do pretty well in England.

If you would care to publish it as a further instalment of my reminiscences I should be very pleased and if you would care to add to that undertaking the publication of the final instalment of my reminiscences in a further book—covering up to say 1930— I should be proportionately further pleased. [. . . . .]

I am sorry not to be able to offer you any of my fiction but I have been obliged to make an arrangement with an American publisher to take all the English language rights of my novels over a prolonged period. If however it would interest you I will ask him to give you the refusal of the British Empire rights.

I should take it as a favour if you could see your way to let me have an answer as to NO ENEMY and the Reminiscences at your earliest possible convenience.[1]

Yours faithfully

To W. A. Bradley

Dear Bradley,

June 8, 1932

I wish I could get you to look at things in a more realistic manner which is the same thing as saying I wish I could get you to understand what I mean. But I am ready to concede that my incoherence may make me incomprehensible. I quite well know that I am in demand in New York. My daily letter bag gives me sufficient evidence of that. But getting paid for my work is quite another matter as I have bitter reason for knowing and I am quite determined that I will not do any more work for America or anywhere else unless I am absolutely certain not only of its appearing but of my getting paid for it. That is to say that I am perfectly ready to do—and do do—a good deal of work for friends for nothing but my friends are not of the same speed as Harpers nor can I by any means regard Mr. Hartmann as a friend. All this is not immediately germane to the matter but it is as well

[1] Victor Gollancz refused both.

that you should not think me more unreasonable than necessary.

There are other reasons why I don't want to write these things. In the first place I don't write articles well and do not add to my reputation when I write them. In addition writing them spoils my style so that it takes me a long time to get back to book writing. If, however, Hartmann would agree to my terms and let me write about what I want as I want, some compromise might be arrived at.

I have long wanted to write a sort of book of travel[1] going over again the not very extensive but quite interesting territory round which I have *patauged* for the greater part of my life, getting their atmosphere all over again as the phrase used to be. This would make a book rather than a series of articles but if Hartmann would like to use the separate chapters as articles I shouldn't mind. They would probably turn out to be something that he liked because my method being anecdotal and, as far as I can see, my stock of anecdotes being inexhaustible he would be getting something like separate units in another book of reminiscences centered round places rather than chronologically and in any case containing a good deal about cookery. What I should propose to treat of, starting from the East, would be Rome and Naples in one chapter, the Italian and French Rivieras in another, Provence around Tarascon and Avignon in a third, Paris a fourth, Strasbourg and the Moselle Country in a fifth, the Rhineland in a sixth, London and the South of England in a seventh, New York in the eighth and the country from Philadelphia to Clarkesville, Tennessee in the ninth. You understand that these are all tracks of country I know more or less intimately and what I want to do is to visit them and contrast their atmospheres of a quarter century or so ago with their atmospheres today. If Hartmann cared to commission three or four of them I should not object, presuming he would pay for them each in advance so as to pay my expenses beforehand. The order of the chapters would not be the same as those I have outlined above. I should prefer to begin with London. Then do the Riviera and Rome and Naples returning through the Dolomites to Munich and the Rhine and

---

[1] The first mention of an idea Ford developed into *Great Trade Route* (New York, 1937).

back through Alsace to Paris. But I don't of course intend to set out on a year of travel but merely to make flying visits to those places in order to look at them again. Hartmann need not bother to object that these places have been done before because they have not been done in the way I should do them and his readers would probably end up with more real knowledge of the original causes of the crisis and of the hygiene of food and methods of preparation of the same than they ever did before. Whereas they would probably know surprisingly little about the ceilings of Michelangelo in the Vatican. If that does not suit Mr. Hartmann I am afraid I can not propose anything else.

I could write the three articles I have mentioned in my last letter for the following reasons. Zionism I have for long been interested in. I mentioned in my reminiscences that I must have been the first person to propose what afterwards became the Balfour declaration as a part of practical politics. My making that claim in my reminiscences has caused me to have a great many communications from Zionists and I am actually at the moment planning out a series of articles on the subject which the chief Zionist journal in America has asked me to write.[2] But I am sure they would let part of these go to Harpers for the sake of the wider appeal. (B.) Cookery, as Harpers know, is a subject about which I can always write with pleasure to myself and profit to the reader. I am always cooking and lately I have invented a new Provençal plât almost every day. Indeed I am actually cooking while I am dictating this letter to you. With regard to the decade of the 'twenties I could write about that because I am studying the period at the moment and have it very much in mind so that I could make what I wrote a study for my HISTORY OF OUR OWN TIMES. Indeed I should not mind writing five lively studies of the decades from 1880 to 1930—but I should prefer to write the travel articles.

You do not seem to realize that as soon as I had finished the novel[3] I began working on the History. Otherwise you would hardly have written cheerfully about my throwing off a few short

[2] There is no trace of the publication of these articles.
[3] Probably *The Rash Act*.

things. Still I suppose people can't get used to the fact that I am rather industrious.

If by any chance Hartmann liked to propose some subjects, there might be one or two among them that might fall in with my present preoccupations. I never was very good at thinking out subjects for myself and nearly all the articles I wrote for Harpers were suggested by Wells.

To Ray Long[*1]

My dear Long,

[Villa Paul, Toulon]
2 July 1932

I am flattered indeed that you and your friends should have taken Henry Martin so seriously. You seem to have entered into his problems as closely as I have myself—but from a quite different angle. You see the RASH ACT is the beginning of a trilogy that is meant to do for the post-war world and the Crisis what the TIETJENS tetralogy did for the war. It is to give the years of crisis from the point of view of a central character, as SOME DO NOT and NO MORE PARADES gave the war from the point of view of Tietjens. Now the chief characteristic of these years is want of courage— physical and moral. We are in the miserable pickle that we are in simply because *no one* has the courage either to spend money, commit suicide or anything else. Henry Martin is the typical man of this period. Far from being in love with suicide Henry Martin would never have committed it. If he had not done what he did he would have found some other way out of death. To kill him would make an old fashioned 'tragedy' of the pre-war 'nuvvle' type. That is not his type of tragedy—or ours. Ours and his is that we do not commit rash acts. It is true that Henry Martin's prototype—the man of whose life I was thinking—did

---

[1] In June, 1932, Ray Long (publishing partner of Richard R. Smith) wrote Ford at length about the manuscript of *The Rash Act*. Though enthusiastic about the book, he tried to make Ford change the ending. Ford had a sequel in mind, but Long could not have known that, for what he suggested was Ford's killing his hero, Henry Martin, by having him "die in bed with a girl, surrounded by the luxury and glitter and ease of his harem villa, . . . Fate's final trick" on a man with a New England conscience, an ineffectual man in love with suicide.

actually commit suicide last month. But he was a great poet, an audacious pervert and a hopeless dipsomaniac.[2] Henry Martin was none of these. He was just a sympathetic nonentity—the world as it is today, amiable but without purpose or faith.

His tragedy is that whatever he does—whatever feeble action he commits himself to—he always finds himself in exactly the same situation. If you consider his situation at the end of the book you will see that that is the only possible close for this volume. He began the book aimlessly married to some one who in no way interested him and in love with a vivid creature who is not for him. He lives on money that he has done nothing to earn, the sum being $5,000 a year. At the end of this volume he is united against his will to someone that does not interest [him]. He has got hold of, but not earned, a capital sum sufficient at five per cent to give him $5,000 a year, and he is in love with a vivid creature who is not for him. So it will go all his life. In the second volume[3] he will lose a considerable portion of his income by the collapse of the pound. To recover himself, at the instance of M. Lamoricière, he will invest the greater part of his capital in a real estate scheme; the dark girl will have coerced him into giving most of his income to Mlle. Becquerel; his capital will disappear by fraud. He will find Mlle. Becquerel dully insupportable and suspect her and the dark girl of being Lesbians. In the end he will finish in Springfield, Ohio, living on $5,000 a year that his father leaves him on condition that he inhabits that city for eight months out of the year.

This is of course the merest outline. There will be plenty of intrigue and of pictures of Riviera and Middle West society of all sorts. I am sufficient of a novelist not to put all my eggs into the first basket and I think if you trust me you will find yourself in possession of a more or less permanent property. A quite respectable portion of my income comes from books written twenty-five and thirty years ago and later. That, I know, is not in the American publishing tradition—but it is not disagreeable to have money coming in for nothing.

[2] On April 26, 1932, Hart Crane took his own life by leaping from the steamship *Orizaba* into the sea.

[3] *Henry For Hugh* (New York, 1934) is a sequel to *The Rash Act*.

If I changed the end of this book in the sense that you wish, it might make a dramatic tragedy of the older type. But that is not what is expected of me. I could not do it well or with any conviction and I should lose my present public which is quite faithful to me. What is more I should lose the support of the press. That is more serious still for with the support the press gives and your admirable knowledge of how to handle books there is no reason why my public should not be enormously and permanently increased. On the other hand if I tried for another public, writing with my tongue in my cheek, I should simply lose it. You cannot, you know, make a silk purse out of a sow's ear. On the other hand, you can make pretty good head-cheese. . . . Brawn they call it in England. A very nourishing food!

I hope, my dear Long, that the above will be sufficient to convince you that the obstacle to the change you wish is practically insurmountable. It is rather long but I put a good deal of it in for the use of your publicity branch. I will go through the last chapter and think about it. I daresay that the introduction of a sentence or two might make a little more plain what is exactly Henry Martin's position at the end of the book—I mean the fact that he is—*mutatis mutandis*—exactly where he started and that that is his real tragedy. In that case I will forward you the changed passages in the course of next week.

There is another point. It is rather late to think of getting the book ready for early this season and if it came out late the presidential election would surely interfere with its chances. I have had too bitter experience of having my books come out in the midst of general or presidential elections, wars and public turmoils to want this to happen in this case. Would it not be better to put off publication till the Spring?[4] I am getting on pretty fast with the HISTORY OF OUR OWN TIME and it is coming out pretty readable. There is no reason why it should not be ready for the Spring if you want it but as far as I am concerned it might just as well wait till the Autumn. But of course you know the situation over there much better than I and I am quite willingly in your hands.

By the bye, the father of my secretary, Mr. Murphy, is a proof-

---

[4] *The Rash Act* was published in February, 1933.

reader for Condé Nast and he says he would be glad to look through the proofs on the RASH ACT if that suited you. He is pretty good and strong on French.

I should be glad to know that you are coming over soon and am disappointed that you are not certain. I have two or three first manuscripts that I want to shew you and was holding them on the chance of your coming. Perhaps I had better mail them to you?

It is getting hot but not too hot here. My green corn, water-melons, squash and egg-plants are all pretty near bearing so if you come there will be plenty of home vegetables for you.

All good luck in any case.

To Ray Long*

Dear Long,   August 8, 1932

Further to your publicity or rather mine.

I enclose two photographs of myself and Ezra Pound. They were taken in Rapallo.[1] One of them shows the base of the statue to Columbus. Columbus landed in Rapallo after committing his indiscretion. Your publicity people might be able to make some-thing allegorical out of that—I don't quite see what. Ezra, at any rate, is the greatest poet the new world has ever sent to the old. Columbus was presumably the greatest explorer the old world ever sent to the new. I don't know quite where I come in but you might get one of your people to work it out. Ezra has just finished his immense poem called XXX CANTOS. It will be published by Farrar and Rinehart in the fall. My principal occupation at the moment is trying to get that book over. In the conspiracy for that purpose against the American peace of mind I am indulging in various and singular malpractices.

As for my other activities I go on working at—or rather work-ing up—my HISTORY OF OUR OWN TIMES. It gets considerably shorter and crisper as I go along. Otherwise I garden—an occu-pation that is considerably hampered by the drought, or sit on the

---

[1] Pound includes a slight but acute record of Ford's August visit in *Pavannes and Divagations* (New York, 1958).

terrace and look at the Mediterranean—an occupation whose pleasures are enhanced by the drought since one can always drink Vichy water.

I can't think of anything more to say but I hope this may be helpful.

To John Farrar*

[Villa Paul, Toulon]

Dear Farrar, [August, 1932]

I hear you are publishing Ezra's Cantos in the fall. I hope you will do well with them, for, as you know, the book is of very great importance and Ezra has been working at it for a very long time. I am trying to get up some sort of campaign in its favour because Ezra is not half as much recognised as he ought to be in his own country. I thought of doing as they do for Proust and people like that when they die—i.e. making up a pamphlet of testimonials from more or less distinguished people and sending it around with the review copies of the book.[1] Of course you would have to do this last. What I want to know is; when do you intend to publish? I hope not too early for the presidential elections are sure to interfere not only with the sales but with the public interest in books. Also I think it rather essential that the book should appear in London before it does in New York—just long enough before, that is, to let you use English reviews on the wrappers. American reviewers as a rule do not take Ezra half seriously enough and he has managed to offend a great number of them.

[1] By mid-August, Ford had organized a fanfare for Ezra Pound's *XXX Cantos*. He had asked Victor Gollancz earlier in the month to take sheets from Farrar and Rinehart, but apparently he refused since Faber and Faber eventually published the *Cantos* in England. The New York edition appeared in March, 1933. By that time Ford had assembled tributes from fifteen of Pound's friends and supporters—letters addressed to Ford in Toulon which he excerpted and edited for a pamphlet Farrar and Rinehart printed and enclosed with review copies. He called the twenty-two pages *The Cantos of Ezra Pound: Some Testimonials by Ernest Hemingway, Ford Madox Ford, T. S. Eliot, Hugh Walpole, Archibald MacLeish, James Joyce and Others.* The others included Allen Tate, Edmund Wilson, H. D., and William Carlos Williams. Their tributes are as varied as their personalities, all of them frank, some flattering, several unusually modest. Ford wrote an expansive introduction, signed D. C. More than likely, Pound remembered Daniel Chaucer.

But if you could quote some good English notices—and I would see that there were some—that might have an effect of brow beating people that don't like him. Also, would you go to the expense of printing the pamphlet supposing I supplied the copy? In the last resort I would pay for printing it myself but this is a year of crisis for me as for other people. Would you mind replying by cable? Yes's or No's would be sufficient. Let us say that question one is: Will you circulate copies of the pamphlet? Question two: Will you pay for printing the same? Three: Will you delay your publication until, say, a fortnight after English date of publication? What is your date of publication as at present arranged?

I hope you don't mind my butting in—but I don't suppose you will.

To T. S. Eliot*

Dear Eliot,

[Villa Paul, Toulon]
[August, 1932]

I suppose you know that Ezra's CANTOS are to be published in the fall by Farrar and Rinehart, in New York. For me as no doubt it is for you—this seems to be an event of primary importance in the tottering world. I am trying to organize in the United States—not in England from which Heaven defend me and where [A. R.] Orage says he's already active—a sort of campaign of log-rolling of which in the circumstances I don't think one need be ashamed. What I want to do is to get together a number of tributes to Ezra in person and if possible to the CANTOS themselves. These I propose to print in a small pamphlet and to let Farrar and Rinehart send this out with the review copies. If you would write a little—or indeed a lot—for this it would be of immense importance and use. I am thinking of brow beating the American reviewer into taking Ezra with the seriousness that ought to be accorded to him. I don't know what may be your opinion of the morality of this procedure but they do it for people like Conrad and Proust when they die and I don't see why poor Ezra should not get the benefit of this. I'd be glad to hear your answer to this as soon as you can bring yourself to write it.

To Hugh Walpole

Villa Paul
Cap Brun, Toulon, Var

Dear Walpole,
August 13, 1932

I am trying to get Gollancz to take sheets from America of Ezra's CANTOS. If you could use any influence on that amiable but singularly dilatory house to make them take a prompt and favourable decision I should feel extremely obliged. I don't know what your attitude towards Pound may be. He may very well have hit you with bludgeons in the past as he has hit almost everybody in the world at one time or other. But the xxx CANTOS is an epic of extreme magnificence and meaning and I am pretty sure that if you have read it you will want to help it on its way or if you haven't you would.

Let me have a line about it at your early convenience. As is always the case with me I have put off this job until it is almost too late and now have to work with cables and by beseeching people to answer me by return.

I see your activities continue to be as valiant as ever. I hope that means that you are prosperous and well—as indeed I am myself for the moment. Look us up one of these days.

Yrs.,

To William Carlos Williams*

[Toulon]

Dear Williams,
[September, 1932]

I am getting out a pamphlet of testimonials to Ezra on the occasion of the publication of his CANTOS. I know you will write something for it and that you don't have to be told why it is right and necessary that it should be done. Let me have something of about the length of a longish letter as soon as you can at this address.

What is the mystery of your publication at le Beausset which is just around the corner from here?[1] I have been to that rather lugubrious place four times since I saw the advertisement in

[1] *A Novelette and Other Prose* (*1921-1931*), published at Toulon by TO Publishers in 1932. Le Beausset is a village northwest of Toulon; the book may have been printed there.

Contempo but no one there has ever heard of un americain du nom de Williams. I hope you keep writing. I come across traces of you from time to time in various sheets and always with pleasure. When I was very young I wrote a poem about myself the last lines of which ran

> Like poor Dan Robin thankful for your crumb
> When other birds sing mortal loud and swearing
> When the wind lulls I try to get a hearing.

That might do well for you—and me—in these prodigious months and years but come over here and spend a little time under this roof and you shall see what le Beausset is like.

Yrs. always,

To A. R. Orage[1]

Dear Orage,

[Toulon]
September 7, 1932

Thank you for yours of the eighteenth ult. What I have been doing is to get together a pamphlet of testimonials to Ezra which his publishers are going to circulate along with the book in America. Paul Morand, Joyce and T. S. Eliot are so far enlisted and of course myself and Allen Tate and presumably Hemingway, William Carlos Williams and others of that kidney and year will come in automatically. I'd be glad, supposing it not to interfere with your plans, if you yourself would write a word or two. But who else is there in England that one ought to ask— I mean someone with some sort of international or at least transatlantic weight. I haven't the ghost of an idea. Enlighten me, will you? The only persons I can think of are Galsworthy and Walpole, both of whom seem inappropriate though I don't want to be in the least exclusive. The back numbers of the N.E.W. have duly reached me. They are not the more recent ones. Thank you. It makes striking and alarming reading and is surely what is wanted and more. I am rather alarmed at the idea of inserting my head between so many flashing shillelaghis but I will send

[1] Editor of *The New English Weekly: A Review of Public Affairs, Literature, and Art.*

you something as soon as I get my book finished. In the meantime
more and more power to your elbow.

To Ernest Hemingway

Villa Paul, Cap Brun
Toulon, Var
6 nov 1932

dear hemingway, (i have cut off the top of my left thumb with
a sickle and so cannot put down the capital stop)

thank you very much for the book on bull rings[1]   i have been
absorbing instruction from it ever since last night when i got it
and shall shortly be able to talk like any aficionado   the best
bull fighting in france is to be seen in nimes in the arena
they have regular dates—the last sunday in may and the sunday
next after the feast of the assumption and so on   i saw maera
kill some of his last bulls there some years ago

i wrote you some months ago asking you to write a word or
so about ezra on the occasion of a sort of testimonial that i am
getting up and that is to be circulated with his cantos   they
are to be at last published in n y next january and i think that if
one could cow the reviewers with authority the cantos might
receive decent attention   i suppose you did not get my letter
but write something now, quickly   you will feel good after
doing it   all sorts of people have done so and i at least should
feel badly if your name should be absent—either about the cantos
if you have read them or just about e p

all sorts of sla[i]nte's!

yrs always

To Theodore Dreiser

[Toulon]
My dear Dreiser,   27 February 1933

I was very glad to see your signature again.

Alas, I am afraid there is no chance of my writing anything for
your organ,[1] spirited as it is and much as I should like to write

---

[1] *Death in the Afternoon* (New York, 1932).

[1] *The American Spectator.*

for you. But I simply can't write anything short, try as I may. Otherwise I should try to do a piece for you and believe, pray, that I am flattered by the invitation.

I am pretty well, thank you, but bothered as everyone is nowadays. But you, I hope, flourish. I wish I could get to New York and come again to Mt. Kisco, but I see no immediate likelihood of being able to leave here for I am buried deep beneath voluminous works. It is a good idea of yours that having a book out should make one feel better—as if, I suppose, it were a tooth!

All good luck!

Yours always

P.S. Do you suppose you would like a little [article] about the state of Jewry, which in Europe has become pretty parlous with the arrival of Hitler and the closing of Palestine? I was a little responsible for the Balfour Declaration and have for a long time wanted to write something about Zionism. There is a great deal to say about the matter but I might be able to boil something down into about 3,000 words if you could let me have that amount of space in two numbers.

To Ezra Pound

37 Rue Denfert-Rochereau
[Paris]
8. 3. 33

Dear Ezra,

Thank you very much: I feel humiliated at having worried you—especially with the dollar collapse which probably hampers your father. Things however are a little better here. I have wrung £50 out of Cape for Stella [Bowen] whose complete pennilessness bothered me more than anything and Lippincotts have paid—with a cheque that cannot be cashed. If you do not mind I will keep your cheque by me till Stella has actually got Cape's money and will then destroy it wiring you the one word "burnt." We can I think dribble along till then in reduced circumstances. I *ought* to have plenty of money for there is plenty of demand for my writing in your country—but it does not work out that way.

I wish I could send you some verse, but except for the BUCKSHEE series which has already appeared I have not written

any verse since 1930. If BUCKSHEE would suit you although it has
appeared I will ask the London publishers—I can't remember
who they were and have not the book here—for permission. It was
in a series got together by some fool whose name does not come
back to me—Abercrombie, I should think.[1] I might write some
verse in a day or two. I have felt the sort of birth symptoms
lately and if the capers of your bankers do not cause abortion
something might come. I wrote the below in answer to somebody
who said I could not find a rhyme for Closerie des Lilas:

> An elderly maid at the Lilas
> Emitted a horrible squeal as
> She found that a male
> With cheeks pink and pale
> Wasn't really a man but a he-lass.

It would be rotten luck if your CANTOS are really to come out on
the 14th before all this financial uproar is settled. My RASH ACT
which is more like what I want to write then anything I have
done for years came out on the 24th ult. and has naturally been
absolutely submerged. Should not have minded if I had not put
more into it than, as it were, I could afford—I mean in the way
of mental fatigue. You will find more in it about your country
than in all the belchings poor Bob ever belched.

Janice [Biala] sends her love. She added something about
your critical activities, but I have forgotten what it was and she
has gone out. It is just as well because she is rather modern.

                                                           Yrs,

To Ezra Pound

                                                        [Toulon]
Dear Ezra,   March 27, 1933

I am ashamed to say that I cashed that check of yours after all
as it took a very long time to get the Lippincott money. Here,
however, is a check for the amount. I do hope it hasn't bothered
you too much to be kept waiting.

As soon as I have found some paper and string I will send you
a copy of the RASH ACT.

---

[1] *New English Poems*, edited by Lascelles Abercrombie (London, 1931).

I have delayed writing this because I have been angling with another publisher to get him to publish the Cantos in England. The matter is still undecided but as soon as it is actually decided I will write to you about it. The publisher is one to whom you have written letters of violent abuse and the chief obstacle is that he is afraid you might resort to violence if one of the letters got printed upside down. As soon as I have convinced him that this would not be the case, I think it may come off.

To Archibald MacLeish*

My dear MacLeish:

[Toulon]
May 1, 1933

I have just seen the Pound pamphlet though Farrar & Rinehart never took the trouble to send me a copy. I think it looks fine and is a tribute not only to Mr. Pound but to the generosity of its writers.

Did I, by the bye, ever express to you my admiration for your HAMLET? It is really a very great book, and my admiration is equally great. If you would tell your publishers to send me copies of your works it would give me great pleasure and I might possibly be of use to them. I ought to buy them myself but I never hear of them in Toulon, so I can't.

Will you ever be coming over here? If so you will find a hard bed and plenty of highly spiced cooking always at your disposal in this bastide, and in the meantime more power to your elbow.

Yours,

To Mr. Mack*¹

Dear Mr. Mack,

19. 8. 33

I have now had your manuscript some days and have read it with a great deal of interest. It appears to have been held up in the douane though why the customs should have been disturbed about it seems rather inscrutable. However, on payment of Frs 4 it was delivered to me.

¹ Ford was eager to help all young writers even when, as here, he knew little of their identity.

I wish I knew something of your circumstances—and temperament. I found the book ingeniously constructed and full of life,
very well written and with admirable character drawing. You
have undoubtedly got the proper gifts for a novelist and a great
deal of knowledge of how a novel should be written. So, if you
can stick it, I see no reason at all why you should not become a
considerable novelist.

The trouble with this book is that the subject is not very good.
It is, that is to say, rather slight for the formidable apparatus of
psychology with which very admirably you approach life and,
though there is plenty of subtlety in the handling and indeed in
the writing, the story is singularly unsubtle. I doubt, to begin with,
whether any one is going to believe that a hard-boiled city man,
like your husband, is going to be taken in for a minute by a
confidence-trickster—and the mere circumstance that your villain
or his pal can imagine that he could be makes both those characters rather unreal. They could not have been so naive as to think
he would be so naive. The subject of betrayal by a war-comrade
is good enough but it would appear that you have not cast around
for sufficiently long for the machinery of the betrayal. You must
remember that material invention is as necessary to the appearance of inevitability of a novel as is any other department of the
art. It is in fact the sine qua non, for without the appearance of
inevitability no novel can stand on its legs. The betrayal must be
something much more from the plane of psychology even if it
had to be a matt [sentence unfinished].

It would even be better—if more usual—if the villain plotted
the seduction of the city man's wife. That would be a real betrayal whereas getting a few pounds out of him by means of the
confidence trick is nothing at all as a device since the city man
would probably make him a present of the money for old sake's
sake. It could not be a matter of more than a few quid. A city
man on a week end does not carry more than that and surely
he would lend as much as that to an old comrade of the trenches?

This may seem to you a rather commonplace way of looking
at the matter—but life is a commonplace affair and it is only by
piling one damn commonplace complication on another that you
arrive at the tragi-comedy or the comic tragedy that life is. . . .

As it is, on account of the inadequacy of your mechanical device you are forced to the bundle of chinese crackers of the last scene— which is a pity because the rest of the book is good stuff.

That is why I say that I wish I knew something of your circumstances and temperament. If you are hard up or impatient or both you might very well publish the book as it stands: it might quite possibly meet with some success and there you might be launched. On the other hand, if you are not in need of money and are strenuous and determined, you might do worse than to consider what I have said and try to find another machinery and a less detonating catastrophe. The book might in that case have less success, for the public and the critics like simple and naive tales that detonate at their ends. So you might be longer in establishing yourself as a novelist—but your position would be more secure and your self-respect enhanced. A third way would be to put the book in a drawer and start another. I am sure that with this apprenticeship you will do something much bigger sooner or later. . . . But perhaps that would be a too heroic remedy.

Don't think that I am unappreciative. The mere fact that I have tried so hard to make plain what I mean should be evidence that your work has interested me a great deal. I do not think I have written so long a letter for donkeys' years—and then more donkeys and years. Perhaps if you ever take a holiday you might dare to look me up here. I should be glad to have a talk with you.

To Gerald Bullett*[1]

Dear Sir:

[Toulon]
24. 8. 33

Anything that calls attention to writing in a world that avoids with disgust all the products of the Muse is to be enthusiastically supported. You yourself must know best whether such matter can attract your readers and, since you do apparently think that it can —why, the Crisis must be approaching its end. In any case accept my blessing on your efforts.

But when it comes to writing about my own work, blushes, confusion and muffled curses are more the order of the day. I

---

[1] An editor of *The Week-end Review*.

have not the least idea what to say. I have for years been writing—
for American and a little for French consumption—an immense
series of works attempting to render our own times. America and
to a less extent France have, thank Goodness, consumed them in
sufficient quantities to keep me going on a Mediterranean terrace
where I continue to work and to watch the fall of the dollar. Occasionally one English publisher or another has published one of
these books in London. Six months after he has written to tell me
that that book has sold from two to a hundred copies, that he has
lost a thousand pounds over it and that his imminent appearance
in Carey Street is all my fault. Then, for my next book he offers
a fifth of what he paid for my last one.

I gather thus that the London public does not like my work.
Nothing is there for tears. Why should a London public like my
works? My constatations of life have dubious international back-
grounds; they contain nothing about British birds' nests, wild-
flowers or rock-gardens; they are 'machined' with a Franco-Ameri-
can modernity that must be disagreeable indeed to the inhabitants
of, say, Cheltenham. To them, on account of the 'time-shift' and
projection instead of description, they must be quite incomprehensible and inexpressibly boring. Between the Middle West and the
Eastern sea-board of the United States as well as round the Pantheon where those devices saw the light they are already regarded
as *vieux jeu*, accepted as classics which you must know of, and
used for Manuals in University English Classes. So I go on writing
in the hope that, a hundred and fifty years from today, what I turn
out may be used as an alternative study in, say, Durham University.
And at any rate I have the comfortable feeling that none of our
entrants for the Davis Cup will have been kept off the playing
fields of Eton by a reprehensible engrossment in my novels. For
goodness' sake do not let me be taken as decrying our recovery
of that vessel. The only two times in years when I have voluntarily
listened to the radio have been when the results of the late Presidential Election and that of that Cup were coming in from Sche-
nectady and Paris respectively. And the election of Mr. Roosevelt
left me relatively cold. If only Kent could win the County Cham-
pionship and we could have a succession of thunderstorms here!

I am sorry I cannot say more about my books. I hope you will take it that that is because I am like Marcus Aurelius' really virtuous man who, when he had put forth his good works, thought no more of them than does the vine when its grapes are gathered.

Yours faithfully

P.S. I remember reading with pleasure one of your books—it must have been in 1923 or four. If I have read none since it is my misfortune for no Literary organs ever come my way. I remember it very much disturbed my friend Mr. W. C. Bullitt, the Democratic mystery man, because he thought it would interfere with the sale of a book he had just published. So I was pleased to see your name again.

To Horace Shipp*

Dear Mr. Shipp,

[Toulon]
25. 8. 33

I am of course much touched by your wanting to dedicate your new venture[1] to me and I feel that I should be churlish to refuse.

At the same time, could you not do better for the book? My connection with England is now so remote and the poor old gleam of my ENGLISH REVIEW shone so long ago upon the waters that, should your readers look at your dedication—I suppose some readers do!—they will say: "Ah, a poor relation!" Or else: "This fellow wants a Tin Lizzie de luxe at reduced rates." A dedication should radiate lustre on a book, not the book on the dedicatee.

Far away and long ago, indeed all that! It is really fabulous how far, and I find myself writing, not on purpose, books merely for Middle Western consumption, and of course a little for the French. At any rate, thank Goodness, the Middle West and some French army messes and the district round the Pantheon consume a sufficiency to let me continue working on this Mediterranean hillside— and of course writing autographs!

Occasionally a daring London publisher puts out one of my books in that city. Five months or so afterwards he writes to me to say that the volume has sold anything between two and a hun-

[1] *The Second English Review Book of Short Stories* (London, 1933). The first collection (1932) had a foreword by Ford.

dred copies, that the expenses of the publication have ruined him —and offers me a fifth of the sum he paid for the last for my next book but two. It is like dropping things down wells so deep that even after years of waiting no reverberation comes to the listener at the well-head.

I do not mean that I am blighted. If one makes no effort to be read in Hampstead why should Hastings read one? (I beg your pardon; I had forgotten that you lived in Hampstead, having the Elgreco's and Toledo in my mind—by the bye do if you can go to Compostella. It is one of the most spectacular places I ever struck.) No, I was merely elaborating on the theme that it is foolish to dedicate books to me. . . . However, I suppose you will in spite of that and I remain touched and obliged.

By-the-bye, too, why not, since you are so far south, come on here and look us up. You can get from Barcelona to Toulon for about twopence and the view from this Mediterranean hillside will beat any view between St. Sebastian and Gib[ralter]—though I don't know the Mediterranean Spanish coast. It may be less arid. In any case I hope you are having a wonderful holiday and remain—in the words of Johnson when he accepted a dedication from a Rev Mr, I think, Kidd—

Your obliged, humble and obedient Servant

To Gerald Bullett

[Toulon]
Dear Mr. Bullett,   October 8, 1933

I shall be delighted to write a notice of the Cantos for you. I suppose you will not mind if I repeat a few phrases of what I have written about Ezra in America. I have written so much about him there that I am afraid it would be difficult for me to say anything completely inédit.

May I put the delicate question as to whether you pay for contributions—if not perhaps you would kindly put me on the free list of the Week-end Review and we will call it quits.

Ref. to that inquest[1] it occurred to me to mention it merely because I imagined there might be going to be a sequel and in that

[1] Probably a reference to a novel or story that Gerald Bullett had sent Ford.

case the fact of there having been an inquest would make a considerable impression on the psychology of the adolescent and things that legitimately and usefully and convincingly make impressions on the psychologies of one's characters are so rare and valuable that it is a pity to omit them. But perhaps you do not think in sequels as I do or rather perhaps you do not think in terms of books so vast that they can only be published in instalments. At any rate acquit me of wanting in intelligence in mentioning that inquest without an ulterior motive. I am myself at the moment engaged on the sequel of the Rash Act and have occasion to curse myself occasionally for omitting in the first volume motives that would have made what I am writing now go very much more easily.

Yours very sincerely,

To Ezra Pound

Dear Ezra,

[Toulon]
October 8, 1933

I am duly writing something about [you] for an apparently high brow review in England[1] and I will also slip in a note about the concerts. As for your kind offer to log roll me I guess I am past log rolling and the activity would appear too suspect—in the line of 'you scratch my back and I'll scratch yours.' But if you wanted to please me you would do what you could to log roll René Béhaine[2] who, in the eyes of Léon Daudet and myself and other worthy people, passes for the greatest living novelist in the world—who also has been writing one masterpiece for upwards of twenty years and who, heaven help us, is quite as unpopular as either you or I. If you think you could do anything effective I will have his books sent to you.

[1] Probably the notice Gerald Bullett asked him to write for *The Week-end Review*. In "Mediterranean Reverie" (November 11, 1933), Ford not so much reviewed *XXX Cantos* as "advertised" Pound to the British public as poet, economist, linguist, sculptor, duellist, bassoonist, and composer—the rhythmic virtuoso of Rapallo, the Dante of the twentieth century.

[2] In *The Saturday Review of Literature* (October 12, 1929), Ford attempted to do for Béhaine in America what Léon Daudet was doing in France and Robert de Traz in Switzerland: insisting that every man who called himself an intellectual must read Béhaine's *Histoire d'une Société*, a series of novels begun in 1908 with *Les Nouveaux Venus* and continued through the 1930's.

Both Janice and I are very glad that your father can get along. Do give him and your mother from time to time the assurance that we do not forget them. We should have sent them some green corn this year but owing to the drought the corn was a complete failure.

Yours,

To Ezra Pound

Toulon
Dear Ezra,   29: 10: 33

I got the review of the CANTOS complete with blurb of the concerts off only last week.[1] It would be better if I had not had to wriggle the subject around to get the concerts in—there would have been fewer personalities and more about the CANTOS. . . . Mais tu l'as voulu, Georges Dandin. One day I will really write something au fond about them.

Your reply about [René] Béhaine reminds me of a day twenty odd years ago when I went round to No. 2, The Pines, Putney and told Mr. Theodore Watts Dunton that a remarkable poet had risen in the West, asking him to log roll said R. P. He replied: "My dear Fordie, you are always umumum discovering these remarkable genuises in umumumsnuffleum remote snuffle deserts. They're never any good; I don't suppose I shall be able to read the umsnuffleum barbaric yawps but I'll ask young Hake andumumum Caine and umumum the other young of the um Circle and we'll see the result." And you did, in the ATHENAEUM. . . . Eheu fugaces Pontifex, Putnibus. . . . Plus ça change plus c'est la même chose. . . . Gweil angau na gwyllyth. . . . Eppur—but no, not that. . . . Displicuit nasus suus. . . . Eripuit caelo fulmen sceptrumque tyrannis. . . . Ex ungue leonem. . . . Io non so lettere. . . . Neque semper arcum tendit Apollo. . . . Sine ira et studio. . . . Atque ego. . . But no! Atque mihi eruditio quaedam!

Yrs,

[1] See note, page 225.

To Caroline Gordon[1]

Dearest Caroline: Toulon
                                                       11. 9. 33

I ought to have written to you long [ago]—though "ought" with its collocation of painful duty is not the right word for, once I get started, it is pleasure enough. The difficulty is really in the starting. At any rate with me it is almost a necessity to have some event or mold out of the common run to start one. I really believe I write, hardened though I may seem, with as much difficulty as any schoolboy who follows his pen round his mouth with his tongue— I don't mean merely letters, I mean everything—and the condition grows. I used to write French with greater fluency than English but lately I have been writing articles and letters in French and found them as difficult as English. I don't suppose it means that I am losing fluency: merely that, as my time on earth may be presumed to be shortening, I am more and more determined to express exactly what I mean. Still I manage to turn out pretty regularly my thousand words a day at the story of Henry Martin[2] who is now really getting it in the neck.

It isn't however any special event or mood that makes me now take up, as you might say, my pen. Things go on here like a tale that is told. The drought destroyed everything in the garden except for the semi-tropical things like melons and pimento. Even the corn felt the drought. We went away for about ten days to Juan les Pins, leaving a man to water and of course he did no watering so when we got back all the strawberries and all the string beans and peas and things of a northern complexion were as dry as paper. From the middle of March till the end of September we had not a drop of rain and water in the pipes only twice a week for an uncertain hour at a time. Now however we have had two or three splendid storms and have just put in cabbages, cauliflowers, leeks, celery and sown carrots, turnips, spinach and the more homespun northern things. There has been too much water for the celery and leeks which have developed rust and there are caterpillars in

[1] American novelist, author of *Penhally* (1931), *Aleck Maury, Sportsman* (1934) and other novels.
[2] Hero of *The Rash Act* (New York, 1933) and its sequel, *Henry for Hugh* (Philadelphia, 1934).

millions on the cabbages which look like fishing nets. Still there you are—the short and simple annals of the damn poor.

Ray Long and [Richard] Smith[3] fell down on me in the spring and I transferred to Lippincott's who seem amiable but only pay me half what L & S did—and that again has to be halved because of the fall in the dollar. They are just publishing IT WAS THE NIGHTINGALE and seem rather pleased with it. So perhaps I have found my earthly home. As H[enry] J[ames] used to say—it would be nice to find one's final publisher but it would be rather like going into an almshouse! I don't think I should much mind that if one has a nice copper kettle on the hob and you to bring me packets of snuff—and it may well come to that yet.

[. . . . .] Julie is in London with her mother who fled before the rising franc—or the falling pound. I don't like it much—for I should have preferred Julie never to learn English and certainly not to go to an English school and become the usual English hobbledehoy.

[. . . . .] And that—as Bon Gaultier says—is all my tale: sirs, I hope 'tis new t'ye: here's your ferry coot health: and tamn the whisky duty. . . . You will say I am getting into my dotage with all these quotations. I forgot to say that Janice and I have been working very hard for some months, she earning golden opinions and selling a picture or two which is why we are not stark naked. As for myself, modesty forbids my saying what I think about my novel—but the RASH ACT has made rather a stir in London and my star there seems to be rising again—which you might call calling the Old World in to redress the balance of the [new]; for L & S declared themselves bankrupt on the day after its publication in New York and it sold practically nothing, which is a pity as it was my best book—more, that is to say, like what I really want to write than anything I have yet done. So that's that.

I should probably have written to you much sooner but for your letter about my work. Not that I wasn't touched and pleased and covered with blushes. But I never do know what to do with praise: if I say "Yes, pretty good!" it seems fatuous and if I say "Pretty damn bad" it is almost worse. And I was feeling as a matter of fact rather bad about most of my old work and had not begun the

[3] Publishers of *The Rash Act* in the United States.

new book—but you know that I must have been pleased—and how much pleased. [. . . . .]

Well, now we jog and stagger through the autumn. It is just about a year since we came back from Germany with the Strasbourg paté and just about two since I was setting out from New York to go down to you. . . . But no, three!!!! Truly the waters flow under the bridge and the little stones find their places as says a Spanish proverb of my own invention. [. . . . .]

So may all nice things be yours.

To John Chamberlain*¹

Dear Sir,   21/11/33

I think you should launch a thunderbolt—I suppose the New York, like the London, TIMES keeps them in stock—at the head of Mr. Horace Gregory. Surely it is *lèse majesté* to mislead the THUN-DERER!

I have procured a real New Yorker to read every word that I ever wrote about Chicago and, as per enclosed certificate, you may be assured that I never stated or suggested that there was a subway in Porcopolis. The probability is that Mr. Gregory reads mud-dledly. In a short article—the only one—that I wrote about Chicago I had occasion to say that I did not like underground railways but there is no suggestion that the tunnels I disliked were in Chicago.² And surely if I wanted to invent anything typical of

¹ In his "Books of the Times" column for October 20, 1933, John Chamberlain wrote a jaunty and complimentary review of Ford's autobiographical volume *It Was the Nightingale.* "The literary portrait which Mr. Ford lights up," he said, ". . . seems to be a compound of a great deal of curiosity, some shreds of Tory philosophy, a little garrulity, some undoubted charm, a bit of Oriental passivity, a liking for good talk, good dinners, and much deference from his fellow-craftsmen." But Chamberlain also credited Ford with founding *The English Review* in 1900 (rather than 1908), of printing T. S. Eliot in its pages (which he did not), and of describing (according to Horace Gregory's memory of it) the subway system of Chicago.

² "Chicago," New York *Herald Tribune Books* (June 5, 1927), pp. 1, 6. Ford found Chicago exhilarating but less comfortable and friendly than New York: "I dislike, for instance, being treated as a moron in subways if I do not know how many cents to put into coin boxes. It is for that reason that I have always

Chicagoan energy it would not be anything so purely Cockney as a tube. Did you never hear of the Tuppenny one? Why, at the age of ten I used to go to school every day—from Kensington to Westminster—by the Underground. So I hope you will correct Mr. Gregory.

Did I, by the bye, publish Mr. T. S. Eliot in the ENGLISH REVIEW? I don't believe I did. . . . More trouble you will have made for me!

Otherwise I have to thank you for an amiable article.

Yours faithfully

To Jefferson Jones[*][1]

[Paris]

Dear Mr. Jefferson Jones, 12. I. 34

I have now had a bit of rest and am thinking about work again.

I have in contemplation two books, the one my history of our own times for which I have been collecting materials for a number of years and the other a book about Provence and the Cote d'Azur. [. . . . .]

The book on Provence is the sort of thing I like writing and usually write with spirit. It will form in one sense a book of reminiscence since I have spent so much time in those regions, in another one of cheerful history since the story of Provence and the Riviera extends not only from the time of the Romans but as you might say from the courts of Love of the Troubadours to the love without Courts of Monte Carlo and Cannes today—though I do not mean that the book will be at all erotic! The contrast of this antiquity and modernity will give me naturally the chance to make digressions on many things from the heresy of the Albigenses to cooking, bull-fighting, the wines of the Rhone, and the Crisis, and all the South of France is so full of international literary and aesthetic memories—with which in later years I have been a good deal mixed up—that the result should be much like that of IT WAS THE NIGHTINGALE[2] with possibly an appeal to a rather larger public since

---

feared the America that is not New York." The statement is admittedly ambiguous.

[1] Of J. B. Lippincott Company.

[2] Ford's impressionistic memoirs which Lippincott had published in October, 1933.

almost everybody with any money at all goes at one time or another to the Midi and likes to be reminded of it. [. . . . .]

In the happy event of your wishing to commission both books I think I should finish the History before beginning on the Provence book since I am in Paris where materials for the last chapter are more handy. On the other hand I should prefer writing about Provence as I am rather mentally fagged and it would be more pleasurable writing. However, as to that, I should be quite in your hands.

Perhaps you would kindly let me have a reply at your early convenience for I shall be rather at a loose end until I know.

With kind regards,

To Gerald Bullett

37 Rue Denfert-Rochereau
Paris
14. 1. 34

My dear Bullett,

I am really grieved to see that the WEEK END REVIEW is stopping.[1] It was a really admirable journal and gave me pleasure with each number—which is more than I can say for any other journal I have lately come across. I hope it does not mean that you lose work that you need or liked—but of course a fatality attaches to work that one needs or likes—and to journals to which the same adjectives can attach and a certain gloom seems always to hang over these months of the year. But I hope you will find luck in other quarters.

Could you by any chance tell me who was editor of the SATURDAY [REVIEW] in 1919? I mention the gentleman in IT WAS THE NIGHTINGALE but can't for the life of me remember his name.[2]

I am addressing this to the W.E.R. office. I suppose there will still be someone there to forward it to you. Let me have news of your activities from time to time and, if you ever come to Paris, look us up. I wish we could get to London but, since this time last year, three publishers—two American and one French—have gone bankrupt under me and in addition there is always the fear of the

---

[1] Founded by Gerald Barry, *The Week-end Review* merged with *New Statesman and Nation* in January, 1934.

[2] W. E. Waltop.

complete collapse of the dollar to keep one from adventurous voyagings.

                                        Yours cordially

The W. E. R., by the bye, still owes me for the Pound article I wrote for them. Tell them not to bother to pay for it if there is any shortage. I know what it is to be badgered when one has difficulty in turning round!

To Janet Adam Smith*¹

Dear Madam,   3. 6. 34

I am flattered and obliged by your letter of the 17th ult. which has followed me about a good deal. I am glad too that you are going to have a series of articles on American literature which is a subject very much calling for attention. I trust that with no firm hand you will check your writers in any tendency to patronise that phenomenon—for one day there will be a war between the two branches of Anglo-Saxondom and it will be caused by someone from a minor Oxford College patronising a writer from Spokane.

I should be very glad to write something for you—but I have written so much about Henry James and the subject is so vieux jeu—and in a sense, dangerous, that I cannot bring myself to write about him any more. Besides, as the years have gone on I have grown more and more antipathetic to the Master of Rye. Why not ask Mr. [T.S.] Eliot himself to do it: he has been reversing my mental processes.

But if you would let me write about something more actual I should be delighted to embrace the opportunity. The greater part of my life since the war has been spent in literary America or in the society of American writers; I pass in that country for an American writer myself and am given credit for having what is called "discovered" a considerable proportion of the better-known post-war American writers. So that, if you would commission me to write for your journal—of which the few numbers that I have seen I have found very sympathetic—something on, say, the American literary scene today I would jump at the opportunity

¹ Assistant Editor of *The Listener*.

and could let you have the article well before the end of this month though perhaps, to avoid repetition, it might be as well if you would let me see the proof of the article by the writer on the American Novel and indeed of that on the Book Market and the Reading Public.

Yours faithfully

To Anthony Bertram

Villa Paul
Cap Brun, Toulon, Var
14 Sept. '34

Dear Bertram;

I fancy I owe you a letter and should have written some time ago but both Biala and I have been slugging away at my book on Provence and things in general.[1] Fortunately we got it off a week ago last Monday—with its thirty-eight illustrations and all and since then we have done nothing but tidy up—the garden and the house and our wardrobes—and letters too. We are having a prolonged tropical spell—which is very agreeable when one has plenty of shade and, momentarily, enough water for the irrigation—at any rate for three days ahead and that is as much as we can expect here. Curiously enough, though we started the garden very late and I have had relatively little time to attend to it we have had bumper crops—enough for ourselves and our neighbors and we still wallow in tomatoes and pimenti and eggplants, though things like haricots and peas and what, in England, are called 'greens' are at an end and we shall not see any more until October when we may expect some rain. They will go right on till next summer. I get three crops a year off my land and could get five if I took the trouble—but three is quite enough. The vintage is just over—we did not get a great many grapes as the vines had the maladie and I never found time to spray them.

If we had not to go to New York pretty soon—which with things as they are is a rather nervous undertaking—we should be enjoying a halcyon time of leisure after a rather harrying spring and summer, for Janice's thirty-odd illustrations meant that we had to go see almost as many places including a very interesting corrida at Nimes at which she made some really startling drawings *in*

[1] Published by J. B. Lippincott in 1935, by George Allen & Unwin in 1938, to the most enthusiastic notices Ford ever received.

situ—which is not very often done. This particular *mise à mort* was interesting because the audience were engaged in hating actively a particularly magnificent *matador* whose performance was so classical and perfect that they yet could not hiss him. . . . And to feel sixteen or seventeen thousand people all actively detesting a single figure was a most curious experience. The last time he had been in Nimes—where he had formerly been an adored performer—he had been off colour—which happens now and then even to the best of matadors—and the audience had hissed him. He had shouted out that only geese are really proficient in that pursuit and that had driven the Neumausians crazy. So he had been trying to stage a come-back. But his second bull—a clumsy beast like a Sussex red—wouldn't fight and that finished his chances, so if we want to see Chicuelo again we shall have to go to Spain.

I don't know why I should deluge you with horticulture and tauromachics except that that's what one has mostly on one's mind here. I read both of your novels with pleasure and admiration for the handling—particularly the one about the castle which I have lent to an appreciative American so that I can't remember—oh yes, THEY CAME TO THE CASTLE. That seemed to me to be extremely skilfully worked out. I can't myself take much pleasure in the contemplation of the extinguishing of disappearing aristocracies and their social distresses. One sees a lot of it here and viewed from near at hand the only wonder is that they have kept afloat so long. But that is not a criticism. Anyone has the right to choose what subject he pleases and the handling, as I have said, is very good indeed. I hope that it, and all your books, do well—and the decorative journal and the servant and the maid and the ox and the ass and everything that is in Sussex.

I often look back with pleasurable memories to the week-end we spent with you, and Janice asks me to say that so emphatically does she. Indeed she often talks of taking a cottage with a thatch and an ingle in the shelter of the South Downs—and having tamed such detester of all things Anglo-Saxon, Bignor and its sunlight may score something to the account of international cordialities.

But indeed we both harbour mild feelings of guilt at the idea that we kept Mrs. Bertram so long in Chi[chester] that your olive branch may have suffered. . . . Still, I suppose if it had been so, she would have sent us an envelope-full of small-pox germs. All good wishes to you.

Yrs,

Oh, Janice saw on your table a copy of a poetry periodical—called, I think NEW POETRY—and in it a poem by Allen Tate which I want to quote for my Provence book's title page. Could you send me the address and correct name of that journal so that I could write to them for a copy? I'd be much obliged.

To Anthony Bertram

Villa Paul
Cap Brun, Toulon, Var
27 Sept. 1934

My dear Bertram,

Thank you very much for your letter that is, like yourself, always charming so that I don't know at which place first to begin. ... Let us begin with the young man from Fleet Street. I haven't got a copy of the NIGHTINGALE handy so I don't know to what you refer. But I am pretty certain that I never guyed you either identifiably or unidentifiably. I was surrounded at Coopers[1] by such shoals of young men of all shades and countries—who have nearly all since "made good"—that I might have been referring to anybody and still more likely to nobody—and I am pretty certain that, if I were referring to you, I should have called you an amiable young [man] from Trafalgar Square which was the place with which at that time I most identified you.[2] Indeed I am quite certain of that. Besides which I probably invented a young man to serve my purpose. Indeed, if the reference was at all disagreeable, I assuredly did.

Certainly I'll accept with the greatest pleasure the dedication of your book,[3] but for goodness' sake don't use any such form of words or all the panjandrums—or is it panjandra since they are certainly neuters?—or the United Kingdoms will throw their bed-pots over you and the book. Something like

---

[1] Ford's cottage at Bedham, Sussex.
[2] Anthony Bertram worked at The National Gallery for a time.
[3] *Men Adrift* (London, 1935).

6 May 1935

TO

F. M. F.

WHO

WENT DOWN THE

DRAIN

ANNO MCMXIV &

SINCE THAT DATE

ABANDONED

ALL HOPE OF

A GLORIOUS RESURRECTION

THIS!

( ) *deprecatingly* ( )

would probably best redound to your reputation.

Thanks also very much for copying out Allen's poem. I couldn't imagine myself taking so much trouble for anyone in the world.

Nothing could be lovelier than the thought of another stay in Bignor, but, alas, Destiny seems to be taking us to New York on business—if you can imagine anything so forlorn as 'business' in N. Y. of these days and years. Perhaps we might take Sussex on the way back. I'm sure I wish we could.

Our best wishes to you all and with renewed thanks I'm

Always yours,

To Paul Palmer*[1]

61 Fifth Avenue
New York City
6 May 1935

Dear Palmer,

For the articles by me that you have suggested I should propose the following subjects

Henry James
W. H. Hudson
John Galsworthy
Stephen Crane
Arnold Bennett
Thomas Hardy
George Meredith
Anatole France
Theodore Dreiser

[1] Editor of *The American Mercury*.

H. G. Wells
Christina Rossetti
Ezra Pound

the articles to be not less than 3,500 or more than 5,000 words in length, the ms. of the first article to reach you on or before the 1st July next and the remainder at intervals of two months at latest, you to pay me or my agent on receipt of ms.[2]

As these articles will cost me a good deal of trouble in the way of getting together and reading books I think you ought to pay me at the rate of $150 per article. I think I ought to stipulate that as the articles will run over a couple of years, in case you or the proprietor of the *Mercury* should give up the editorship or proprietorship respectively the contract should continue to bind your successors. . . . But I hope you will not give up.

What would you think of ALMS FOR OBLIVION as a general title for the series?[3]

Let me have your observations on above at your convenience

To Julia Ford*

Dearest Julie: Cap Brun
                                                       11 Sept 35
It is sad that you shd. have so far forgotten yr. French as no longer to be able to write a French letter: [. . . . .] At any rate I'm glad you seem to have enjoyed yourself at Hennequeville in spite of the rain.

It rained even here, after you left. There was a true cyclone with immense rain from the East & then ten minutes of complete stillness & immediately afterwards tremendous rain from the South & West, wh. shewed that we were in the centre of the gyration

[2] Ford eventually omitted Bennett, Meredith, France, and Rossetti, substituting Turgenev, Swinburne, Conrad, and D. H. Lawrence. The article on Pound was written but never published. "Conrad and the Sea," the first of the series, appeared in June, 1935; the eleventh and last article, an impressionistic portrait of Theodore Dreiser, in April, 1937.

[3] When collected for book publication in the United States, the series was called *Portraits from Life* (Boston, 1937). It was published in England in 1938 by George Allen & Unwin under the title *Mightier Than the Sword: Memories and Criticisms.*

. . . just like the cyclone I described in the *Rash Act*. . . . However, as you know, the more rain we get here the better we like it. As a result, we ate our first peas immediately afterwards and indeed ever since we have got all our vegetables & fruit from the garden wh. means a certain saving of money & still more of Janice's time—for since she does not have to go to the market she can paint &, since yr. departure, has done three pictures of New York. . . . That, you see, is *l'Art Moderne*—you paint New York from Provence & the shores of the Mediterranean from New York. . . . Indeed it's the way I write.

The vitrier who has been putting in my window in the study has left, so I can get at my machine again. [. . . . .]

I think I am going to write a serious letter to you because I am in the mood and because it is possible that we may never meet again—though that will not be my fault. You suffer under various difficulties as regards myself. You don't I think doubt my deep affection for you any longer but there are other queernesses about me that no doubt puzzle you. Politics no doubt have a great deal to do with it. You live apparently amongst the middle-class Left in England and I live about the world with no politics at all except the belief—which I share with Lenin—that the only thing that can save the world is the abolition of all national feelings and the prevailing of the Small Producer—and the Latin Tradition of clear-sightedness as to what one means oneself.

Why I lay great stress on the French and Latin languages for you is this: Anglo Saxondom is a hybrid collection of human beings all of whose refinements and practical sense comes from the Latin Tradition and all of whose vaguenesses and self-deceptions and worship of the Second Class in trains, arts, cuisines, vintages and personal habits comes from the Teutonic strain. In the late war—which was mostly engineered from the Right in England—the national feeling swung towards the Latin Tradition; in the reaction, as I am tempted to put it, and with the insurgence of the middle-class Left, the national feeling, like a dog to its vomit, has returned to the vaguenesses and self-deceptions of the Teutonic strain. That is natural and can't be helped; you can't make a silk purse out of a beefsteak and kidney pudding cooked without condiments. But just because you are in the middle of that show and have, out of politeness, to agree with the people who surround you, I want you to be trained to some sort of clearness of mind so that you may be able to take care of yourself when that sort of mental Walpurgisnacht finds its inevitable Armageddon—and French and Latin are the only lifeboats for the maelstrom that is coming.

England is admirable on account of its legal system—which is why I wanted you to be trained as an international lawyer in Paris. You would thus have got the best of both mental worlds—which could only have helped you in whatever subsequent artistic career you might espouse—because only clear thought can help you when you approach artistic problems. The logic of painting or writing or music is just as clear and is provided by the same mental processes as that of the Law whether of England or the Code Napoléon.

That of course will not help you materially in England; but it will give you things that no amount of second class travel will ever give you. It will keep your interest in life alive till long after what it is convenient to call Pumblechookishness has overcome the adiposities of most females—and that is the best thing that the arts, if you are a real artist, can do for you. [. . . . .] Our sort of *vie simple* is however not merely the product of clear thinking; it is an elected form of life. Clear thinking it is true is the cause of indigence because the immense lower middle class that has latterly defaced the surface of the globe shudders and screams when thought is presented to it—but in spite of that we might have a little more comfort than we have if I had not long ago come to the conclusion that material comfort deadens one's interest in life—and extinguishes self-respect. It fills you, let us say, with horror to take a bath in the open air whereas I do not like the bother of taking baths at all and, if I do so, prefer to take them surrounded with trees and birds and tomato plants, in the sunlight—rather than in a steamy and too small room. . . . These, you see, are matters of points of view that it is little use arguing about.

[. . . . .] But use what clarity of mind you have to prevent your taking sides until you are sure what side your essential temperament will force you to take. You made, for instance, the violent pronouncement the other day: "I de*test* the pre-Raffaelites," [. . . . .]. But consider for a moment the inexpediency of the pronouncement. You cannot really know very much about those direct and collateral ancestors of your own whilst you are speaking to one who passes for the greatest living expert in that particular matter. I am indeed usually called the last of the pre-Raffaelites and you, if you practise any of the arts—as I hope you will—will inevitably in time inherit that sobriquet. And with some justice. Consider for a moment. The pre-Raffaelites are the only English artists who cut any ice at all outside England. They are admired in these other countries for a certain dogged sincerity—and they are not more admired than they are because they were muddle-headed beings born into a very bad period. That is another reason why I lay so much stress on the Latin strain in your up-bringing.

I imagine that when you have passed your present smart-Alecky phase your inheritance from the pre-Raffaelites will give you your share of dogged sincerity in the Arts. Then as you have been born into a very bad period indeed it is very necessary that you should not be muddleheaded.

Or again, you related an anecdote of some dreadful French people who made a noise on a *plage* to the horror of your companions. That is all right from one point of view. There *are* people who think that the sea beach is a place on which to display all the morose silence and *renfrogné*nesses that distinguish their suburban breakfasts. But there are other schools of thought. The motto of Provence whose civilisation has outlasted all other civilisations for thousands of years is *fen de brut*—which means that when the moment has come for letting oneself go one should forget the standards of Balham. After all a *plage* seems to be a pretty good place for making a noise since there is plenty of room.

I recall these instances of your table-talk more in order to explain what I mean when I say that you live among people who de*test* all that I stand for than to criticise yourself. In the natural course of things you will eventually react so violently against your present phase that your present phase, if I find it rather trying, is nevertheless a thing to welcome.

[. . . . .] But I think that, by now, you have achieved a better understanding of how I feel towards you. If I don't cover you with the flattery that you are accustomed to and consider your due it is because I do immensely want to be able one day to be proud of you for yourself and not merely to say that I am enraptured at your on dits in the style of some one else. You inherit certain duties from people who for generations have ended their lives in indigent circumstances. So that, not only should you not be so abhorrent of indigence—which nowadays is a thing rather to be proud of; but to carry out those duties you should eschew all easy triumphs. . . . That first of all. And then eschew all triumphs at all. The victor is always contemptible and to hurt people's feelings by words is the most contemptible of all human employments. My grandfather who—as time goes on you will discover to have been not a person to de*test* [. . . . .]—used to give as a rule of life: Believe nothing: hurt nobody. It is a very good rule. Try to follow it now and then.

There was a time when you used to say je tème de tou mon queur é encor beaucou plussss and then I was proud of you because it was an expression of yourself. Your present phase is good enough—for just anybody and I am not reprehending. But I write in this way because your present phase will not last much longer. You are old enough now to understand what all this is about and when you are a real grande personne you will realise the truth of it.

You see, if you will think of it, I am the kind of person whose truths eventually swim up the surface. They seem silly to you now as they seem to the press and public of your country. But if you think of the persons whose truths, historically, have eventually swum up to the surface of public consciousness and have prevailed you will see that it is the lonely buffaloes, ploughing solitary furrows who have generally produced those truths. So [. . . . .] consider that, in the bottom of your purse, you have a ticket for a lottery which may eventually draw one of the gros lots.

I should not pay much attention to M. Marcoussis. I daresay you may one day write something good—you probably will if you can come across anyone who knows what English is for and how it should be handled. Why I do not like your writing it to me is because your English is full of redundancies and unnecessary phrases and that gives me pain.

"Did I mention the fact that it goes on raining? Well it goes on raining and Madeleine goes on singing which I am sure helps it a lot. She also plays the guitar all day long and breaks a string every five minutes." . . . Don't you feel the little shiver going down my spine? Because that is what is called journalese. A writer would have put it:

"It goes on raining and Madeleine goes on singing. Sometimes she plays the guitar and breaks a string every five minutes." . . . There is no sense in saying "which I am sure helps it a lot." It means nothing—and if you are sure of a thing you do not have to say so. That is the way you should criticise yourself—before you write.

Good bye, my dear. Janice did not win any kind of *lot* with any of her five tickets, alas! Otherwise what *brut* we would have *fén* on the plages of Spain. She is now thinking of taking part in the sweepstakes. She sends you bundles of love—which is the phrase used by her favorite sister-in-law in her last letter, so perhaps it is the latest New Yorkese which, I know, is always welcome in Hampstead. Say thank you!

And as for me if you put it that jer thème de tou mon qhueur é enchor boocou plusss é ke je toubli jamé you would not be so far from the truth.

Your old

To Paul Palmer*

[Toulon]

My dear Palmer: 11 Sept 1935

That is quite correct about Mrs. Aley; I move about so much that I had to have somebody to collect things for me.

I have just forwarded to her for you my article on STEPHEN CRANE. I hope you will like it as much as the HENRY JAMES your appreciation of which I much appreciate.

Yes, thanks too, things are pretty good here. We have since seeing you visited Spain, Portugal, Monaco, the British Empire at Gibraltar, Italy and now sit in our garden. We have been here two months today and have already eaten—three weeks ago—peas of our own planting, string beans, leeks and sorrel—as well of course as grapes, figs and pears—so vegetably we are already self-supporting which is pretty quick going, though of course this is a favoured spot. Janice has produced three pictures of New York and other work; I have written about 30,000 words of my new book[1] as well as the Crane article; we have been in one near-revolution with bloodshed and all; one cyclone; and have seen Italian troops entraining for Africa. I can't say that the populace were particularly enthusiastic; we seemed to be the only people who cheered the troops—and that of course only because they are probably going to very nasty deaths, poor devils. But the populace just stood about with their jaws hanging down and doing nothing. Things are pretty bad in Italy; the greater part of the population near the frontier [is] on the edge of starvation.

I am glad of all your good news—especially the Montrachet.

Our best to you both

To Anthony Bertram

My dear Bertram:

[Toulon]
27/9/35

I am overwhelmed by the dedication of your book[1]—which I received a few minutes ago. . . . So little I ever did to help you!

I am sure it represents a real development on your part. I am up to the eyes with work to send off to New York and though I shall read it almost immediately it will probably be rather muddledly, as, even from merely glancing at it casually here and there after unwrapping it, I can see that it needs attention. So I shall not write to you seriously about it till next week.

I don't suppose you read some friendly references to you and yours in a latish chapter of my PROVENCE. No-one will publish it in England though it was a best seller in America—which is funny[2]. If you can get hold of a copy take a look at it. The references to yourself—though not by name—occur in the early chapters of the Third Part. They will at least serve as a hospitable-roofer

[1] Probably *Vive Le Roy* published by Lippincott in 1936.

[1] *Men Adrift* (London, 1935).

[2] George Allen & Unwin published it in 1938.

and prove that neither Janice nor I forgot you in spite of the oceans that roared between.

She had rather a successful exhibition in N.Y.; sold several pictures—which is rather a miracle there now—and earned the plaudits of a bewildered press which took her to be the latest thing in Paris extravagances.

And so à tantôt with renewed thanks and many kind wishes to Madame and the olive branch,

Yrs,

By the bye, wouldn't it be better if you dropped over here for a little and we could talk about the book. We'd love to have you. The weather at the moment is absolutely divine and will probably so remain till about Christmas and the view from our terrace—which is about the most beautiful in the world, whatever they may say about Naples or Sydney or Valparaiso and the other resorts of the lesser breeds without the Law—is at its best. But even if you don't come—which I hope you will, you can believe that your book will be devoured in circumstances of great beauty.

To Jefferson Jones[*1]

c/o The Guaranty Trust
Paris, France
Dear Mr. Jefferson Jones,   3 Oct. '35

I have had a communication from you through Bradley's ref. VIVE LE ROY. Personally I think mine is a better title than the one you propose. The "Disappearance of Walter Leroy" suggests something mid-Victorian and is not easily memorisable—a proposing purchaser will go into a bookstore and ask for a book about a disappearance and the clerk will at once plant on him Mrs. Lindbergh's memoirs by a process of ratiocination that will be apparent to you, especially as he will have overstocked said memoirs.

I recognize your point, but the D.O.W.L. does not seem to meet it very well. However, as I suppose you will not be publishing the book very soon, there will be time to think of something neater. Of course you know what your travellers can sell better than I; on the other hand I should rather dislike having

[1] Of J. B. Lippincott Company.

such a title in the list of my books; it would suggest that I had
become a nice old grandmother of Wilkie Collins' day.

I hope you flourish. It is rather disagreeable here with wars
and rumours of wars; we are so near the frontier that one might
wake up any night and find the house full of Italian gas. So we
shall probably move up to Paris, but the above address will always
find us.

Yours faithfully

To Anthony Bertram

Cap Brun
15/10/35

My dear Bertram,

I have now read—but indeed I did a week or so ago—*Men
Adrift* with a great deal of pleasure—pleasure because it was fun
reading it and at being able to think that you have found a form
that is really suited to you and have managed your subject with a
great deal of skill. It is certainly a great advance on anything else
you have ever done and I really congratulate you. The book is
full of good things, moving steadily forward altogether—and, if
that progression of effect doesn't end in final illumination that is,
I suppose, because there is no illumination to be found in the state
of being adrift.

But I imagine—indeed I am pretty sure—that when you do get
hold of a really good subject that is really suited to you you will
now do something authentic. The Christ progression is, you know,
really too *vieux jeu* and too provincially Middle Class English.
You *must* shake that off, if only because it is a source of continual
slackness. When the Englishman—who is almost never a Christian
but always, or almost always, a Christ-ist—takes the Christ saga in
hand it means that he is treating a subject that is already more than
half written for him and, being able to do without invention in
that particular, he permits himself to slacken off in all the Christ-
cum-Magi or Christ-cum-whatever-else-he-pleases passages and
then he is in the greatest danger of going slack all over the shop.
In the end he is really only embroidering on a fairy tale—and
there are now in the world so many people who don't even know
the fairy tale, that at once you get provincialism. We as English-
men have gone on for long imagining that if we as individuals

model ourselves on the English ideal of the Redeemer we shall have a good time—for so long that we expect the Redeemer to touch his forelock like a good footman and give us supernatural market tips and advantages even when we are doing no more than writing a novel. The process is wanting in respect to the Son of God.

Obviously you have carried the matter a little further than that—but to attain the really authentic you must cut loose altogether from that sort of thing; you must give up being a Christist and become a Christian or something else that is fierce and bitter as Christians have to be. Christianity isn't you know a Sunday supper with the maids given the evening off; it is eating flesh and drinking blood. When you do that the legendary caboodle—all of it—grows so dim that it is unrecognisable and can't be used for progressions of effect in books. If you had been—as we've just been for the last few days—in Geneva what I mean would appear to you with startling effect.

But objecting to a fellow's subject isn't objecting to his texture or his writing or anything but just the subject—and subjects are extraordinarily a matter of luck, environment, accident and perhaps a little laziness or lack of having suffered. You just keep on with the same texture and writing and when you have pioché enough you'll get the right subject and then you will be all right right through. I am really immensely pleased and impressed with the book; the feeling of a crowd going forward like a slow tidal wave is really admirably achieved. Keep it up and you will be all right.

However on looking the book through, I see that there's rather less of the Christ legend than I had thought. Still see what you think of what I have written about it.

As to finding an American publisher, I do not think I could do much with it from here, but when I go back in the Spring I daresay I can do something with it by word of mouth. It is less than no good writing to American publishers; they never read anyone's letters. In the meantime if you have not got an agent there why not send it to my agent: Mrs. Ruth Aley, 510 West 89th Street, N. Y. C. saying that I asked you and that I will give it all the backing I can if she finds a publisher. She's pretty good.

It's too bad you can't come here before December for I don't know where we shall be then—in Paris or Spain or even back in N. Y. if things get too unpleasant here.

As for PROVENCE I don't know what you can do unless you put it down in the B. M. as a wanted book. They sometimes get them.

In the meantime I garden and write and write and garden and Janice sends her best regards to you all and I'm

Yours, always,

To Paul Palmer*

Toulon, Var
France
17. 11. 35

Dear Palmer,

I daresay you are right about the *Hudson*[1]—though I think every educated American knows about the Fabian society because of the big part they have played in Left Developments in both branches of anglo-saxondom. I was asked to write an article only last week about them but turned it down because I don't like them and don't want to be associated with them in the public mind except in these articles for you where they must come in from time to time because every writer in England was—and indeed is—associated with—or against them. As for the presentation I daresay you are right: at any rate Janice agrees with you and I know I do exaggerate my method now and then. I'll look it over again and turn it round a bit.

I think I will do Galsworthy next, if it's all the same to you. I dropped him out of my last letter accidentally, meaning to have put him before Lawrence and Swinburne. I want to reflect about Lawrence a little longer because, although he was my 'discovery,' I'm not a hell of a lot in sympathy with him and find him difficult to re-read.

I'm afraid I must ask you to let me have the cheque for the *Hudson* now. These articles cause me a dreadful amount of work and expense for buying books and they are very long and worth more than the money. By the bye, would you ask the publishers— I suppose Scribner's—of the official life of Galsworthy[2] that is

[1] The article "W. H. Hudson" which *The American Mercury* published in March, 1936.

[2] H. V. Marrot, *The Life and Letters of John Galsworthy* (New York, 1936).

just coming out to send early sheets as soon as possible; that will save me something. Harpers always pay me in advance for any articles they commission. I didn't ask you to do this as being a friend but I can't afford to wait too long.

I haven't, by the bye, had those copies of the MERCURY with my articles in them—nor indeed any of the others. Do shake your people up, will you? I want the small-holding article—and indeed the anti-propaganda one—for the book I am writing for the Oxford Press and I have no copies at all in ms. and your people have not sent me any copies of the review.[8]

Things are still like a seething pot here and a plague of myriads of small snails has destroyed nearly all my vegetables!

Yours,

To Paul Palmer*

Dear Palmer,   11 Dec. 1935

I have sent Mrs. Aley the reconstituted HUDSON article. I have practically re-written it and imagine it will now suit you. I hope you will not keep it to the last of the series. I have tried to avoid giving these articles the aspect of a serial; all the same there is a certain mental connection between them. Conrad, Crane, Hudson and James constituted a group of foreign writers living in England who exercised an enormous influence on English—and later, American writing, all of them but Conrad having been American and all more or less intimate the one with the other and I want to keep them together so as to accentuate the difference between them and the outer ring of English writers like Wells, Galsworthy, Lawrence and to some extent Arnold Bennett who were all propagandists of a Fabian complexion rather than straight novelists.

You are I daresay too young—which is a good thing to be—to remember the immense sensation that GREEN MANSIONS, the PURPLE LAND and FAR AWAY & LONG AGO made in the United States, but you would be wrong to think that among educated Americans and writers Hudson is at all forgotten and it is one of the func-

---

[8] In addition to the literary portraits, *The American Mercury* published "Hands Off the Arts" (April, 1935) and "The Small Producer" (August, 1935) which Ford incorporated into *Great Trade Route*.

tions of a review that is at all literary to call the attention of the large public to great writers who, mostly by accidents of publishing, are not at the moment very much to the fore.

Think about it a little, will you?

I shall be sending you the Galsworthy article in a day or two. I have got the advance sheets of the biography from Heinemanns!

I hope you will have a good Christmas and that weather is not as cold in Gotham as the papers make it to be. Mrs. Ford sends her regards to your wife.

To Paul Palmer*

Dear Palmer,   19 Dec 1935

This is of course an impasse. You are practically asking me to submit articles for your approval, a thing I have never done in my life and don't propose to do now. I will if you like propose a compromise: I will write the remainder of the twelve articles you commissioned by letter and you will pay for them on receipt of MS according to your promise. If you then want changes in the articles I will, if I agree with them, make them without extra payment. This seems to me to be fair. It is a thing I have never done before because no editor ever asked me to change anything except a word here or there and I have never before considered the matter.

I don't want to make a song and dance about the inconvenience this has caused me; you can think that out for yourself. I told you again and again that I did not want to do these articles, but now that I am launched on them I have got to finish them. I make a living by writing and these articles have taken up all my time since I saw you besides putting me to a great expense for books by now rare and difficult to obtain.

I more or less agreed with you about the Hudson article; as to the Wells one I don't so much. It is a perfectly good article. You object to the personal tone—but you asked me to write personal articles. Indeed the James article was the most personal thing I ever wrote. But in order to oblige you I will make the Wells one more impersonal. I should do so in any case when the articles appear in book form because I disapprove of personal writing myself.

I am obliged to you for saying that you are sending me a cheque—it has not yet reached me. Let us then take it as representing the Hudson article. If you will send me one for the Wells I will at once let you have one on Galsworthy which [I] have nearly finished and will set to work on changes in the Wells.

I should be obliged if you would let me know by cable if [you] accept the terms of my first paragraph and I will then go on with the work

To Paul Palmer*

c/o The Guaranty Trust
Paris

Dear Palmer,   5 June '36

Yours of the 27th ult. just received.

You are, you know, treating me very badly. When I was an editor I would not have behaved in such a way to the meanest worm amongst the people who wrote for me.

It was quite definitely established by yours of the 14 Jan '36 that you were definitely commissioning these articles yet here you are back again at saying: "the final decision will be made after I have read the articles" . . . this ref. the Pound and Dreiser articles of the latter of which I have already written over five thousand words after over two months' hard reading.

It was also quite definitely settled that you would take the Pound and Dreiser at our conversation at the Plaza. You said that both writers had insulted you; you however waived your objection on my pointing out that Dreiser and Pound, each in their separate fields, were the only two American writers—and except for the President of the United States, Mr. Ford, and Public Enemy No 1 for the time being the only Americans—of world wide position, fame and esteem; that after you and I and the remainder of the 119,999,999 of your compatriots were only so much dust as would fill a few cups my articles about those writers would still be read, and [illegible] to write about English literature of the last half century and leave out those two writers would be like writing about the French Wars between 1790 and 1815 and leave out Napoleon and, say, Nelson. And all that remains perfectly true because Dreiser as novelist and Pound as poet completely changed the aspects of their arts.

On the other hand you put me to a great deal of trouble by suddenly asking me to substitute for George Moore, about whom I could have written with ease and enthusiasm, the antique figure of my godfather [Swinburne] who presents for me about as much interest as the once celebrated John Brown, Queen Victoria's ghillie—and I consented, to oblige you, though it has meant reading all through *Songs Before Sunrise* and hundreds of thousands of lines like ASK NOTHING MORE OF ME, SWEET, ALL I CAN GIVE YOU I GIVE so that I shall probably never again be able to write any vers libre.

Moreover I want the money. I write these things for my living and they have held up all my other work for over a year. I ought to have delivered the first volume of my HISTORY OF OUR OWN TIME before now.

If you definitely don't want the Dreiser and Pound I don't want to pile them in on you, but as the Dreiser is nearly finished you may as well see it. But I will do in addition the Swinburne and the recapitulatory article—which of course I shall hitch onto the others and you can pay me $450 whether you take the two or the three. In that way I shall not feel I have any grievance against you and you will not suffer much for even at that they will be the cheapest copy you ever handled. I don't mind dropping Pound for I have written a great deal about him already—but you will lose a good and amusing article.

If this suits you please let me have a cable to that effect.

I'm sorry your gardening has not turned out so well. I have not done any at all this year and, as we are going to England at the end of this month and sailing for New York, probably from there, I don't see much chance of doing any.

Thanks for your invitation which sounds good. We'd accept with enthusiasm except that these vexations and uncertainties will probably prevent my coming. . . . I mean you wouldn't probably like to have a coffin delivered on your person.

                                                    Yours,

To Paul Palmer*

from
FORD MADOX FORD ESQ
THE NUNNERY COTTAGE
PENSHURST . . . . KENT

My dear Palmer,   July 2 436

As you will see from the above address[1] (I put the ESQ in not to lay claim to my legal style as one of H.M.P.B.—His Majesty's Poor Bloody—Foot-sloggers, otherwise the Forty-First Infantry of the Line, which as you are aware takes precedence of the Black Watch which is only the Forty-Second, but so as to make a nice looking square slab of type)—as you see then I have taken—on receipt of your lamentable letter—Hamlet's advice and gotten me into a Nunnery . . . the 4 being a mistyping for ', I having just changed my machine.

It is intensely tragic. . . . But do me the justice to acknowledge that I prophesied that you would find paying me so long and so regularly all sorts of a burden. I know. I know. *Don't* I know! On the other hand I am overburdened with an enterprise that is slowly driving me to the grave. Can you imagine what it is to try for six weeks to read SWINBURNE? to try and try and TRY, like Bruce's spider . . . and to fail. . . . I got up at half past five again this morning . . . as every morning . . . to face those printed pages to which the mind will not adhere. And read

> ASK NOTHING MORE OF ME SWEET ALL I CAN GIVE YOU I GIVE
> HEART OR MY HEART WERE IT MORE MORE SHOULD BE

And when will that damn girl bring my coffee? And would it be better to buy pounds sterling here or wait till we get to Penshurst. And I think Eileen had better go to Vienna by way of Basel and not pass through Hun-and-Hitler Land

> LAID AT YOUR FEET
> LOVE THAT SHOULD HELP YOU TO LIVE SONG THAT SHOULD HELP
> YOU TO SOAR
> ALL THINGS WERE NOTHING TO GIVE ONCE TO HAVE TASTE[2]. . . .

[1] The Fords were visiting Edward Crankshaw, novelist, critic, and reader for George Allen & Unwin.

[2] The poem is "The Oblation" in *Songs Before Sunrise*. Ford misquotes a few words.

Oh Hell! Stick it, the Welch.... What a row the ordure gatherers make. Why do the Beaux Arts students choose six in the morning to make that noise.... It was of course the Quartz Arts last night. They've been up all night. I THAT HAVE LOVE AND.... Do you remember the Quartz Arts of '97 when they.... NO MORE GIVE YOU BUT LOVE OF YOU SWEET.... All together now, men. Get it over. HE THAT HAS MORE LET HIM GIVE ME THAT HAS WINGS LET HIM SOAR MINE IS THE HEART AT.... God, let's try another page.

> EIPATE TO BASILEI? XAMAPESE DIADALOS AULA
> OUKETI PHOIBOS EXEI KALUBAN. . . .

Of course that's better.... It's Aeschylus he's quoting.[3] ... And damn true, too. Phoebus has no cabin here. The rats have holes and the sparrows gutters to block with their nests, but the Son of Jove. . . .

And so I go on trying and trying. . . .

Ah, but each heart knoweth its own bitterness. "The ENGLISH REVIEW," say you, "found a ready market among people of taste and intelligence." Don't you know that people of t&i all expect free copies and blackmail you if they don't get them and that millionaires and pimps and porters all go to the free libraries to read so that one copy serves five hundred? Hence all our tears.

It's very kind of you to ask us so insistently to Ridgefield. Listen.... We propose arriving in N. Y. two or three days after what is going to happen to your President happens . . . say on the 11/11/36. If you would put us up for a couple of days while we look for an apartment, it would be a lovely thing to be able to look forward to, because the friend we usually stay with on such occasions will then be here. But perhaps that will not suit you? Or you will not be there, having been nominated Secretary of State in the new Administration . . . or lynched? In any case we will meet about then if time, envy, want, the patron, or the gaol shall not previously have disposed of us. We have just got over moving from one apartment to another prior to leaving for the Nunnery . . . and what with that and this damn new machine—

---

[3] The lines are half of the epigraph Swinburne used for his poem "The Last Oracle." They are not Aeschylus' words but the "last oracle" of the Delphic god, said to have been delivered to the Emperor Julian.

unaligned a's and all which means that it will have to go back
to the shop—we are fair moidert . . . qnd and q's where the q's—
I meqn a4s—no, i meqn q's . . . no, damn, a's;;; ought to be.

Well, the best be yours

To Eugene Pressley*[1]

Villa Paul
Cap Brun, Toulon
20. 8. 36

Dear Gene,

Would you please save my reason if not my life—or both, and
my fortunes and those of my descendants to the uttermost generations—by retrieving these parcels from 49 rue de La Boëtie 8 and
forwarding them to the above address registered up to the teeth?
When I explain that said parcels or packets contain not only all
the proofs but the only complete manuscript of my immense
book[2] on War and Peace and Chattanooga—not to mention
Shiloh—and that I have already written over and over again to
the s.ng..n.ry Bulgar called the RECEVEUR P.T.T. BUREAU N° VIII pray-
ing him to send the parcels—prayers of which he takes no more
notice than does the obelisk in the Place de la Concorde—here to
me; and when you consider that I do not know another single
soul in Paris who could retrieve it, saving only you, all being on
their congés, payés ou non; and when you further consider that,
let alone the fact that I do not want to lose my ms., I am just
on the verge of litigation with the Oxford University Press over
modifications they have arbitrarily made in my pacificisms quasi-
communism and other outrages that they have committed and
are continuing to comit and that, unless I can get my ms. I cannot
check up to the full their militant-b'joice (*bourgeois* as pronounced
by London Printers) . . . well then, I say, I do not believe that—
in the full conviction that I will do at least as much for you when,
in the metropolis of my birth, you shall have attained to my
years, for I am convinced that when said metrpls gets hold of
you it will not willingly let you go . . . in short, I hope you won't

---

[1] An officer of the American Embassy and husband of Katherine Anne Porter.
For his labors in deciphering the holograph manuscript of *It Was the Nightingale*
(Philadelphia, 1934) and typing copy for the printer, Ford dedicated that book
to him.

[2] *Great Trade Route* (New York, 1937).

mind my asking you, but whether you do or don't for God's sake do it because what with one thing and another—gout which has completely crippled me, ever since we got here, leading to as complete sleeplessness—not one wink of sleep last night at all!—the whole being conduced to by the really very bad behaviour of the O.U.P.—I shall really op off me bleedin cokernut if you don't. . . .

So we have done nothing hitherto either for the LEAGUE OF PEACE or the garden or anything else, Janice's time being entirely taken up with waiting on me, walking backwards and forwards the two miles to Toulon Market, there being a Grève des Tramways here just to make things cheerfuller and so on and so on as is apt to happen when you re-fit yourself into Earthly Paradises, Lands of Cokaigne [*sic*], Gardens Atlantidean or Hesperidean . . . and my eyes are so bunged up with sleeplessness that I cannot see to correct this only hoping this finds you as it finds us in the pink I *don't* think.

And our love to the remaining Organiser(s) of the L. O. P. and send us any news.

I ought perhaps to explain that I have been occupying the long nights in making a mental comparison of Imperial Roman (i. e. Pompeian) Empire State and British Imperial Slang, with a touch of argot and the Memphite dialect thrown in . . . and of course Proust as sentence-maker.

Do please attend to those parcels quick, to relieve my mind!

To Allen Tate

Dear Allen,

Toulon, France
6 Sept 1936

I have just got your MEDITERRANEAN[1]—and it's lovely. I suppose I may be pardoned for liking the first poem best since it brings back the occasion[2] . . . which was a happy one. . . . And after

[1] *The Mediterranean and Other Poems* (New York, 1936).

[2] Allen Tate supplies this note: "Ford had some Parisian friends who had a summer villa at Cassis. Invited to a picnic that his friends organized, we went by small fishing boats to a *calanque* about five miles from Cassis. The setting is described in the first two or three stanzas of my poem. There were about twenty people, and we drank and ate all day. On the way back to the village, Ford

that AENEAS AT WASHINGTON, and then PASTORAL and SHADOW AND
SHADE; and then TO THE LACEDEMONIANS and THE MEANING OF DEATH
in, I think, that order. But they are all astonishingly level in quality.
You have got hold by now of a sort of lapidary sureness and hard-
ness that puts you, I should think, alone among the poets so that,
the quality being almost equal all through, it becomes the subjects by which we appraise the different poems. Landor had a
little of the quality . . . in his prose, but in verse I don't know
anyone else who equals you. I think if Ezra had not spoilt the
term IMAGISTE, you could appropriate it and wear it all alone.
Such lines, I mean, as

> "When the night's coming and the last light falls,
> A weak child among lost shadows on the floor,
> It is your listening. . . ."[3]

That is beautiful and marmoreal and yet tender. . . . It's, that is
to say, your unique gift. I hope it will bring you fame, though
it probably won't; but at least it gives you the right to say that you
stand alone. I like to think of the immortality I shall get from
having my name on its forehead. . . . But it's astonishing how
your method has strengthened itself without changing its essence.
. . . One could say to every one of these poems Agnosco veteris
vestigia flammae and yet you have grown stronger and more
simple and deeper. I should think you ought to feel happy when
you think of the little volume. . . .

And are you all anyhow happy and prospering and in beautiful
weather? I know it's useless to expect you to write. But why not
pick up one of the cardinal's feathers from your lawn sometimes
and put it in an envelope addressed as above. We'd then at least
know you were living. One hasn't indeed the least idea of where
you are or whether letters will ever reach you. I wrote you a
month or so ago to Memphis asking several questions to which
I got no reply; so this time I shall try Benfolly.[4] I heard vaguely

---

remarked that in some such cove the refugees from Troy must have stopped
for refreshment. In the next few days I found a copy of the *Aeneid* in a book-
stall in Toulon, and read it for the first time since prep school. The result was
the poem."

[3] "The Ancestors."

[4] The Tate farm in Clarksville, Tennessee.

in Paris that you had given up professoring and were having a
sabbatical year. I'd be glad if you found it possible to do it, though
I don't think you were unhappy at Memphis and you have managed to do some work. . . . We most of us have so much to over-
write ourselves to get the little thin oatmeal. I don't believe I should
mind a similar job very much; at least I am tired of writing for
the pot . . . though I suppose I shall have to go on.

We have had our usual ups and downs, being for the moment
very down indeed and not likely to get up again unless we could
get to New York to look after my business and not likely, as far
as I can see, to be able to rake up the fares for years. We went to
England and managed to fix up a lot of things, among them a
collected edition, a one-volume TIETJENS, and all my books for
good. It's satisfactory to have done that but what little money
there is in it goes to Stella and Julie so that it does nothing for
us. . . . It's with Allen & Unwin who're a very good house—my
first publishers. They're starting by the bye a series of 15 to 30,000
word stories, so if Caroline[5] has anything of that sort lying around
she might very well send it—to

Edward Crankshaw, Esq.
The Nunnery Cottage
Penshurst, Kent

. . . where Sidney wrote the ARCADIA. I've naturally prepared the
ground. Crankshaw is a good boy: he liked PENHALLY very much
but the other[6] much better. He made the curious remark that it was
one of the few—perhaps the only—books he had ever read that
held you so much that you never bothered to wonder where the
writer got his knowledge. I took the occasion after he'd read it to
re-read it myself. It's an exquisitely beautiful piece of work. I don't
know—and don't particularly care—where Caroline gets her
knowledges [*sic*], but I wish I knew where she got her gift so that
I could drink of the same spring.

Janice said, this morning: "It's odd, you know, the Tates seem to
be the only friends or family we have in the world" . . . quite out
of the blue, like that, when we were discussing what to have for

---

[5] Caroline Gordon Tate. Her first novel, *Penhally*, appeared in 1931.
[6] *Aleck Maury, Sportsman* (New York, 1934).

dinner. (There has been a tram-strike here ever since the very day we got here—so everything we eat has to be carried by hand on foot from Toulon and the problem of what will most nourish four people—we've got some guests stopping here—becomes more of a subject for discussion than you would believe.) However, I so thoroughly agreed with her that I came straight in and wrote this. It's true that we haven't any more got any *real* friends—in the sense of people one can talk to without having to explain every second word and both Janice and I are pretty good at making enemies. . . . So it's absurd that we should not even know where you are laying your heads and whether you are professors or even breathing. It is true we had your p. c. signed and countersigned by Carl Sandburg the other day. But mightn't we argue from the fact that Caroline says she is going to write a long letter on the morrow —and knowing how reliable she is in these things I don't think— that you had been shot in one of the secessionist riots that make the French tourist papers—copying their transatlantic confrères— declare that folk had better stay at home? Mightn't we?

I'm afraid there's little or no chance of our getting together this year. We had planned arriving at Baltimore on the 9 November, but my unspeakable agent has not sold my book,[7] so we shan't be able to pay the fares. Indeed we're giving up this place on the 1st October and going to live in one room in Paris . . . the end, alas, of a phase! Life is really so dear here that we intend to go and live in Majorca as soon as their troubles are over—if ever. . . . We hear the guns from the Barcelona front when the wind is in the right direction—but that is as near to the anarchy, murder and disruption that your papers swear are going on here. Janice's friend, Eileen's husband, has cabled her—she's in Tcheko-Slovakia —not to go near the South of France because of the horrors being there enacted. . . . I mean Eileen is in T. S., not Janice. . . . It's the sort of sentence I ought never to try. I suppose it ought to have begun The husband of Janice's friend, E., has cabled the latter . . . or, no, 'the last-named'. . . . What a language!

Well, I suppose we shall one day beat the buggers as we used to say in H. B. M.'s Army . . . meaning not the Hun but the gory Staff. But I wish I knew how or when.

[7] *Portraits from Life* (Boston, 1937).

Oh. . . . Do a little log-rolling for my COLLECTED POEMS, will you all? I wouldn't ask it, as you know, if there were any money in it or if I cared twopence about them. My heart sank into my boots when I saw the immensity of proofs, and half of them I could not even read for correction. But I don't want to be harmed by people calling me a lousy old wasser which they might well do. I have at last adjusted my lunatic strife with the Oxford University Press—you know, either I must be mad or they. They are really unimaginable people. No wonder Roger Bacon invented gunpowder to blow them up when they contracted to publish his works.

I enclose the proof of my last poem.[8] It appears in the LONDON MERCURY for this month. It's certainly me if it's anything, but I don't know that there's anything more to be said about it. Warren[9] could use it if he liked if it isn't already out in volume form. The O. U. P. say they are going to publish this month, so I don't suppose they will get it out before next mid-summer.[10] But you never can tell.

Good bye, my dears, may the cooling breeze blow softly upon you—we've had one hell of a mistral in painfully bright sunlight for the last few days with 104° in the sun where it's sheltered. So I can not think of any kindlier wish. . . . Janice also yelps, like a young swallow in the mouth of her nest, not so much for flies as for news. So it's up to you to prolong this friendship.

Is there, by the bye, any decent translation of the XELIDON song?[11] If there isn't, I think I'd have a shot at it. Isn't it the most beautiful thing that was ever made . . . or is that one of my sexagenarian delusions?

Always yours,

[8] "Latin Quarter."

[9] Robert Penn Warren, then one of the editors of *The Southern Review*.

[10] Oxford University Press published *Collected Poems* in October, 1936.

[11] *The Vigil of Venus* (*Pervigilium Veneris*), a poem of unknown authorship, preserved in the Latin Anthology, in which in the last stanza the poet uses the Greek *chelidon* instead of the Latin *hirundo* for swallow. Encouraged by Ford in conversation to translate it, Allen Tate published his version in 1944.

To Ezra Pound

Toulon
6 Sept. 1936

Dear Ezra,

On the occasion of your want of generosity ref. [René] Béhaine I swore on the bones of St. Gengulphus, some of which are handy in the cathedral here, that I would never write to you again. I herewith break my vow. I cabled you because one of my intrigues to get you a settled job in the U. S. A. appeared to be maturing— said [Paul] Palmer having undertaken to print any one I told him to, and I thought I had better go to Rapallo and censor anything you wrote him. . . . But, as you expect when I have got so far, I desisted when I got a letter from Palmer, a cable saying that he would rather die than print anything that you wrote or even to print your name in his magazine.[1] He said you had insulted him in a manner no human being could be expected to stand and, as he is a very mild and forgiving person, I guess you *must* have done something to him. I daresay I could have overpersuaded *him* —and indeed I very nearly did—because in matters literary he will do pretty well what I tell him; though I don't do it any more because I am tired of being kicked in the face by people I get printed. But then the Capitalist behind the Machine sailed in and swore that *he* would rather die than let a word of yours appear in his periodical. And he wouldn't quit.

As for Palmer, he has the merit of thinking me the greatest writer that ever put pen to paper and he gives me as much space as I want or if he cuts me does it with reverence and skill. So you can make what you like of his maternity. The only fly in the jam is that his proprietor does not give him enough to let him pay too well; nevertheless we have lived for the last year on him, but it's unfortunately now coming to an end owing to alterations in the format and staff of the paper. For the rest we have been in your country, my country, Portugal, Spain, Monte Carlo, Geneva and have in consequence enlarged our minds and I have written a book[2] that is practically one long philippic against your ancestral city and the Keystone State in general. . . . Nothing you ever wrote

[1] *The American Mercury.*
[2] *Great Trade Route.*

was quite so wounding—because I know how to do it and as a rule something about my subject. . . . I got hold of some publicity for Penna that pointed out that she was the only State in the World who had never felt the Crisis; that she led the Universe in the production of rubber pants, and linoleum that outbeautied the famous rugs of Khorassan; and led the U. S. A. in the production of underpants in shoddy, whilst, round her coal dumps can be seen standing more men thrown out of work by improved machinery than anywhere in the created universe.

So, having renié'd mes dieux by writing on public affairs I feel myself sufficiently a pariah to reopen a correspondence with You.

Not that I have anything in particular to say. My collected poems are being published in September by the Oxford University Press. I wish they had been selected ones because there's an awful lot of bilge among them. But they insisted on all or none . . . and then when they read them were so appalled that they tried to get out of publishing them at all. They don't like you to mention the Deity except in devotional verse and, when you insist, remind you tearfully that they were the original publishers of Roger Bacon's treatise on gunpowder and Dr. Watts's Little Hymns. So I insisted on their carrying out the contract—not that I particularly yen to mention the Deity but that I believe that publishers should be as sadistically punished as possible. . . . And they *were* and continue to be pained . . . what between pain at letting the letters GOD come out of their forms and the thought of the dishonour that would attach to them if it appeared in litigation that they had refused to carry out a contract. So after a delay of a year they really appear to be going to bring them out. Their youngest and newest director, it appears, is my second greatest admirer in the world and foisted me on them before their eyes were clear of sleep. . . . But it's been a wearisome transaction.

I have also arranged for my collected edition, the TIETJENS books in one volume and all my work past and to come with Allen and Unwin of London. That is satisfactory in a way; there is very little money in it and what there is goes entirely to Stella so it does not help us much. Indeed things are pretty low here and likely to remain so. We are having to give up this place and go and live in one room in Paris. It's impossible to make a living outside New York, one's agents are always so incompetent and we'd both die if we had to live in the U.S.A. for good.

I don't suppose you're any better circumstanced. No one is that one knows. We shall beat the buggers yet—but not soon. . . . Oh, looking through this—when I said "censor what you wrote Palmer" I meant see that you wrote Esq after his name on envelopes and the like—not interfere with your style and content. . . . Indeed I'd asked him to subsidise you as a poet, not prosateur; but I was afraid your epistolary-lapidary manner in an initial letter might make him believe that you were not a poet.

Janice sends her respects: she's engaged in painting a series of all the cavalry battles of the Civil Wars—yours—in a neo-pointilliste manner. She'd switch over to the Spanish War, I think, only they do not appear to have any cavalry. We hear the guns from Barcelona here on a still day with the wind in the right direction; the rest of the air is filled with practice for the resisting of your crowd when you come to annex the Riviera française. . . . 'Cela vous donne une fière idée,' as Maubougon used to say, bowing, 'd l'homme.'

And so Yechi dachi . . . I must write to the Oxford people again.

Yrs

To E. C. Cumberlege*[1]

c/o The Guaranty Trust
Paris
19. 9. 36

Dear Mr. Cumberlege,

You may be right about the Literary Agent . . . but I'm inclined myself more to the opinion that it's a poltergeist that is the main cause of these confusions, if not Old Nick himself. I ought perhaps to have told you at the beginning that my earliest known—apart from legendary—ancestor was fined ten crowns and ordered to stand in the pillory for printing, in the XV century, insults to the Sorbonne, and ever since my forbears have been occupied in making themselves disagreeable to and in being persecuted by Universities—the most egregious of them being the Famous Dr. John Brown, inventor of the Brunonian System of Medicine. Him Frederick the Great invited to be his body surgeon but the invitation

[1] Of Oxford University Press.

being sent to the University of Edinburgh, that body preferred to send out a John Brown of their own whom that sovereign, on discovering the imposture, threw into gaol and kept there till his death.

I am moved to these historic reminders by the fact that the agreement you have sent me is quite different from the one that I last signed and sent out to you—which may be the work of the aforesaid Literary Agent. But how do you account for the fact that the copy of the POEMS that you have kindly sent me has neither title-page, h.t.p. nor roman signatures but begins at p. 49 and after p. 63, returns to p. 3 and so continues? That I think must be the work of the poltergeist for I don't see how the Literary Agent *can* have had a hand in it. Anyhow I am reduced to the condition of the lady who said she was past keering and can only faintly hope that the review copies did not all go out in that state. . . . Otherwise the book is very handsome and one that one might be proud of.

I think the 'blurb' of the *Great Trade Route* at the end of the dust sheet might be a little more spirited, although I am aware that my own phraseology is mainly responsible for its high notes. I will when a little recovered try to put together some suggestions for a publicity which, whilst not outstepping the bounds of good taste, might make someone want to read the book.

What by the bye would you think of *A Mirror to Life* as a sub-title? Or does it seem too inflated? Yours faithfully

To E. C. Cumberlege*

Dear Mr. Cumberlege: 27. 10. 36

I attach herewith some notes that might be of use to your advertising manager.

When I see your advertisements of the POEMS in the Herald's BOOKS I fair blush, I do! But I don't *object*!

Yours very sincerely

Notes for publicity for GREAT TRADE ROUTE

There is a fairly satisfactory biographical notice of the author on the back dust-wrapper to VIVE LE ROY (Lippincott). The last sentence should however be amended to read: in 1922 Mr. Ford, whose health had been severely affected by the War, took up his permanent residence in the south of France. And the rest as in text.

The point to be made about the GREAT TRADE ROUTE is that it is not the book of a meditative gentleman who stands before ruined temples and pours mournful soliloquies on old unhappy things, but as it were the testament of a man usually of action who has spent a long life not only on writing and study but on digging, editing, carpentry, cooking, small holding, fighting both literally and metaphorically and in every kind of intrigue that could advance what he considers to be the cause of good letters . . . and particularly on running round the part of the world here treated and observing with disillusioned eyes politicians and public men of every type and shade. In the series of books to which this belongs—which besides this includes PROVENCE and one which will deal with Burgundy, North France, the English South Coast, the Southern States below Baltimore, returning to Marseilles by way of all the Mediterranean coasts from Jaffa north and westwards—he deals with a certain erudition of most of the things that make for the happiness of mankind . . . cooking, reading, farming, fighting, the Fine Arts, the Stage . . . how they all—and particularly politicians—should be handled if the civilisation which we know and which is founded on the civilisation of the Mediterranean is to have any chance of continuing. It is in short a book of advice from a man of wide experience and a remarkable memory who is without any illusions and no irons in any fire to men of reason, good will and common sense who desire that the present tumults which overfill the world should be suppressed so that they can get on with their jobs in peace. And the series of books contains passages of equal enthusiasm for the Greek Anthology, the Maison Carrée as for the sea food of New Orleans or Marseilles, the painting of Clouet, the military genius of Stonewall Jackson, the intensive cultural possibilities of the Tidewater and Piedmont districts of the Old Dominion and the climates of the countries that run round the world along the 40th North parallel. It is in short what in the old days would have been called humane literature.

To the Editor of *The American Mercury*[1]

Sir:
[November, 1936]

Mr. Carl J. Weber and I stand at opposite poles of the Universe. There is really room for both of us. I write for the reader already educated; he for the instruction of the ignorant.

As for his paragraph I, I cannot see where he differs from or corrects me. I say: "At the pressing instance of his bride-to-be, he had launched out into the occupation of the commercial novelist"; Mr. Weber puts it: "She (his bride-to-be) urged him to 'adhere to authorship' ". . . . If it is wrong not to write like Mr. Carl J. Weber, then I am wrong. But alas, *dis aliter visum!*

I pay your readers the compliment of believing that they know a little about novel-writing and life. I took it, that is to say, that your readers could work out for themselves that before Miss Gifford could have "urged" Mr. Hardy "to adhere", he must have given some beginner's proof that he could, let us say, wield a pen. He was a practicing architect making a modest living by restoring churches; he wrote some unimportant pieces on the side. . . . Almost everyone who knows anything or has given the remotest thought to the literary career, knows that that is the sort of thing that happens in the case of almost every novelist. He writes pieces on the side till he has courage to earn his living by his pen. There was neither need nor space for me to say so.

Mr. Weber's (2). Mr. Hardy told me that he began revising *Jude* before the version for serial publication began to run. "Years" is the colloquial expression that he used. If Mr. Weber will re-read the Official Biography—which I did for the purposes of the article —he will see that Mr. Hardy must have begun his revision very early. . . . Or, if Mr. Weber has ever to revise a very long novel, he will find that a sedulous revision lasting nine months may well in the retrospect seem a matter of years. He will then feel prostrate for a long time. But to cure mental prostration, one goes precisely to dances and gives teas. One desires to forget the stress and torture through which one has lately passed.

[1] See vol. xxxix (November, 1936), xx, xxii. On pages xiv and xx of the same issue, Carl J. Weber attacked Ford's essay on Thomas Hardy, citing four inaccuracies in a generally unflattering warning against Ford's "distortions of fact."

Mr. Weber's (3). I am afraid Mr. Weber has me there . . . but he also has Mr. Hardy. You cannot see Winchester from Stonehenge; you can see Salisbury Spire from quite close to that monument. I have described it several times myself. I confess to having read *Tess* carelessly. It is a book I don't like and find painful to read. So I took it that Mr. Hardy knew what he was writing about and meant Salisbury by Wincanton. I suppose the black flag to have come down. Or is it still flying?

Mr. Weber's (4). Mr. Hardy told me succinctly and in so many words that no one could have persuaded him to change a word of his poems. This was in connection with the *Cornhill Magazine's* having refused to publish *A Sunday Morning Tragedy* unless he would make changes in the poem. He may have meant "no editor" ever persuaded him, but he said "no one" . . . and with considerable force of expression. The general sense of his conversation at that date was to the effect that he did not care who made suggestions for altering his novels, but you would have to look out before you dared to do as much for his poetry. Of course, that did not mean that he would punish his own head if he made alterations himself. . . . Which is all that Mr. Weber proves by pointing out that the first published drafts of Mr. Hardy's poems differed from the final versions.

The fact is, sir, that as I sufficiently announced to you before writing this series of articles, I have been trying—to the measure of the light vouchsafed me—to preserve the memories of a body of men to whom I, as must be evident, was much attached . . . but to preserve them as I saw them, not as Mr. Weber deduces them from Official Biographies. [. . . . .]

But you know, sir, as well as do all of your educated readers, what takes place after the physical dissolution of a distinguished writer. For a year or so his publishers flog the sales of his collected editions and breathe on the dying fires of his memory. But then comes the Official Biography . . . and the poor man dies, sales, memory, and all in perpetuity or till the time comes, years after, for some creative artist to have a try at re-breathing life into their dead bones. If that effort coincides with a swing of the public taste towards the great man's works, he will again step all glorious onto the public stage and take his place beside Shakespeare, Heine, and the author of *The Song of Solomon*. If the public are not ready he must continue in Limbo till they are. The Official Biography kills in two ways. Inexpertly written and constructed, it spreads boredom round the great figure; and then, no man being willing to read an author's books when he can read salacious, moral, or merely imbecile details about the Great Man's . . . say, affection for his doggie-doggies, while the Biography lives the man must remain dead. Who reads Johnson? Who would read the Swan of Avon had he had a Boswell? [. . . . .]

To George T. Keating[1]

Dear Keating: [December, 1936]

   The history of that item called in Scribner's catalogue SOME REMINISCENCES by Joseph Conrad, New York, Paul R. Reynolds, 1908, is as follows.

   As you know I coerced Conrad into writing that book, with friendly and at times quite angry violence. It was a matter of getting him over from the Pent where apparently he could not work, to my place at Aldington about seven miles distant, where he just had to. He was at that time convinced that nothing that he ever wrote would ever pay, and that this thing in particular wouldn't but as [Arthur] Marwood and I paid him, for the performance in the English Review, more than he had received hitherto for anything he had ever written, I did not pay much attention to that plea. I may make a note that Jessie Conrad was even more hostile to Conrad's writing the Reminiscences than Conrad himself. I had lately refused to let them buy—which would have meant my paying for it—a pair of trotting ponies and a phaeton of sorts with scarlet wheels, and Jessie never forgave this till her death about a fortnight ago. Neither, indeed, I fancy, did Conrad. I would, then, walk up and down on my terrace which looked right over the Channel into France—walk up and down in front of Conrad who would groan, extended in a steamer chair. I would say: "Well now, what about the *Tremolino*" or "What about the diamond mine you owned in the Transvaal?" and, after exclaiming a dozen times: "Nonsense, no one will want to hear about that," he would

---
[1] American bibliophile.

begin to talk about the Ukraine of his uncle's day and Palmerston's Emissary with a sledgefull of gold or about Venice when he was a boy or about his exile in Siberia or, of course, if I suggested that he should talk about the Ukraine or Venice or Siberia, he would insist on telling anecdotes about the *"Tremolino"* or his Transvaal mine. In any case, once he was started, he would go on for a long time and as I wrote shorthand very fast, I could take him down without much trouble.

The trouble really came when I had to transcribe my notes by means of an appallingly primitive typewriter, called the Blickensderfer which had a little cylinder the types of which struck the paper exactly as if it were a hammer, and indeed you had to hit the keys almost as hard as if you were knocking in tenpenny nails. This pain was increased when you had to make a carbon copy and it was still worse, as I can well remember, when you had to make two. The third copy was destined for America and must have formed the original script for the item in Scribner's catalogue. I rather think the idea of setting up portions of a manuscript in this country was my own. I certainly used it in the cases of several pieces of work that appeared not only in the English but also in the Transatlantic Review and it might amuse you, if you had time, to see if you could trace any of the other items thus copyrighted at Washington.

Or perhaps I got the idea from S. S. McClure who may have used it for the purposes of his magazine. Paul Reynolds of those days was the most distinguished New York literary agent of his time and he was the correspondent here for J. B. Pinker who, as you know, was from first to last, Conrad's agent.

I do not think that there could be any possible question of these copyright samples being used fraudulently—I mean unnecessarily printed for the purpose of making collectors' items. Certainly that was not so in this case. In those days Conrad items would have appeared unlikely to be worth very much, if anything at all and certainly as far as I was concerned, it was a perfectly bonafide attempt to preserve Conrad's copyright in this country for him, since, though the rest of the book would remain uncopyrighted, and therefore at the disposal of pirates, it would have no value if they could not pirate the first two or three chapters as well.

To the Editor of *The American Mercury**

Dear Sir: January 19, 1937

I don't understand exactly what Mrs. Lawrence wants.[1] My impressions differ from hers but they are quite as strong as hers. It is comforting to know that Mrs. Lawrence did not share in the civilian reaction. It appeared so to me at the time, but I absented myself, as I have said, at an early opportunity from the scene. The rest of Mrs. Lawrence's letter does not seem to me to be interesting enough to your public for me much to discant upon it. I was early taught to avoid the example of Addison's moon. You know perhaps, sir, that remarkable passage

> "Soon as the evening shades prevail
> The moon takes up the wondrous tale
> And nightly to the listening earth
> Repeats the story of her birth."

I can't help it if I am descended from barons. I am. So is Mrs. Lawrence. My barons were, however, not Rhinelanders but Ruthenian Galicians. I can't believe that Miss Hunt whom Mrs. Lawrence doesn't like said "Russian descent." I have been called in my time French, English, German, Polish, Welsh, Scotch, and Galician Ruthenian, and more often than anything, American, but never, oh never, Russian. Mrs. Lawrence is incorrect in saying that I prefer to be an Englishman. That also I could not help. I was born in England. One does not preside at the destiny of one's birth.

I think I was in uniform. Mrs. Lawrence thinks I wasn't. I think Lawrence received a small sum from West Kent County Council. Mrs. Lawrence thinks he didn't. I was with Lawrence at the time. Mrs. Lawrence wasn't. But whatever may or may not be the truth of all these things, there is one frightfulness, Mr. Editor, that I swear upon all that you or I hold divine, I never committed. I will not protest if you accuse me or Mrs. Lawrence accuses me of almost any imaginable or unimaginable crime. It is

---

[1] In June, 1936, *The American Mercury* published Ford's essay "D. H. Lawrence." Frieda Lawrence probably took exception to certain details in Ford's reminiscence and wrote to the Editor. Neither her letter nor Ford's reply reached the "Letters to the Editor" column.

against my principles to protest. But this I never did, waking or sleeping, beneath suns or snows, or in over steamheated apartments. Never did I attempt to gore the gentle bosom of the German language by turning it into verse.

I have the honour to be your, sir, obedient servant.

To Ezra Pound

31 rue de seine
[Paris]

Dear Bertran de Struwwelpeter y Bergerac,   17. 2. 37

I was taken seriously ill with heart trouble shortly after getting your last and am not much better now, but just able to write.

This is the point on which I wish you would focus your opinion. Both Janice and I spend a large portion of our very occupied days —from time to time—in trying to get you permanent writing jobs with editors—and are always put off with the information that you have long since tried to blackmail all the editors in question and that they'll be damned to Hell etc. . . . Under my contract with one of them I wrote an article booming the Cantos: he refused to print it: I have lost my contract which I could ill afford to! . . . having to take myself to the FORUM.

A point, however, has arrived at which through me perfectly firm admirers of yours are ready to offer you a permanent contract —to fill a job I'm filling myself[1] and if it's good enough for me it's damn good enough for you, concealed son of the authoress of John Halifax Gentleman though you be. It means of course going to America: but that would give you an opportunity of getting rid of the cobwebs from your blackmailing instruments.

In short, you are invited to stroll for eight months of a year— or several years—about the philosophers' groves of Olivet. I personally give a couple of lectures a week to classes because I like lecturing. You would not have to if you did not want to. You would be conferring obligation if you talked to any youth or youths you thought intelligent. There the duties would—or could —stop. The real point is that you would have complete leisure to

---

[1] As visiting writer and lecturer at Olivet College, Michigan.

write whilst earning a living wage. They pay me slightly less than a living wage but would pay you more and with your greater skill in expenditure and ability to eat bleeding beef you would of yourself it draw very well. (French idiom: too tired to think of English for same). They also pay boat fares from Europe and back.

The point about Olivet is that here is a college of old establishment that under its new management[2] has for professors exclusively practitioners of the arts. Literature is looked after by me; music by a pretty sensible orchestra conductor who has several composers writing music for his orchestra to work out. (You would have his orchestra at your disposal. There is also a pretty good library and they get me all the books I want.) Painting by a rather indifferent painter—though for all I know you might think him pretty good . . . and so on. The point is that the aim of these people is not to turn out youthful genius but to get into the heads of the general public what the arts are about. The music students for instance try out any passages that the composers want to experiment with—one of them is pretty good—and in that way the pupils get some idea of forms, orchestration and so on. You may of course jeer at this or try some other form of blackmail but observe that that would be rather more unprofitable than even your normal unprofitalia because you are offered a complete finger in the pie, so that if you don't accept the offer . . . I shan't finish the sentence because I am tired of finishing sentences. But if you did choose to go to Olivet you would have a working, model educational machine to play with. . . . A man said to me the other day that he did not care for your CANTOS because of their umer [*sic*]—or rather that he detested the umer of your CANTOS so much that he never opened them for fear of coming on some of it. "But," he added "no-one can deny that Ezra is the greatest Educator in the world." You will I suppose refuse the offer and throw *bâtons* in its *roues* when occasion serves. That would be a pity because it is difficult to get good teachers for the place and your example would probably bring them . . . and the enterprise is a good thing because the eccentric Principal, Brewer, who once humorously sub-edited —or rather literary-edited the SPECTATOR for three weeks and then

[2] Joseph Brewer was then President.

was summarily retired because my influence on him was too great and who is also one of the best clog-dancers in the world, is quite impressionable and youngish and ready to learn.

Of course I know that one cannot expect a man of your age to change his habits or renier his material gods. But you have arrived at an age when few men save themselves unless they do change their habits and travel a little.

There are two other points about Olivet. It ought to continue because it is perfectly ready to become a refuge for good writers who are down on their end-bones, which in itself is valuable. AND then, you have no idea how extraordinarily many prostrate admirers you have in the U. S. And if you add the people who are avidly curious about you, you would arrive at a pretty good figure. . . . It is one of my normal worries thinking about your material prospects and I can assure you of this that if you did go to the U. S. you could, if you would lecture or radio or something, make enough in a few months without going out of the Detroit district to keep you for the rest of your life in comfort.

Still I know all this is beating the wind. The main point is that I should like to see you. I don't take myself to be an educational panjandrum and would like to talk the subject over with you. We have now added to the palatialness of this apartment, kitchens, baths, eau, gaz, électricité, open wood fires and most of the things demanded by the Victorians. So you could safely come here and we'd welcome you after March 4th when Janice's exhibition opens. Or, would it suit you to meet us at Bandol which is a regular Mediterranean Coney Island, complete with plages, gramophones. I could get as far as there and there is there a man, a painter, whom Janice wants to see . . . equally after March 4th, but before the 23d when our boat sails. I am not quite certain that we can do even this—but if you can fall in with it we will try. Bandol is the next station but two or three before Marseilles.

To the Editor of the New York
Herald Tribune Books[1]

Sir,   [March, 1937]

In one little word your critic of my *Great Trade Route* goes just too far.[2] He speaks of my "vilification of the name of Lincoln." This is a very serious charge. A vilifier is a vile person who uses untrue allegations in a tone of hatred. I trust I have never in my life vilified anybody; certainly the accusation of your critic is the first of its sort to be made against me. I trust you will induce him to withdraw what must have been written in haste, for the charge is likely to do me a great deal of harm. It should do so if it were warranted.

I have taken the trouble to re-read every word that I have written about Lincoln in the book in question and I cannot see one that could be taken as in any way unfavourable criticism of that great organiser of victory ... unless you choose to twist the meaning of one passage (pp. 316-317, English edition, there being no index in the Oxford's edition). There, poking fun at a guide book's phrase about Chatham, "where Washington courted Martha Custis, Robert E. Lee courted Mary Randolph Custis and Abraham Lincoln visited the Army of the Potomac" I indulge in the fanciful speculation as how Lincoln would have felt if he had there met the great shade of the Father of his Country. ... I say, it is true: "You would have thought he would have chosen some other place in which to visit his legalised murderers. . . ." And I imagine he would have had he been able. (Throughout the book I use the term legalised murderers for soldiers of whatever Army—Lee's, Stonewall Jackson's, Napoleon's, my own comrades in the late war

---

[1] See the issue of March 14, 1937, p. 28.

[2] In his review (February 21, 1937), John Patton argued: "It matters very little, for example, that Mr. Ford emphasizes a point of philosophy by an unfair aspersion on the name of St. Dominic, but it matters more that he seeks to drive home a theory of vilification of the name of Abraham Lincoln." With the unfortunate word "vilification," Patton unfairly overstated his charge against Ford. The subject of Ford's letter moves from Lincoln to the whole Civil War probably because Patton also wrote "[Ford] has tried to express and explain his philosophy of moderation and tolerance and good will by indulging himself in a rage of controversy over the American Civil War."

—and by implication of myself so that the phrase has no special application to Lincoln.) In other passages I either shortly state a historic fact such as (p. 356), "On November 1860 Abraham Lincoln of Illinois was elected the first Republican President of the United States"—a statement to which your critic can surely find no objection, or (p. 350) I quote from his speeches, or, as on p. 359 I compare him very favourably indeed with Davis as an organiser of victory, saying: "Compared with Lincoln as the defender of a cause he (Jefferson Davis) was a dyspeptic pettifogger-pedant as against . . . a sharp lawyer and one who knew instinctively every rule of the game of the dreadful court in which their suit was tried." It is true that just before I wrote: "Compared with Lincoln he was a gentleman and, if you will, a half-saint as against a sharp lawyer" and your client if he will may dislike the form of the comparison. But in that dreadful game there is no room for gentlemen and in that conjunction the term sharp lawyer carries no sense of contempt. Lincoln was selected by his constituents because he was a sharp lawyer who would do a certain job of work. He performed it admirably except for his hesitations over McLellan [*sic*] and blunderers of that kidney . . . those hesitations prolonging the war that in any military sense should not have lasted any longer than, say, the Franco-Prussian one. . . . But that criticism is the only one I have ever made of Lincoln.

The position is very difficult with regard to Grant. I find it difficult to think of him without almost abhorrence . . . but for a reason that, unless your correspondent has been responsible for the lives of men in the field, he may well find difficult to appreciate. Grant for me is a detestable butcher, not of the Confederate troops but of his own men . . . your critic's own men. An unsurpassed commissariat officer, a cunning and capable strategist he was, as a tactician—speaking militarily—the greatest villain the world has ever seen, the villain on the greatest scale! Vicksburg is one of the most impressive victories of its kind to be found in recorded history. But that is not enough. The great General is not the one who gains the most victories. He is the one who accomplishes his victories or retreats with the smallest loss of life. . . . But think of Shiloh; think, if you can stand thinking of it, of the Battle in the Wilderness and the days that followed it . . . the mercilessly prolonged hurling of mass after mass of miserable men against impregnable positions—day after day until the whole appalled army refused any more to advance. That is—military—villainy. Even bare statistics are eloquent against that man. During the War the Union Army lost in killed as many men as the Confederates put into the field during the whole course of operations. Yet on top of that so awful were Grant's losses during the closing scenes of the war that no official enumeration of them was ever published for fear of public opinion.

No, Sir, a great general who was also a good man would have realised his limitations as a tactician—"tactics" means the handling of troops in contact with enemy forces, "strategy" is conduct of all the operations of a war—and, retaining the strategic command, would have handed over the whole of the minor branch of those operations to some real soldier—to Pope, say, who never had justice done him. . . . Then, as against his whole achievement of hundreds of thousands of souls hurled wantonly into the presence of their Maker, what is the worth of the inexpensive gesture of returning a sword or two to their possessors or of giving over a few horses so that the enemy fields should produce crops of which the victors were later to take advantage enough? War has become—and had even then become—so terrible an occupation, that a facile gesture or so, will no longer save a man's soul from hell.

I have the honour to be, Sir, Your obedient servant

P.S. It is a pleasure to be able to suggest a correction to a writer who has wielded a Rhadamanthine rod over so many hundreds of thousands of poor wretches who have committed topographical or dialect lapses. But my governess was not, as suggested by Miss Paterson in your last issue, a Southern lady; she came from the shire of the Swan of Avon. It is true that she once sang in Memphis; but to sing by the Mississippi does not make you of necessity of the F. F. V.

27 March 1937

To Ralph B. Wright*[1]

Dear Sir: March 27, 1937

I am glad you have called my attention to the matter of your letter of March 23rd. I don't exactly know how to answer it without a great deal more thought than I have hitherto been able to give to the matter. I am, of course, completely favourable to organized labor, in every department. But this matter would seem surely to be one between yourselves and the publishers. I, at least, in the course of something like fifty years of writing have never been consulted as to what printer a publisher should employ. And I don't know how I could go about it now. The author, you must understand, is merely like the printer, an employee of the publisher. He has no trade union and if he tried as an individual to strike in sympathy with the printer, he would be at once snuffed out. I will, however, ask the publisher of the book[2] in question whether or not the Riverside Press, which prints this book, is or is not a union shop, and will suggest to them that, if they publish my next book, that I should like them to have it printed by such a house.

There is however another side to the matter, and that is that your unions, or rather the copyright laws which are passed in the interest of your unions, are in two ways exceedingly oppressive to authors—and like all other protective measures do no good to yourselves. That is to say, that the refusal of copyright to foreign books—particularly of foreign learned books unless they are printed in this country—is extremely detrimental to American learning and extremely hard on authors themselves who have already a sufficiently hard struggle to live and whose earnings are on an average considerably lower than those of the working printer. If it were merely a matter of refusal to American copyright, it would be relatively unimportant. But, in revenge all other foreign countries have taken similar steps against American writers, which practically means that in one way or another a writer writing English is deprived of at least half his possible income un-

[1] Of the New York Typographical Union.
[2] Probably *Portraits from Life*.

less he happens to be of sufficient position to be simultaneously published both here and throughout the British Empire—the English author being in an exactly similar position with regard to this country and I do not see that your constituents profit in the least. It is true that English books printed in England by the British Empire, if they could be sold here, would deprive the members of your unions of a percentage of employment. But on the other hand since American books cannot be sold in England you lose that not inconsiderable market—therefore the printers are not in any way profited, the authors are exposed to considerable loss, the learning of this country suffers along with the transport trade and no one in the world has profited. I do not mean to say that these facts will prevent my doing what I can to persuade any publishers that I have in the future [to have] their printing done by union houses. But I think that before you make any large appeal in that direction to my brothers of the pen, you ought to consider whether you should not yourselves, firstly, make some concession with regard to the copyright law.

Yours very sincerely,

To Stanley Unwin[1]

c/o Mrs. Allen Tate
Clarksville, Tennessee
May 29, 1937

My dear Unwin:

[. . . . .] I have just got back here after the ferocious but relatively triumphant course of lectures and interviews and all the usual ballyhoo at Chicago. Before then I had an even more ferocious course of the same thing at Boston, where I was offered an LLD. and, incidentally, two professorships, one of which I may take.

Mr. Greenslet,[2] who must have at least twelve Scottish great, great, grandparents, refuses to offer me more than half what I want of the *History of Our Own Time,* though he goes on making timid offers of a little more every few weeks. So that work remains in abeyance for the time being. And in the meantime I am writing something else for another publisher as to which I

[1] Head of George Allen & Unwin, Ltd.
[2] Ferris Greenslet, editor of Houghton Mifflin Company.

will write you in a day or two when I am a little less exhausted
by my travels—during which to soothe myself I read fifteen
works of Aristotle in the original and eleven detective stories—
the Aristotle being really the more entertaining of the two. He
actually knew more about things like the breeding habits of the
cuckoo than all the ornothological societies of the British Empire
put together until a year or two ago. On the other hand, he
asserted that in Trinacria there were gold mines worked by
mice—that is to say, that the mice made holes in the ground and
ate the gold, the Trinacrians afterwards catching them and burn-
ing their bodies, thus obtaining the gold. . . .

Yours very sincerely,

To Dale Warren*[1]

c/o Mrs. Allen Tate
Clarksville, Tennessee
June 11, 1937

My dear Dale Warren:

In premis our addresses will be as follows: here until July the
15th. From the 15th to the first of August at Olivet College, Olivet,
Michigan and from the 1st of August indefinitely at the University of Colorado, Boulder, Colorado. We may stay on a little
while in Denver, Colorado after Boulder because Mrs. Ford is
having an exhibition of her pictures there. Perhaps you would
hand those details over to your mailing clerk. I have not, as a
matter of fact, had any mail at all through you and don't know
that I frightfully want any unless by sense of touch or smell
you could tell whether any of them contains a million dollar
check.

As for our activities, Heaven knows what they will or won't be
because consorting with the Tates is like living with intellectual
desperados in the Sargoza Sea [*sic*]. We have just concluded an
attack en masse upon the University of Vanderbilt, Nashville,
ending in a glorious victory for the forces of intellect. Nevertheless I write my daily thousand words with regularity of a grandfather's clock. Mrs. Ford is less industrious. Nevertheless she has
done a certain amount of work including some drawings of
Boston which will shortly rejoice your eyes in some of the public

[1] Of Houghton Mifflin Company.

prints. So, on the whole, we are in health and spirits though I wish I could contrive for it to be a little warmer here. . . . Oh, by the bye, I meant to say that after Denver, Colorado it is our intention to proceed to Los Angeles by way of Salt Lake City and Sante Fé and from there to take the boat by way of the Suez Canal to Marseilles.

Very, very good wishes from us both.

To Ferris Greenslet*

c/o Mrs. Allen Tate
Clarksville, Tennessee
June 12, 1937

Dear Greenslet:

Mrs. Ford mentioned to you, I think whilst we were in Boston, her project for a book of drawings to be called PORTRAITS OF CITIES which she wants to do, text by myself. She has now got the project fairly well mapped out. She proposes to do about three or four drawings of about fifteen cities—Boston, New York, Washington, Natchez, New Orleans, Chicago, Detroit, Denver, Salt Lake City, Los Angeles, San Francisco, Panama (?), Havana (?), Marseilles, Dijon, Paris, Strasbourg, London. I should purpose, myself, to write from two to three thousand words about each of the said cities. I should imagine the whole would make a book that you might like to handle. If the idea should appeal to you, you might let me have a note and we could then go further into particulars—I would, I mean, send you a Portrait— say that of Boston or somewhere else and you would see what you think of it.

I hope Boston is being kind to you. We live here in sylph and greeneries with, on the whole, less sun than we could do with and the most extraordinary symphonies of mostly cacophonic sounds. But nevertheless my pen continues to travel regularly over the paper and Mrs. Ford's brush on her canvases. She sends her kind regards.

Mrs. Ford asks me to add that as she told you before, if you like losing money over a book like Mr. Schreiber's, you might just as well try making some with a good one.[1]

---

[1] *Portraits and Self-Portraits: Collected and Illustrated* by Georges Schreiber (Boston, 1936). Two pages are devoted to an autobiographical blurb by Ford and Schreiber's sketch of him.

To Paul Palmer*

Olivet College
Olivet, Michigan

My dear Palmer,   July 29, 1937

Certainly, as soon as I get a moment from the absolute madness of work that I have on hand I'll send you some articles to look at. We leave here Saturday for Boulder, Colo. (c/o Writers Conference in the Rocky Mountains) where we shall be until the middle of August, then we return here. I quite understand that you must be very full up.

By the bye, I have consented to give a course of lectures on comparative literature to a class here until the beginning of December. We shall have a little house and some room so if you and Mrs. Palmer would care to run over and stop with us for a while it would be something pleasant for us to look forward to when we are in the dustbowl. Janice says please, if you come, to bring a pheasant—or even a brace.

Yours always,

P.S. If you would care to let me write something about Zionism in which for many years I have taken a great deal of interest, I'd put off everything else to let you have it—I mean on approval.

To Paul Palmer*

My dear Palmer,   [September? 1937]

I am getting into a complete muddle about those articles—in addition, I cannot find the copies of my letters to you on the subject. I will therefore begin again.

I am getting ready—or contemplating—two sets of articles, the one that I am doing with Janice to be called provisionally, Portraits, or Profiles of Cities, she illustrating them in pen and ink. A good many of these—five or six—have been commissioned by magazines that carry illustrations. I suppose you could not carry illustrations—but I could write you one or two of these articles that Janice does not want to do drawings for. The articles are on the whole siteful [*sic*]. . . . I explain that I don't know why such cities—like, say Denver, Colorado—should exist at all.

Indeed I am in rather a spiteful as well as a muddled mood. Contact, for instance, with the (rather wealthy, middle class) students of this institution where I am due to take a chair of Comparative Literature, as well as with students from half a dozen other State Universities where I have been pottering about or lecturing, has given me such an appalled view of the secondary education of this country, that I feel that nothing can save it but something like a revolution in the whole country's educational methods. . . . And crisscrossing the eastern states from say Baltimore to the Rocky Mountains has given me a good many other causes for appalment so that I don't really see what is to become of this—let alone European—civilisations.

Now a magazine to whom I am under no particular sense of obligation wants me to do for them a series of articles with a title something like: *What is the matter with America?* I would much rather do them for you—on Education; the Periodical Press; the tyranny of publicity and the other tyrannies under which the nice inhabitants of this country lie prone. . . . I don't say that I could keep Politics out of it altogether. I should try to, but I don't quite know—I don't believe anybody does—where the dividing lines between politics and domesticity here come in. . . . It seems to me, for instance, that just as the Colonies are the final curse of the British Empire so the Pioneer Cult is, outside New York and, possibly, Chicago, completely smirching the civilisation and ambitions of nearly all the inhabitants of this country. Why should one be proud of and emulate the frame of mind of a pawky double-crosser like [Davy] Crockett when one's ancestry numbers anyone like Cotton Mather? Cotton Mather wasn't nice, but he was at least—if over-ripe—at the least the product of a tree of civilisation.

Obviously I am not going to write from the point of view of the snooty European.

I'll probably do one or two of these articles right off if you feel any curiosity about them and will give you the refusal of them if you like.

You see I can't really figure out whether you really want the products of my pen. . . . Why should you? You have had enough of them to swamp any ordinary MERCURY.

But drop me a line. I shall be here lecturing on COMPARATIVE LITERATURE—the only course of the sort in the United States—till December—when we contemplate taking a holiday on the Riviera. I wish we might meet somewhere en route.

Our kind regards to your family.

Yrs always

To Stanley Unwin

Olivet College
Olivet, Michigan

Dear Mr. Unwin:

5. 9. 37

After criss-crossing the whole continent from East to West, we have arrived once more here where I shall be lecturing on Comparative Literature until December 1st when we hope to return to Paris, possibly via London. The Post Office here is not very good or obliging so I find a great number of letters and proofs from you and your House waiting for me, some of them having done so for quite a long time.

I will send the proofs of MIGHTIER THAN THE SWORD[1] as soon as I can run through them; I do not suppose there will be anything but literals to correct. . . . I notice you say that VIVE LE ROY is meeting with a mixed reception, *chez vous.* I don't see why it should; it is surely a very harmless performance. [. . . . .]

PROJECTED "HISTORY OF OUR OWN TIME":

I do not make much progress with the American Edition of this. Mr. Greenslet's ideas of what an author should be paid differ so vastly from mine that although we have been negotiating desultorily almost to the present moment I do not think we shall come to any agreement—nor indeed will any other American publisher that I know venture money on a book of history not exclusively occupying itself with American History and written from the American point of view. They might tomorrow or they would have ten years ago—but the Trade here is pretty shaky and alarmed. So if you would care to see if you could find a New York publisher I should be very pleased. I cannot afford to hawk my own books about here because it puts down my prices. . . . The least terms I could accept for the U. S. A. rights would be

---

[1] When George Allen & Unwin published *Portraits from Life* in 1938 they changed the title to *Mightier Than the Sword*.

$1,500 in advance in two instalments—$750 on signature and the rest on receipt of ms., on acct. of a royalty of twelve and a half % rising to fifteen after sale of two thousand copies.

In the meantime I have been forced into accepting a commission from the Dial Press for a HISTORY OF LITERATURE.[2] I really don't know anything about the Dial Press except that they pay me very well and regularly and that their manager, Grenville Vernon, is a very old friend of mine. In addition they guarantee me *very* large sales and they seem to have immense sales for the usually educational books that they publish. The capitalist behind the undertaking is a man called Salop, a man with a very good financial standing and a sort of flair for books that will sell here. He sold a quarter of a million copies of Jowett's PLATO in one volume, but I don't know anything more about him.

I have got about a third of this written and it seems to be turning out pretty well. It should make from 200,000 to a quarter of a million words—covering, comparatively, the whole of Literature from the Chinese to, say, Mr. Hemingway in a not too, but yet sufficiently, erudite manner. I hope to have it done by a little after Christmas as the College here has a very good library and working conditions are most favourable.

Would you care to substitute this for the HISTORY OF OUR OWN TIME? Or would you make a separate contract for it? Or what? I think you can trust in its being a pretty good book from the point of view of writing and criticism. Nothing else occurs to me to say except that I hope you enjoy life and a good digestion. When you have to live on the food of the Great North West you realize that nothing else counts in the world.

Twelve miles from here is the largest Indigestion Hospital in the Universe, a place uniting the proportions of Windsor Castle, the British Museum, the Vatican and the Kremlin with traces of the architecture of the lot. It is ornamented by two two-hundred foot towers for the use of patients who do not get cured fast enough and prefer to end it.

Yours very sincerely,

[2] The Dial Press published the longest of Ford's books, *The March of Literature*, in 1938; George Allen & Unwin published it the following year.

27 September 1937

To The Editor of *The Forum*[1]

Olivet, Michigan
Olivet College

Dear Sir:

27. 9. 37

I have listened so often and with such complete concurrence to Dr. Lin Yutang's delightful conversation and public speeches on the subject of diet that I cannot find anything to which to object in his delightful paper on the Stomach.[2] One can only wish more power to his elbow. For unless he will come to the rescue of our Western civilisations, in things gustatorial, what will become of us? What *can*?

You will perhaps have seen a film lately released by H. M.'s War Office to this country—I can't imagine why, unless it is to be taken as a horrible warning to people here. It represents average specimens of the 80 per cent of British recruits to whom the British Army has been forced to refuse enlistment—because of ill- or under-nourishment! This does not mean that the parents of these rickety, undersized or tuberculous poor wretches have not had the money with which to purchase for their offspring a sufficiency of victuals. It means that the food has been ill-selected, sterilised with preservatives and prepared with a hopeless slovenliness. It was stated in a return lately that in the immense majority of English urban homes the children were never given bread and butter—because it was troublesome to spread and cut the bread. They were given instead a pinkish substance called cake which consisted of steel-milled flour faintly sweetened—with glucose!

And do not believe that things here are much better. They are not. Spend some months zigzagging from the coast to the Rocky Mountains; look at the crowds leaving factories, the young men disporting themselves about their colleges anywhere between Boston and Detroit, or in the Solid South or in the Middle West. . . . And eat the food of the share croppers and poor whites . . . yes and the food in the homes from which come the students. . . . If it were only a matter of the immortal sourbelly and beans stewed in pot liquor it would be tragic enough. But it is more tragic still. . . . It seems to me to be the most devastating thought

[1] See *Forum and Century*, xcviii (November, 1937), xi.
[2] "On Having a Stomach," *Forum and Century*, xcviii (October, 1937), 195-199.

of today that 80 per cent of the urban inhabitants of Anglo-Saxondom in both its branches never taste fresh food . . . and almost as great a percentage of the non-urban populations not employed in farming or small-holding. Yes, by all means call in Dr. Lin Yutang as Food Fuehrer. And quickly. . . .

I have only one correction to make in his article. Did the Chinese study the habits of beasts or had Dr. Lin Yutang read me, he would not have uttered his paean to the mildness of manners of the non-carnivore. For, as I wrote only the other day and have been writing for some years, the fact is that the five most gratuitously ferocious of the beasts—those who mangle for the pleasure of mangling, not in the course of hunting for the pot—those five then, the bull, the stallion, the rhinoceros, the gorilla—and Mr. Hitler—are all vegetarians.

I have the honour to be, Sir, Your obedient servant

To Ezra Pound

Olivet, Michigan
Dear Ezra,   Nov. 13, 1937

I am sorry about the Odyssey of your cantos and sorrier still not to get them. We move about such a lot. And after all it is hardly my fault or even the bank's if you mislay the address I gave you.

As things are at the present we expect to leave these climes by the Lafayette on the 4th December and to be in Paris for some little time, returning here on the first of April.

As I'm writing a history of the world's literature from Confucius to Gertrude [Stein], not to mention Joyce and as I'm involved in certain measures for changing the incidence of cultural education in this realm I sort of feel that we ought to get together and discuss these high matters. The attempts to change the said educational incidence here are much more widespread than you have any idea though I don't [have time?] to write about them.

I am getting rather stiff in the joints and the worse from traveling. But we shall probably be in Toulon early in the new year. Could you possibly come along there for a day or two? Or, if you could find us some *really* cheap lodgings and if you can protect us from all possible assaults of Kerensky[1] we might come and spend a week or so at Rapallo. I think this is the point at which you ought seriously to consider taking a hand in things. Don't answer this until you hear that we have arrived in Paris and then answer to 31 rue de Seine 6. Of course if you happen to be in Paris it would be all the better. But whether you come to Toulon or we to Rapallo is simply a matter of which of us is the harder up.

Our love to Dorothy.

Yours,

P.S. I enclose a copy of a lecture delivered by Janice at various cultural centers in this place.

To S. Bagnall[1]

31 rue de Seine
Paris, VI

Dear Sir,

16. 12. 37

The book I am at present engaged on is not the HISTORY OF OUR OWN TIME which I shall probably not reach for a year or so but A HISTORY OF LITERATURE which I hope to have finished by about April and which the Dial Press of New York contemplate publishing in August, you, I suppose, doing it about the same time. This is a book which I have been thinking of and making studies for—like my ENGLISH NOVEL published some time ago by Lippincotts and Constables—for at least twenty years until it was commissioned by the Dial Press and yourselves last year whereupon I began actually to write it, having to date written 157 pp. or so, 170,000 words. This takes the book up to the Shakespearean era. It should be finished in another 130,000 words.

It is written from the aesthetico-critical rather than the annalist's point of view and forms a sort of comparative history of creative writing from, as you might say, Confucius to Conrad. I don't know of any other book of the kind in English, these things being usually written by professors rather than by creative writers and consisting of a plethora of instructive rather than educative matter. . . . I find by the bye in the course of several years now

---

[1] Ford and Pound agreed it was wise to use this pseudonym for Mussolini during their chats in Rapallo.

[1] Of the Publicity Department, George Allen & Unwin.

of intensively reading the classics that it is astonishing how my
tastes have changed since I was not merely twenty but forty and,
except in the case of Boccaccio, Vergil, and Catullus whom I don't
care for as much as I did in 1913, always in the direction of
finding them more readable and, as it were, jolly, than I ever did
before. I found myself for instance reading the *Book of Job,
Orlando Furioso,* or Chaucer's *Palamon and Arcite* as if they
were say Mrs. Agatha Christie and, trying to rest my mind with
light literature, I found myself turning to Dante's *Paolo and
Francesca* as being more restful company. . . .

If you can use any of the above as publicity, pray do so. I can
think of nothing else to say.
                                        Yours faithfully,

To Henry Goddard Leach*¹

31 rue de seine
paris vi
18/2/38

Dear Mr. Leach,

I am very glad you like the cooking article . . . or rather the
food one.² I will, if you please, take a little time off to think about
something else to write about. The international situation here
is rather too newsy to write about immediately. There are two
"lines" that I am maturing in my mind: A: A point that is not
taken into account by even the good journalists who write about
the above things is that the Late War in destroying Fine Illusions
has destroyed them. The War, that is to say, got rid of Faith,
Loyalty, Courage and all the other big words as motives for
human action. . . . But in doing that—which nobody denies
that it has done—it has very much gotten rid of the danger of
wars. You can't flog into enthusiasm for wars people who are
sick of the very idea of martial virtues. This is at least true of
England, France, Germany and the United States. In Italy there
is an enthusiasm for war because, the average daily wage being
four lire, the pay of the private soldier is twelve, per diem. There
does exist the sort of business patriotism that makes for Protection
as a way of heaving half a brick at the foreigner: there *are* patriots

---

¹ Editor of *Forum and Century.*
² "Food," xcix (April, 1938), 241-247. This was the last article Ford wrote for
this magazine.

of that kidney. But that is not the sort of thing that makes for wars other than civil ones. The business man hates the working men of his own country—and the working men the business man in each case with much more of blood lust than he devotes to the foreigner. If you had lately spent as much time in rural Michigan—or in Paris—as we have lately done you would see how true that is. Governor Cox told me that almost every house in Grosse Point is an arms depot, and if you have followed the proceedings here against the C.S.A.R. which is undoubtedly supported by Mr. Hitler in part, you would see that the extremists of the Right here would prefer German rule to Left rule even if established at the price of blood. At any rate there is one subject.

Another I meditate treating very soon is simply the fact that France—from the point of view of culture and the arts—manages everything so infinitely better than either branch of Anglo-Saxondom that the sooner we acknowledge the fact the sooner we shall be out of the wood. Both England and the United States have *got* to provide insurance for France: the world has to. If the United States invaded France she would find Germany, Turkey, Poland and the Republic of Andorra at her side. If then the two branches of Anglo-Saxondom, bracketed equal, publicly and once for all acknowledged that they—because of a certain expertness in physical comfort and steel products—claimed the second place in civilisation, most international troubles would settle themselves. They would go on realising as they do today in the subconscious—and particularly as was the case in '14 and '17— that because France is expert in elegance, moderation and knowledge of the values of life—that France must be preserved because those strains *must* be represented in modern life. And they would with no uncertain voice declare that fact to the world—as if it were another Monroe doctrine. War would then cease in the Western hemisphere—for no European power would want to go to war if the possible spoils did not include the French shores of the Mediterranean and the Burgundy wine district. We on the other hand should have the reward of being now and then slapped on the back and told: "C'est vous qui avez sauvé la France." That has happened to me more than once in my capacity of ancien combatant—and I assure you the experience is sweet. We in short should have the aspect of inveterate drunkards who should vote for Prohibition. We are savages or so near it it makes no difference, we Anglo Saxons, but we know that, with very little of a slip back towards barbarism we should become naked gorillas, barely able to walk sufficiently erect to keep the steel mills going. On the surface we detest elegance, moderation, and knowledge of life—because we do not know how to enter a room, how to hold our hands, how to construct a single decent sentence in our own languages or how to order a meal that will not in its menu proclaim us barbarous as gorillas. Among the whole four hundred millions of us we cannot properly support one decent periodical . . . for without knowing the figures I will bet that you do not get one tenth of the support you should have and there is no one else. So, vaguely conscious of all that, under the shouts of the Chauvinists we know that the counterbalances of ourselves must be preserved. Once we have it officially acknowledged for us that our arts, prose, murals, thought, wine, beefsteaks, wit, manners, drawing-room behaviour are all hopelessly second-hand we shall give over vain strivings, rely for good in the future on our cushionings, interior decorations after Kate Greenaway and steel and cellophane and hard liquors and consider that we have one claim to be distinguished mentally from the duck-billed platypus in that we once saved—and shall continue to go on saving—France.

I'd like to write something along those lines if you'd let me and I think it would be worth while. Perhaps you would think it worth while to let me have a cable care Garritus, Paris as to what you think.

Perhaps also you would tell Miss Moir, and thank her for me that her version of the Food article seems to me to be perfectly all right.

Yours very sincerely,

To Ezra Pound

Paris
Dear God, Father Divine. . .   9. 3. 38

I know that Your awful face must be veiled to the lesser mackerel nuzzling between Your toes in the ooze. Indeed this lesser mackerel knows also how it turns Your divine stomach to have to communicate with lesser ones at all. But in this case it would be a convenience if Your Divinity would communicate directly to this l. m. the nature of Its exactions. Should Your Godhead write to the tops of Olivet—and *sure* Its communication should only be with the tops—the message would only be forwarded to this lesser mackerel to decide on—except on the financial requisitions which will have to be referred to the Trustees. But for all other purposes this l. m. here may be regarded as tops too and thus time will be saved and confusion avoided. And your petitioner shall ever pray. . . .

To Ezra Pound

Dear Ezra,
[Paris]
16. 3. 38

Do exercise a little imagination and try to understand the situation. I am an *extremely* sick man and your incomprehensible scrawls are a torture to me—to read and to have to answer. Get the waiter at your hotel to write your letters for you; he will at least write comprehensible dog-English. Your 1892 O. Henry stuff is wearisomely incomprehensible by now.

The situation is this: I am offering to give up my job at Olivet to you because you have been making noises about Universities for a long time and it would give you a chance really to do something. I have already answered your question about a press. They have already a press at Olivet. They print a paper. They would no doubt do any necessary scholastic printing you needed. But they probably would not print Mussolini-Douglas propaganda for you. They might. But it would be up to you to persuade them. They do not, as I have already told you, use your books as text books because "They" are I and I do not approve of the use of text books. At the same time I constantly recommend my classes to read your books. You understand I do not approve of making any reading compulsory. If a boy tells me he does not like Vergil I tell him to find something he does like & read it with attention. That gives results that satisfy me. If you wanted to revert to text books you could.

With regard to salary etc. Olivet pays me $125 a month, say 1500 a year. They would pay me more if I wanted it but their endowment is not very big and as I find it quite possible to live on that sum there and have plenty of time to do my own work I do not think fit to do so. In addition, last year, I made about another $1,200 by lecturing in the neighbourhood. I could have made a great deal more but I am pretty feeble these days. (They also pay my round trip fares to Europe). Ref. all this: You will probably want more than that salary. You can take either one of two courses: Either write direct to Joseph Brewer, President, Olivet College, Mich. and tell him how much you want, or write to me and I will do my best to get it for you. All I am empowered to offer you is the $1,500 and round trip fare as above. It would be better in any case to let me know what you are asking because I shall probably have to explain to them (the Trustees) why you want so much. For myself I should certainly think you would be wise to ask more. You will probably be let in for extra expenses as not at first knowing your way about—and, anyhow, you should ask more on principle.

We expect to leave here today week for N. Y., going on to Olivet after I have lectured at N. Y. University on the 5th August. If you want to ask any more questions do so before we leave here. But try to understand. Disciplinary and other matters in the English section are entirely in my hands & the faculty consult me as to the other branches that interest me—i. e. music, painting, history. There are other departments—several science branches, municipal law and other things that I am vague about because they are no affair of mine. The number of students at the moment is 305—the capacity of the college; the number of faculty is 45. The system is tutorial, each teacher having so many students to boss for study and discipline—that not applying to me & not to apply to you unless you wanted it to. I teach what I want to— i. e. comparative literature from the beginning of time to the moment of speaking. No one interferes with me in the slightest degree. Nor would they with you. I don't know just what they would do if you tried to introduce your politics into your teaching—nothing at all probably unless you were too loudly communist in which case the local farmers would shoot you.

Please understand: I am not a confidence trickster trying to induce you into some disastrous folly. *I am not trying to persuade you to take the job.* You would probably turn that pleasant place into a disastrous sort of hell. But it is my duty to say that there the place is for you & the College authorities want you because they admire you as a poet and teacher. Nor is it part of a sinister conspiracy on my part to rob you of your claim to be the greatest discoverer of literary talent the world has ever seen. I don't care a damn: I wish to God I had never "discovered" anyone. . . . The only conspiracy I am in is to get you the Charles Eliot Norton professorship at Boston to which Olivet would be a stepping stone. The snag as to that is that the Professor ought to be an Englishman—but I have tried to persuade the Boston authorities that you are English enough.[1]

I do not know if I have any Olivet prospectuses. If I find any I will send them on.

Please again: If you want to ask any more questions get someone to put them into comprehensible English.

To Julia Ford

31 rue de Seine
Sunday
[March 20, 1938]

Dearest Julie,

This is by way of being a farewell letter, for we expect to be sailing by the NORMANDIE on Wednesday. I am sorry not to have seen more of you. It is a pity you could not have been here whilst Janice's exhibition was on, because she had to be at the exhibition most of the day and I had to sit here alone and should have been glad of your ministrations for I am still pretty feeble, practically unable to walk and so on. Still, it was not to be. I shall hope to see more of you when we come back—whenever that will be. But I have got back to work again, which is a good thing, though I cannot do much—which is not so good because lots of money won't flow in unless I work hard and we shall not be able to realise the project of your coming to Olivet unless lots of money does flow in.

---

[1] Pound never taught at Olivet or Harvard. He saw Ford in New York during his 1939 visit, but he stayed in the United States only a few months, then returned to Italy.

One piece of news is good and that is that Janice's exhibition has been an extraordinary success. The State has announced its intention of buying one of her pictures—either the BATTLE or the KENTUCKY DAY—for the Jeu de Paume, and she has sold a couple of others and the praise she has received on all sides has been almost unprecedented. And Montparnasse says she has restored painting to its proper functions—whatever that means. And on the strength of her sales I have been able at last to buy myself a new sponge bag so I shan't have to be ashamed when I go into the washing places on Pullmans! . . . Otherwise the amount of money realised by said sales has not been extraordinary—working out in time spent at about two hour per sou. So that is that.

I hope you are shouting a bas Chamberlain good and strong at any demonstrations that are going. It makes us ashamed to be leaving Paris now that Mr. C. has brought his friends the Huns so near. But I guess I should not be much good when the city is bombed. . . . Think of the rue de Seine in ruins, like Barcelona, and me in a gas mask pouring water on the ashes of my manuscripts and Janice trying to save the cat—which is the first thing she would think of.

I hope you have got a good hide hole in a lonely place in the country for when they bomb London. It does not make me very comfortable to think of you there, I can tell you, and us across the sea!

Goodbye, my dear MONSTER. I am too tired to write more. . . . By the bye if you would get two or three more razor blades and put them into an envelope and mail them here right away—or perhaps better still to the NORMANDIE at Havre I should be obliged. They are a great luxury for me.

Your quite old

To Alvin C. Hamer[*1]

Dear Mr. Hamer: May 11, 1938

I have reflected carefully over your letter of the 8th and have

[1] Hamer's Book Service in Detroit requested support in a defense of Ernest Hemingway's *To Have and Have Not* which had been banned by the Wayne County Prosecutor from all commercial distribution channels. Alvin Hamer wanted either a letter or Ford's presence in the court room.

come regretfully to the conclusion that I don't think that even in the interests of your cause I should do any good if I entered the arena. I have made it an absolutely rigid rule not to enter into any controversy about the public affairs of this country and your affair seems undoubtedly to fall into the category of public ones. And, believe me when I say that if I did so it would do more harm than good. On the few occasions when I have entered into merely literary controversies here it has invariably been said, even in New York, where xenophobia is at its lowest: "Hello, this fellow is a foreigner. How dare he mix himself up in our affairs. Let us beware of foreigners even if they bring gifts." And the effect on Detroit of a foreigner entering in this quarrel would surely be bad. All foreigners are not only lecherous but aim at corruption of the morals of American youth. That is too well known to need any contradiction.

If the censorship were likely to do Hemingway any harm I might dash in—but all censorships invariably defeat themselves and the only effect of this one will be to increase Hemingway's sales so please leave me out of the matter. I would gladly do anything I could to be of service to you in this matter but in this particular case I should do you no good—particularly in the witness box where I should make a horrible muddle of things under cross-examination and I should get myself accused of publicity seeking. I don't have to tell you that I am heartily on your side in the struggle.

With kind regards to Mrs. Hamer.

Yours very sincerely,

To George T. Keating

Olivet College,
Olivet, Michigan
June 1, 1938

My dear Keating:

[. . . . .] Yes, *Memories and Impressions* is the same as *Ancient Lights.*[1] I don't quite know what information you want about *Henry for Hugh.* It is the sequel to a book called *The Rash Act* which was published in America by that Smith Company that

---

[1] *Memories and Impressions: A Study in Atmospheres* (New York, 1911) is the American edition of *Ancient Lights and Certain New Reflections, Being the Memories of a Young Man* (London, 1911).

disappeared, and in England by I really can't for the moment remember whom.[2] *Henry for Hugh* itself has not yet been published
in England because I thought the time has not really come to
publish it. It will be published by Allen & Unwin as soon as I want
them to do so. I consider these two novels are my best books—
at any rate they fill exactly my ideas of what a novel should
be. Of course the much better known *Good Soldier* is equally correct in handling, but I think it is relatively rather thin and timid
in handling. I do not suppose this interests you very much as you
can form your own opinion for yourself. I hope you are quite
over the ill effects of your Middle Eastern disaster—Jugoslavia
is the Middle East isn't it—or no, I suppose it is really the Near
East. For myself I am now so crippled with rheumatism that I
can't even dress myself or brush my own hair. It is the cussedly
damp climate of this place and I may not suppose I shall ever
be even nearly well again until I can get to Provence. As Cunninghame Graham's old Shellback said, "I ought never to have left
them islands." But I can't get away from here before August first
and then shall be pretty well bound to somewhere near New York
until December. Some fellow wants me to do a lecturing tour
which is a thing I despise and detest, but if he offers me a sufficiently attractive program I shall have to accept it, though I expect
the winter travelling will finish me off. Verily, peace hath her
perils greater than in war. But anyhow I am getting [along] really
fast with my *History of Literature,* which (d.v.) I have to finish
on the anniversary of the taking of the Bastille.

As I have said, if you happen to be in this neighbourhood before
the first of August, we would be delighted to give you our hospitality.

Yours,

I appreciate yr. concern in asking me to go to the older publishers but they are no good for my type of work. Lippincott was
a defeat; the Oxford University Press a disaster; Houghton Mifflin
complete ruin for a reason I will explain when I have more time.
Allen & Unwin, who are two very old firms amalgamated, can
sell me in England because I am a classic but this country won't buy
classics so it is only irregular publishers who can sell me here.

[2] Jonathan Cape, in 1933.

To George T. Keating

My dear Keating: June 28, 1938

I am extremely obliged to you for getting Yale University to send me ZEPPELIN NIGHTS so promptly. The book was never published in this country and I want, if I can find a publisher, to reprint one or two of the little historical sketches which I think are some of my best writing.[1] Certainly I will put some sort of little inscription in the book before returning it. I don't know whether I am more proud to have your collection of me in Yale or more sorry. I think it saddens me a little not to be able to think of you pottering about your treasures by what we used to call the warm hearth stone. And I don't quite see why you shouldn't have left the things to Yale in your will. However you know your own motives best.

I hope you are going to have a really nice holiday this year without any near Eastern operations. I am pretty well myself, nearing the end of my book[2]—only about 75 pages left to write out of 900. But the weather is frightfully treacherous here and my rheumatism gets worse and worse so that at times I can hardly move at all and can neither dress nor shave nor brush my hair by myself.

The doctorate was conferred upon me by this college, and I can tell you I looked swell in my robes. I have always wanted to be a cardinal because just think what a fine expanse of scarlet that would make! But this is nearly as good. However if you ever address me as doctor again, I shall return the letter unopened and marked "addressee unknown." Many thanks again.

To W. H. D. Rouse*

Dear Mr. Rouse: July 13, 1938

I am indeed flattered that you should have sent me your Iliad, and by the nice things you say about MIGHTIER THAN THE SWORD.

[1] Subtitled "A London Entertainment," it was published by John Lane in 1915 as a collaboration between Violet Hunt and Ford. Actually the bulk of the book is composed of historical sketches which Ford had published in *The Daily News* and *The Outlook*.

[2] *The March of Literature.*

Certainly your ILIAD and your ODYSSEUS are achievements of which you can well be proud.[1] The language is impressively clear and simple and you certainly get your Homer over, as the saying is. I am taking the liberty of quoting the passage about Nausicaä's picnic in your Odyssey parallel to Chapman's translation, in the HISTORY OF LITERATURE that I have just sent to the printers. I hope this will meet with your approval. I cannot get over the almost adoration that I have always had for Chapman, but obviously it is of the first importance that children and simple minds should be acquainted with Homer, and they could not go about it better than by reading you. Wouldn't you think it possible to turn your attention to Froissart, who for me has always stood somewhere near Homer? And Berners' translation, magnificent as it is, is also beyond the reach of the young. I have found indeed that many of my students in this country find him difficult enough to read to be discouraged at the task. It is curious indeed, the difficulty with which quite well educated young men here read Elizabethan English. It is, I suppose, because they don't read here the Bible or the Book of Common Prayer as they do in England, but I may tell you that several of the children of my colleagues here already have long passages of your ODYSSEY by heart, which obviously makes the world a little better every day. Your letter only reached me about ten days ago because my life is so extremely peripatetic, and since I got it I have been so buried in what Carlyle calls the belly of the ugly enterprise of finishing my book that I could not answer before.

By the bye, has not it struck you that Homer was a personage something like Froissart who travelled to all the courts and blacksmith shops in Western Europe trying to get details from eye witnesses of battles in which they had taken part, and is it not significant that his activities should have taken place at just about the time when the alphabet was replacing ideographs and things of the sort? Still, you know so much more about that sort of thing than I. I received yesterday a manuscript of a book purporting to trace extraordinary parallels between Homer and the

[1] *The Story of Achilles: A Translation of Homer's "Iliad" into Plain English* (London, 1938); *The Story of Odysseus: A Translation of Homer's "Odyssey" into Plain English* (London, 1937).

Hebrew prophets, written by an old lady of over ninety who lives near here at a place called Grand Rapids. Her name is Cornelia Steketee Hulst, and she seems to have won approval for previous books on Homer from all sorts of people, from President Hutchins of Chicago University and Gilbert Murray and Valdimir Vedel, Rector of the University of Copenhagen. I wonder if you happen to have come across her. If I come across anything really striking in the book, which doesn't seem in the present state of the book trade very likely to get published, I will take the liberty of notifying them to you. Thanking you again for your kindness, I am

Yours very sincerely,

To Stanley Unwin

Dear Mr. Unwin: August 4, 1938

I am returning herewith the marked proof[1] with the best answers I can make to the enigmas there set me. I simply do not feel well enough actually to correct the book as, in spite of the fact that I am supposed to be on holiday, various odd jobs completely overwhelm me. Yesterday I had to go into Detroit to world broadcast over short wave an account of the History of Literature that I've just finished and it takes me about four hours a day to answer the letters of Michigan ladies who want to send me in Mss. for my comments. Would it be any good trying some of these on you? I have turned up one mss. in particular which I think is the best first mss. I ever read—excluding none—I would send it to you in any case, except for the fact that it is a m[in]ute, if singularly ironic projection of life in one of the richest suburbs of Chicago and as such might not interest the London public. I have also turned up one of the very best detective stories I ever read and an extraordinarily beautifully written historical novel about Egypt. This might very well suit you and I think I will tell the writer to send the mss. to you in any case when it is finished.

The writer is a lady of I should think 45 with five children living in a tiny village right away to the devil in the forest and she writes every morning from 4 to 7. That is the sort of phenomenon that

---

[1] Probably of *Provence*, which George Allen & Unwin published in November.

confronts you all the time in this extraordinary literary middle west where every farm hand and every mother of family and every spinster and every policeman writes books. Oh, and then there is Maureen Whipple,[2] another of my pupils to whom Greenslet has just given his literary scholarship for the year. If you are writing to him you might suggest that he let you look at the book.

By the bye, is it really advisable to put my LLD which is really a D.Litt on the title page of Provence considering my long and strenuous anti-academic career? It is all right with me either way but you might think it over.[3]

Your stern proof reader rather spoils my story by cutting out the bloodys which in this country are regarded as merely harmless eccentricities. The one in particular reminiscent of the cockney recruit in Canada who being asked which London he came from— as for instance London Ont. London N.Y. London Mich. London Ky, replied London the bloody world! is too good to be spoilt. However if it must be it must be. I hope you've had a pleasant holiday.

Yours very sincerely

To Stanley Unwin

Dear Mr. Unwin: October 13, 1938

Thank you for the kind things you say. I was, myself, very much against the title MARCH OF LITERATURE but could not think how to better it and the Dial Press were very anxious that that should be the title. The objection to calling it a History of Literature is that that would imply a history of all literature whereas practically I only treat of those literatures that have had an influence on the European and American literatures of today. I mean that I have only just touched on Persian, Arabic, Japanese, Polish literatures, etc. and not even touched on them because they seemed to me to lead no where in particular as far as we are concerned so that if you could think of a better word than *March,* I should be very much pleased. Anyhow, the book is marching very well here and meets with practically no opposition in the press which is rather

---

[2] *The Giant Joshua* (Boston, 1941) was her Houghton Mifflin fellowship novel.
[3] The title page reads, Ford Madox Ford, LL.D.

disappointing because the book contains a good many attacks on the professorial school and one would expect that the professorial school would hit back but they haven't.[1] And I suppose it is not a thing really to grumble at. I don't know whether it would not be a good thing if you got somebody professorially minded to look through the book before its English publication and formulate objections. But perhaps that would be asking for trouble.

I am having some trouble myself in formulating the plan for the international book which, let us, for the purposes of identification call "And There Is No King"; but as soon as I have got the plan at all satisfactory in my mind I will send you a sketch of it.

We are having something like a heat wave here which I find deadening to the intellect.

To the Editor of *The Saturday Review of Literature*[1]

Sir:— [October, 1938]

You will perhaps permit me to diagnose as amiably as possible for the benefit of your readers the case of your David, Mr. Ernest Boyd,[2] as against that Goliath, "The March of Literature." It is an eternal fight which in the case of this present writer has been going on now for nearly half a century and in the case of this writer's family has persisted for something like four hundred years. His earliest noteworthy ancestor was an apprentice of Gutenberg and, setting up for himself as a printer in Paris, he wrote and printed a pamphlet declaring that the University of Sorbonne did not know how to teach Latin and so was fined five hundred crowns in the year 1490. His great-great-grandfather was expelled

---

[1] Ernest Boyd condemned it in *The Saturday Review of Literature* (October 8); Peter M. Jack praised it highly in the New York *Times Book Review* (October 9). Later in the month George F. Whicher (*Herald Tribune Books*) and Cuthbert Wright (*Commonweal*) raised objections to its superficialities, while other reviewers praised its amiable enthusiasms.

[1] See vol. XVIII (October 22, 1938), 9.
[2] His review appeared on October 8, 1938.

from the University of Edinburgh for telling that University that it did not know how to teach medicine and his father was expelled from the University of Berlin for telling that University that it did not know how to teach Romance Literature, whilst his grandfather cut this writer out of his will, at any rate temporarily, because he proposed to go to the University of Oxford. Today this writer has written a long book to prove that none of the universities of the world know how to teach literature. Mr. Boyd naturally resents this.

The first review that this writer received appeared in the London *Athenaeum,*[3] a periodical, *mutatis mutandis,* almost exactly parallel in weight and literary position with the SRL of today. The writer's book was a novel all about love and such stuff, as the saying is, and the *Athenaeum's* review was as follows:

"From the fact that this author employs the phrase *heroesia anglicana* on page 47, the worthlessness of this effort may be perceived. On page 92 the word mucilage is misspellt."

Observe how exactly your reviewer, the Erse paladin and protagonist of all the universities in the world, parallels with his review of this writer's last book that first of all academic sallies against the infant product of this pen. His review is some hundred and forty lines in length, of which sixty are given to finding fault with index and tables and to lamenting the author's quite wily omission of the table of contents so dear to reviewers whose overcrowded tables preclude the reading of books submitted to their censure. The *Athenaeum's* reviewer being an Anglican resented, as it were regionally, any allusion to Anglican heresy. Mr. Boyd as a good Scotch Protestant Irishman resents the fact that this writer, coerced by considerations of space and proportion, did not devote much attention to the products of the Scotch Protestant Irishry of whom Mr. Yeats is the chief living ornament. Mr. Yeats is indeed a lovely poet but "The March of Literature" concerns

[3] Ford's first book, *The Brown Owl,* had its initial review in *The Times* of London (October 7, 1891). *The Athenaeum* commented three weeks later in a mild review. When it came to assess Ford's first novel, however, in November, 1892, it spent one paragraph in describing the "singularly repellent situation" of the book and ended: "Such blunders as 'lusi naturae' are venial trifles in comparison with the errors in taste and temper which colour the whole story." The spirit of these objections rather than the text remained in Ford's memory.

itself with poets who had an effect on the march of literature rather than with those who were lovely in themselves, and Mr. Pound is there mentioned eight times to Mr. Yeats's one because firstly this writer made six quotations from Mr. Pound's translation from the Chinese and twice called attention to the very considerable influence that Mr. Pound, in conjunction with other American writers, exercised on literary mainstreams between 1892 or so and the present day.

The actual influence on the course of literature of the Irishry of the early years of the century would appear to be exactly nil except that perhaps the actors and actresses of the Abbey Theatre, Dublin, have had considerable influence on the school of naturalistic acting but that hardly comes within the scope of a work devoted to literary tendencies. Mr. Boyd also resents the fact that this writer considers that Americans from the days of the *Yellow Book* onwards—the days of Henry James and [Henry] Harland and [Stephen] Crane—exercised a main influence on the literary stream ever since their day. So his Irish regional patriotism exceeds his transatlantic allegiance. That is a thing that this writer cannot help; only, he being neither Irish nor American, his judgment may be taken to be relatively unbiassed. The influence of Messrs. James, Harland, Crane, Pound and T. S. Eliot on today's Anglo-Saxon literary stream seems to have been paramount. On the other hand, the critic of the local equivalent of the English *Thunderer* soundly berates this writer for not having accorded sufficient weight to the American literary product. He, however, unlike Mr. Boyd, unrepentently confesses that he has made no attempt to read the book in question. There is in fact no pleasing all the people all the time and no pleasing the academic critic with any type of creative esthetic work.

Mr. Boyd complains that "The March of Literature" is not a work of reference. It isn't. He concedes, however, "that as talk to students, some of the material might be useful if they were near a library with good references and bibliographical facilities." That is all that, modestly if in proportions elephantine, it set out to be.

I have the honour to be

Your obedient servant,

P.S. Mr. Boyd may be interested to be told that the devoted compiler of the admirable tables that complete the "March of Literature" was as duly stated in the book Miss Olive—*not,* as stated by him, Mr. Oliver—Carol Young. *O quis custodiet ipsos custodes?*

To Irita Van Doren*[1]

Dear Irita:

October 25, 1938

I am both astonished and grieved that you should let that fellow write as he did about me in your last issue.[2] Surely, surely, you know me well enough to know that I am neither ignorant nor indifferent to the claims of American literature considering that I discovered and printed at my own expense and saluted with loud praises quite a large percentage of the present literary lights of this country—*including* Robert Frost, long before this country was ready to receive them. There is nothing, I suppose to be done about it—I mean I'm not going to write letters to you officially but that silly sort of xenophobia which is too rampant both here and in England ought to be checked. But perhaps, the article escaped your eagle eye before publication—and indeed Isabelle[3] fairly contradicts it with her amiable note with her "third hatching of swans."

I hope you flourish.

Yours affectionately,

To Sinclair Lewis

ten fifth avenue
new york city

My dear Lewis,

25 Nov. '38

I was so struck all of a heap by your reference to me the other night[1] that not to mention the omission of all tribute to Miss Pearl Buck—to whom I had prepared a quite nice little one!—I omitted

---

[1] Editor of the New York *Herald Tribune Books.*

[2] Professor George F. Whicher reviewed *The March of Literature* on October 23, 1938.

[3] Isabel Paterson commented, in her column "Turns with a Bookworm," on Ford's "generosity to other writers and the scanty credit he has received for it." He was at work, she said, on his third generation of "discoveries."

[1] At a P. E. N. club dinner.

any thanks to yourself or expression of admiration for your work—for which the merest decency would have called!

The fact is: I first fell wondering who could be the phoenix you were lauding and then concluded that Thomas Mann must be somewhere in the audience and that you were talking to him. So when you dropped out my name I clean forgot everything I had prepared. I am not, you see, modest but you went so far beyond any praise I could allot to myself that I clean forgot all manners!

But please accept this as a testimony at once of my appreciation of your generosity & my real admiration for your renderings of our world and time.

With many good wishes I'm   Yours very sincerely,

To Edward Crankshaw*

My dear Crankshaw: November 26, 1938

I was very glad to have your news from which I hope we may gather that you are fairly prosperous. I am very glad that you have made the change to Sandhurst which I know quite well and which is certainly likely to be more dry and airy than your Penshurst place.

My editorial projects will have been rather held up by the fact that I couldn't get on with the Dial people but I am making arrangements with an old publisher which I think will materialize next week. In the meanwhile Stanley Unwin is taking up the whole subject with enthusiasm and it looks as if we might in one way or another start a rather imposing international project taking in not only this country but England and France and occasionally some refugee Germans. I don't want, as a general rule, to publish anybody who has been published before but this is not an absolute law—I mean, it would not exclude writers whose first books have been absolute failures but it would rather exclude people who have already made some position like Ralph Bates, Elizabeth Bowen or Sean O'Failann [*sic*] simply because I want to give as much chance as possible to writers who have no chance at all. Yes, Isherwood is quite well known in this country, at least in circles where he could hope to be well known. I have just got your novel and will read it right away. From the first two or three pages, I fancy that I shall like it quite well.

I am so extremely glad that you are doing another Béhaine and that the reception of *The Survivors*[1] is sufficiently good to encourage Stanley Unwin to go on with publishing him. The reception here wasn't too bad but not nearly as good as it seems to have been in England. Perhaps you would send me one or two of the best English notices. Have you, by the bye, found a publisher for *La Conquête de la Vie*? I think it rather a pity that *Les Nouveaux Venus*[2] hasn't got published because it seems to me to be more of a complete book than the others which all bear the marks of either being or calling for sequels. Still, I expect you and Unwin know your business better than I do.

Thank you. I am gradually getting a little less limp than I was after finishing that book, but I am beginning to make little dabs at a new work and shall, no doubt, be at it full time very soon. *The March of Literature* certainly has had an amazingly good reception here and I receive almost unbelievable tributes from one quarter or another. The night before last at the P. E. N. club, Mr. Sinclair Lewis in announcing me as a guest for the evening declared that I was not only the greatest novelist writing in English that there had ever been but one of the outstanding literary figures of all time. And he was dead sober too. It astonished me so much because I thought he was talking about Mr. Thomas Mann, that when he finally mentioned my name I was so astounded that I completely forgot the speech I had made up to congratulate Pearl Buck on her reception of the Nobel Prize and had to content myself with talking about my grand-aunt Eliza— the famous lady who said: "Sooner than be idle, I'd take a book and read," which was the only thing that came into my head at that moment and the above is always in my head and for the moment, too, so I will ring off. Let us know from time to time how things go with you.

Janice asks to be kindly remembered.

[1] Ford wrote a preface to Edward Crankshaw's translation of René Béhaine's novel *The Survivors* (London, 1938).

[2] The first novel (1908) in Béhaine's multi-volumed series, *Histoire d'une Société*; it was republished under this new title in 1928. *La Conquête de la Vie*, the fourth of the series, appeared in 1924.

To Richard Hughes*

My dear Hughes: November 26, 1938

I have had *In Hazard* some six weeks now and having read it
with enthusiasm in the first two days, I have been wondering what
to write to you about it. Because, the book being a masterpiece, it
demands some sort of at least coherent comment. And my brain
has been so limp since finishing my last enormous book that co-
herence is the last thing to be expected of it. However, my wife
has for the last thirty-six hours been doing nothing but saying that
In Hazard is the greatest and most amazing novel ever written
and that seems to be the best thing to say about it. And I really
don't know what to add. Your gift is so individual and it is profit-
less to attempt to form judgments of individualities when they express themselves in writing. One can write about *Typhoon* because
it has literary skill and poetry and obviousnesses; but if *In Hazard* has literary skill—and possibly even obviousnesses, though I
haven't observed any, both are completely obscured to the reader
by the extraordinary overtones of your temperament. I certainly
know of no other book—or temperament—in the least like it. It
is rather as if the book itself were a ship in a hurricane—and the
hurricane be overtones of which I have just written. I hope this
has some sort of sense for you; it seems to me to be so essentially the
note of the book that there is hardly anything to write. You stand
really quite apart from any other writer known to me—I mean,
any other writer in the whole history of Literature. That comes,
perhaps, from your foreignness from things Anglo-Saxon. The
little dark persistent race might see better where you get it from
but they couldn't admire more. There is, for instance, the episode
of the birds. I don't suppose you invented this but I am quite certain that no other writer—no other writer would have rendered it
with such extraordinary vividness or have given it one half of
its significance.

So, I will leave the matter there. I don't know how the book
has done here. I have seen one or two notices that quite miss all its
points and resolve themselves into saying that it is or isn't better
than *Typhoon*. It isn't, of course, better than *Typhoon. Typhoon*

was written by a great writer who was a man. *In Hazard* is written by someone inhuman—and consummate in the expression of inhumanities.

I haven't been able to write any reviews of it because I am not at the moment in contact with any papers that do reviewing but I have mentioned it—and I don't need to say with how much enthusiasm—in a great number of radio talks and lectures and to every human being who seemed to have any intelligence at all.

And when is a third book coming? And what is it? I'd appreciate it if you would keep us from time to time posted as to your activities and vicissitudes.

Mrs. Ford asks me to say that she repeats with emphasis the fact that *In Hazard* is the most amazing masterpiece that has ever been written and she will go on repeating that to her dying day. And in the meantime, I am always, believe me, the most sincere of all your innumerable admirers.

To Stanley Unwin

10 Fifth Avenue
New York City
January 18, 1939

My dear Unwin:

Ref. young American writers: I have had sent you in the last week by their authors (1) *Forward, Children* by Paul Alexander Bartlett and (2) *White Mule* by William Carlos Williams, the latter published by Laughlin of Norfolk, Connecticut.

Bartlett seems to me to be a young writer of very considerable merit and one whom I expect to see go far. In this particular book he gives the best rendering that I have ever seen of mechanical warfare and I think that for that reason alone, if for no other, it should be widely distributed and I should think it ought to appeal to an English audience almost more than to an American one. Anyhow, I hope you will like it.

William Carlos Williams is quite another pair of shoes. For at least a quarter of a century he has been regarded by every American and most English writers of any perception as being the best prose writer and one of the acutest minds alive. His work is completely unpopular here and is practically only published by small firms making a specialty of exceptional writers. His first book was published by John Lane at my recommendation in 1913;[1] it attracted very little attention except from poets but it was not a very mature work and I do not think that he has since been published in England at all. *The White Mule*, however, shows Williams at his extraordinary best and so many American writers have received their first real recognition in England—and not unusually on my recommendation—that I should think that the book might have a good chance of at least a literary success in England. For that reason I do hope you will see your way to publishing it. I shall be sending you some more manuscripts in a little time but my health has been so poorly so long that I have not been able to do much in that department for over a month or so and my own work is quite at a standstill. However, I shall be beginning a new sort of treatment next Monday and that may restore me to some sort of activity. I shall be mailing you the final scraps of *The March of Literature* in a day or two.

I hope you are well.   Yours very sincerely,

To R. A. Scott-James

My dear Scott James: January 19, 1939

It was nice to see your signature again. (Would you get your mail clerk to observe that my quite permanent address is 4 Place de la Concorde, Paris and that letters will always reach me from there with at most a day's delay?)

It is nice of you to ask me to write for you and I certainly will as soon as anything to write about presents itself. My only trouble is that I write so long and your space is so limited—and then I don't quite know what you want. If you would suggest anything you would like me to write about, I'd certainly manage to do it. I am at the moment engaged very slowly in writing a novel of which I've got the first chapter written. Outside that my mind is mostly given to speculations as to what I will call The Intellectual and Cultural Real Wage of Life in this country and in Europe,

[1] William Carlos Williams' first book, *Poems*, was privately printed in 1909 in Rutherford, New Jersey. Elkin Mathews, not John Lane, published *The Tempers* (London, 1913), with an introductory note by Ezra Pound.

e.g. England and France mostly. The subject is extremely complicated and delicate. One is accustomed to say roughly that class for class in terms of the real wage mechanical and material conditions here are superior to those in Europe, whereas on the cultural and all the more enjoyable sides of life, the advantage is enormously with Europe; and both propositions are probably true in the large but the distinctions are apt to vanish as soon as you make anything like minute studies of conditions.

I shall probably be writing a couple of articles on these lines for Harpers Magazine and, if you like, I could forward them to you. Or if there is any subject on another line that you would care to have me write about for you specially, I will try to do that.

Thank you for thinking of me.

I hope the passage of the heavy years leaves you unscathed. For me with all sorts of handicaps, I manage to get along one way or another.

Yours always,

To E. S. P. Haynes*[1]

10 Fifth Avenue
New York, N. Y.
January 24, 1939

My dear Haynes:

I was glad to see your signature again after all these years. Chateau Pavie is usually esteemed one of the big cru wines but the domain is very small and the output insufficient, therefore, to pay for the usual publicity. You come across it from time to time in restaurants but I rather think the whole crop is usually bought up by Nicholas and disposed of privately. I get mine from them. It is *red*.

Ref. garlic—I have written a great deal about this from time to time and in various places and I will see if I can dig up an article or two on the subject to send you. I am personally convinced that without a reasonable amount of garlic in your diet, you cannot be completely whole either mentally or physically.

We pass our time as a rule almost equally between Paris, le Côte d'Azur and here, though a couple of years ago, we were in London

---

[1] A staff member in 1916 of Cecil Chesterton's weekly, *The New Witness*, Haynes had supported Ford against an attack by "J. K. Prothero" (Ada E. Jones) in a review of *Zeppelin Nights*.

for four or five months. I didn't find it very exciting. There did not seem to be anybody there to talk to and those one could talk to didn't much understand what one said. The year before last we spent thirty-two days in Penshurst[2] and it rained for thirty-one and a half. On the half day we went to Canterbury Cricket Week and had the dissatisfaction of seeing Lancashire beat Kent after a much too early declaration on the part of Kent. So that on the whole, little old New York remains good enough for me.

I hope you flourish.

To Stanley Unwin

10 Fifth Avenue
New York City
February 3, 1939

My dear Mr. Unwin:

You should be receiving about this time two manuscripts whose authors I recommended to send them to you. The first is just called *Stories* by Eudora Welty. As the title implies, they are short stories and I know the usual objection to them. But they seem to me to be of such great beauty and so beautifully written that you might possibly make an exception for them. I am bound to admit that the only publisher I have been able to find for them here is a quite uncommercial publisher of new writers but Miss Welty is quite well known amongst writers in this country and the first short story in this volume is for what it is worth in O'Brien's selection of the best stories of the year.

The second manuscript is called, I much regret to say, I can't remember what. That is to say, that I had it carefully wrapt up to send to you and can't for the life of me remember what the title is because the author has changed it so many times and I shrink from unwrapping the parcel all over again. It is, however, by Mrs. William (Wanda Tower) Picard so that you will be able to recognize it, more particularly, if you tell your mail department to look out for a manuscript coming from me and addressed personally to you. I really think so immensely highly of this manuscript that I won't tire you with superlatives, about it.

Mrs. Picard has been writing for quite a long time but has only hitherto published short stories, this being her first novel. I am

[2] Visiting Edward Crankshaw and his wife at The Nunnery Cottage.

bound to confess that she has found some difficulty in getting an American publisher for them though our friend Greenslet seems very likely to take it if he can get Mrs. Picard to accept his rather exiguous terms—which I don't think she will. So my patriotism makes me hope that this may be yet another case of an American writer being recognized in England first.

It is really astonishing how many cases of this there are. Indeed, almost every American writer of literary prominence today falls into that heading.

I am trying very hard to place Béhaine but here again I am afraid we shall have to fall back on a non-commercial publisher.

I am slowly picking up from a bad relapse. I got pretty well about a month ago, then began to work again and went about and lectured and dined and went to receptions and then had another collapse so that I've only just begun to think of work again—that is to say, I have written very slowly the first two chapters of a novel but when I shall get to the international book I simply don't know. I shall certainly have to go slow for quite a time.

My best wishes,
                                                                Yours,

To The Rt. Hon. Malcolm MacDonald*¹

Sir: February 27, 1939

I take the liberty of intruding on your attention on the subject of Palestine as a national home of the Jews. In 1915 in common with a number of historians and economists—amongst them being Profs. Gooch, Hobson, Hobhouse, Sir C. P. Scott of the *Manchester Guardian* and others—I was approached by Mr. C. F. G. Masterman, then Chancellor of the Duchy of Lancaster—in his capacity, I think, of the Chief of Ministry of Information—and asked for what proposals I and they thought should be made for terms of peace by the Asquith Ministry. Amongst my proposals which included the creation of a Rhenan [*sic*] Republic to act as a buffer state between France and Germany was the creation of a National Jewish Republic in Palestine—which amongst other things would

¹ Of the Colonial Office, Whitehall, London.

act as a buffer state between the Turkish Empire and Egypt, then a British protectorate. In that proposal I called Palestine the Jewish National Home, using, I think, the phrase for the first time. Since that date I have paid very prolonged and earnest attention to the Jewish world problem.

Permit me to say that I am of the opinion that the only possible solution *is* the creation of a Jewish Republic, whether independent or as a British protectorate is immaterial as long as it can be represented at the League of Nations and be capable of sending properly accredited diplomatic representatives to powers committing atrocities against Jews. I will spare you my reasons for this conclusion; you must be aware of them yourself at least as well as I. And sir, you must be at least as well acquainted as I am with the physical and mental atrocities which are being committed against Jews in every nation whose territory lies between the Baltic and the Black Seas. That being so, I do not see how you can do anything but agree that if the public opinion of Christendom—and I use the term advisedly—could be really made aware of these things, an immense movement determined to ameliorate the Jewish world-lot must eventuate. But to bring this about the Jews themselves must be in the position of a sovereign authority having power to obtain publicity for those same atrocities. It is a question of concentration of effort. Today individual reports from press correspondents and others of atrocities such as take place daily, and particularly in Rumania, are simply suppressed by the press of almost every nation whereas a diplomatic report addressed from the Jerusalem Government to the White House or the Court of St. James's or an authoritative speech before the League of Nations must attract some attention.

I am aware, sir, that in your official capacity it is no part of your function to ameliorate the world condition of the Jews but that desire must exist in the heart of every civilized man and it must be of benefit to our country should she conduce disinterestedly to that end. I am aware that it must be prejudicial to the Empire to create in the Arab and Mahometan sections of the Empire a feeling of hostility to the Empire but I beg you, Sir, to give weight to the consideration that it must be infinitely more prejudicial to

Great Britain to earn the reprehension of the whole of the civilized world.

When on the third of July, 1914, Sir Edward Goschen addressed to Bethmann-Hollweg the proud words: "When it is a question of the observance of treaties, it is not the custom of His Majesty's Government to count the costs."—I am quoting without the White Book—England at once stood higher in the estimation of the comity of nations than she ever stood or than any other nation ever stood. It is all important for the very existence of our Empire that you should not at this juncture find yourself under the necessity of saying—like Lord Randolph Churchill—that you had "forgotten Goschen."

It is perhaps not exactly pertinent for me here to advert to the policy of the Government to which you belong when it "forgot Goschen" at Berchtesgaden and Munich. It causes us—whether deservedly or no—to stand today in the estimation of nearly every moderate, instructed and liberal minded man in this country, a little lower morally than perhaps any nation ever stood. And I do not need to tell you that the Prime Minister's declaration yesterday in the House of Commons to the effect that he has recognized the Franco regime without sufficient guarantee for the protection of the Republican population has roused in this country a feeling of horror that has probably never been paralleled. They see in the Prime Minister a dictator with no one to control him, who, at the bidding of the totalitarian dictators, has delivered infinite thousands of innocent humanity to a certain butchery. I may add that in the view of a great many political thinkers in this country, the Prime Minister's surrender of Spain to the totalitarian powers renders Great Britain for strategic reasons of almost infinitely diminished value as an ally in case of war. I am talking now of people who would otherwise have been willing to engage this country in a war on the side of her former allies.

I ask you to understand that I am not here expressing my own views but those of, I am convinced, almost the entire thinking and working class population of the United States. And I ask you to believe, sir, that in writing this letter I am attempting to make you aware of a situation as to which you are probably little instructed. I think that until yesterday, the majority of the population

in this country would have favoured aiding the European democracies in the struggle against totalitarian powers. Today, that
chance has diminished nearly to the vanishing point. In giving
you that considered opinion, I think myself, therefore, to be
performing a patriotic duty.

> And I trust your daily Fate may not be as mine is to hear
> such men, who till yesterday were the friends of our
> country, averring every day both in public and in private,
> that the British Empire is a concealedly fascist organiza-
> tion in the hands of venial, commercial interests and
> under the dictatorship of a ruler who is known to a great part
> of the world as "Judas, the son of Judas." And how much
> more will that accusation not be heard if you proceed to a
> further betrayal in Palestine itself.

I will however add, for what it is worth, my own private opinion on the Palestinian situation. We inveigled these unfortunate
people into that country by a promise, at least inferred, of protection, unhindered immigration and [a] measure at least of independence—for what other meaning could the words "National
Home" be taken to bear? There is, sir, a Nemesis that attaches
to nations—a Nemesis in no way supernatural but as much a matter of cause and effect as is the force of gravity. That equation can
be thus expressed: If a nation earn the detestation and contempt
of the public conscience of the world, it shall find no one to come
to its assistance in the moment of extremity. And, living as I do
amongst the class that forms public opinion in this country and
in France, I am, I take the liberty to imagine, more aware than
you how near we have already come to having earned the op-
probrium and contempt of the civilized world.

I have the honour to be, Sir, Your obedient servant,

P.S. I am sending copies of this letter, omitting two sentences of
Paragraph [seven], which I have indented, to the *Times* and
Manchester Guardian with the request that they publish it. I
presume that if you consider that the publication could be of any
national disservice, you can take steps to prevent its being published.

To George T. Keating

My dear Keating: March 13, 1939

I should esteem it a favour if you could give me an hour or so of your time. I am thinking of re-starting the TRANSATLANTIC REVIEW—indeed, the project has already taken serious shape—and I am extremely anxious to have your advice as to various business details. The original TR collapsed owing to its business affairs having been so badly managed in this country and I am anxious to avoid having that happen again. Almost any time will suit me and I would call off practically any date to keep one with you.

My success in England has now become so marked that I think I can afford to give time to this project which, as you know, I have long wanted to do and I am sure you could be of great assistance to me in putting me on to people I could trust for the formation of a company and the making of agreements. I don't so badly want capital as it looks as if I could find it fairly easily —but some time ago you said you knew a lady who might find money for something of the sort—specifically at that time for the purchase of THE DIAL—and if she was still available—I should not mind raising some extra money. Let me have an answer at your convenience, will you?

Yours,

To Edward Crankshaw*

My dear Crankshaw: March 14, 1939

Once again this isn't going to be a serious letter about your book. I am really kept in such a continuous whirl making up for the time lost during my illness that I haven't got the brain to write anything with even the most minute degree of subtlety. But do understand that I am completely on your side—or at your back, if you prefer it—and that I very much admire your really subtle and indefinable gift.

What I am writing about now is a quite different pair of shoes. I am trying to restart the TRANSATLANTIC REVIEW as an Organ of the Seven Arts and the Three Democracies to be published in New

York, London and Paris simultaneously and I would like to know
if it would interest you to look after the London affairs of the
Review—i.e. to take a first glance through any manuscripts that
might come in, possibly, if you felt like it, giving a little attention
to circulation, advertisements, etc. We shall probably employ an
in and out publicity agent but those fellows want occasional looking after. I propose to propose that Allen & Unwin take over the
actual publishing at the usual commission rate. That is to say,
I should deliver free at Charing Cross as many copies as A & U
think they might dispose of and they would take a commission
on sales, the size of it depending on how much work they would
like to do—like sending out copies for review, etc. As for remu-
neration for yourself—that will have to depend on how much
capital I can get together. But you can be certain of occupying a
certain space in the pages of the Review and on being paid at
the usual—rather meager—space rates.

Just think this over, will you and let me know how you regard
the idea? I will write about it more definitely in a short time.

Yours always and as always in frantic haste,

To W. H. Auden*

Dear Mr. Auden: March 23, 1939

If you could find it convenient to attend the dinner of the Society of the Friends of William Carlos Williams—as to whom I
enclose some documentary matter—it will give myself and my
committee great pleasure; if you would also consent to become a
member of the Society the pleasure would be immensely increased.[1]
I fancy that in this matter of literary politics you and I must think
very much alike. At any rate, in this country the necessity to drive
a powerful wedge into the solid wall of obscurantism, that is the
commercial publishing of today, must be as obvious to you as it
is to me. How it may be in our own country I don't really know;

[1] In *I Wanted to Write a Poem* (1958), Williams says Ford "had the idea of
founding a literary society called *Les Amis de William Carlos Williams* after
the Parisian fashion. But it should, I always thought, have been called *Les Amis
de Ford Madox Ford* . . . for few of the members and practically none of my
countrymen knew anything about me."

I have every reason to be satisfied with my own publishers and I imagine that there are one or two firms there that are not completely hardened in commercialism.

At any rate, if you will come to the dinner you will meet probably a number of the better and younger writers and painters of this country, so I hope you will manage it.

I heard your speech at the foreign correspondents' dinner and was much impressed and touched by your earnestness and the admirable way in which you martialed your arguments. Let us hope that the day shall not be far distant in which you will be able to devote the whole of your energies to your delicate and admirable art without any call upon you for other activities. Please believe me,

Yours very sincerely,

To Stanley Unwin

Dear Mr. Unwin: March 29, 1939

I have just been re-reading my HENRY FOR HUGH and it strikes me, after not having seen it for some years, as being by far the best written and the best constructed of all my books. At the same time, I could quite see that it might be "difficult" for the normal reader. Would you, perhaps, get your novel adviser to take a look at it? I don't, of course, think it would be advisable to publish another non-paying novel at this juncture but I have the feeling that its literary quality might all the same add to my reputation in England and if your adviser thought the book could be improved from the point of sales by the addition of one or two explanatory passages, I'd be quite pleased to add them. I think you could probably get a copy of it from Lippincotts' London house or if not, Mrs. Bowen[1] will probably have a copy that she can lend you. Perhaps your adviser might also take a look at THE RASH ACT which was published by Jonathan Cape some years ago without, however, setting the Thames on fire? It will cast a certain light on the other book.

As soon as I have got my agreement finally settled with the

[1] Stella Bowen, who was then living in England.

Frederick Stokes Company, I will send you particulars of the books they want me to write.[2]

Yours very sincerely,

To Allen Tate

10 Fifth Avenue
New York City
May 3, 1939

Dear Allen:

Could you let me know what has happened about the Chapel Hill project? I want as far as possible to fix our movements for the next three months or so. The only actually fixed date we have is that I am going back to Olivet at the beginning of October for a fortnight but I could shift this if Chapel Hill decided to want me then. I was at Olivet for a fortnight just lately and it was extremely gratifying to see the progress the English students there have made both in the matter of knowledge of literature and manners in the last three years. The whole tone of the place has been changed and much for the better. It's a great triumph for Brewer and, incidentally, for the tutorial system in this country. By going there twice a year for a fortnight I can get things run pretty well as I want but the late fortnight in perpetual snow didn't do my health much good so that my doctor says I ought to have a sea voyage which, however, we can't very well afford. The alternative seems to be a sojourn somewhere on the seashore. Do you know of anywhere on the coasts of either North or South Carolina or Virginia where it would be not too hot for May, June, July, and August, and what is always more important, where we might find some sort of agreeable companionship—I mean do you know of anywhere in that range of country where there would be someone pleasant to whom you could give us introductions? The only idea I have on the subject is a small sea-bathing place I once went to near Wilmington, Delaware but I don't know anybody there. I'd be very much obliged if you could give us any information. The only alternative would seem to be the New England coast and I don't like New England. I hope

[2] *The March of Literature* (New York, 1938) was Ford's last published work. He never wrote for the Frederick Stokes Company, though they announced a novel for publication "dealing, in a New York setting, with the swing of the intelligentsia towards the political left." He wanted to call it *Left Turn*.

you all flourish. I hear rumours that you are going to Princeton in some capacity. Can this be true? And what is Caroline doing in the way of writing? I'd be glad of answers to these questions.

Carlos Williams saw Ezra by accident in Washington the other day. He says the author of the Cantos seems very mild and depressed and fearful. That is all I know about him. He had made no sign to me. The Society of the Friends of William Carlos Williams is going quite strongly. We sat down forty-seven people to dinner last night, the dinner being in honour of E. E. Cummings who didn't attend but whose poems were read at great length and brilliantly by Williams himself. The attendance included Sherwood Anderson, John Herrmann, Louis Zukovsky, Higgins, Mendes and lots of other young poets and prosateurs. I wish you could get to one of the dinners. They are pleasant and friendly occasions and really produce some results because publishers turn up there and actually commission books.

All good luck.

Yours,

To Harrison Smith*[1]

My dear Harrison Smith: May 10, 1939

I am quite ready to write the six articles for the Saturday Review for which you have asked and treat of literary subjects as they arise in the course of my next month's travels.[2] Thus, the first which will be dated from New York will deal with the disappearance of the classics from the American bookshops. The second will be written on board a Norwegian tramp steamer and will probably deal with the Sagas interspersed very likely with passages about Norwegian food; the third will come from somewhere in Normandy and will probably contain a comparison between French and American regional literatures—i.e. between Maupassant's peasant stories and those of Messrs. Caldwell, Penn Warren, etc. The fourth will come from London and will deal with the dearth of young writers in England as compared, say, with the

---

[1] Of *The Saturday Review of Literature*.

[2] Only one appeared: "Travel Notes. I. Return to Olivet," *The Saturday Review of Literature*, xx (June 10, 1939), 13-14.

plethora of the same between Detroit and New Orleans . . . and so on. But it must be understood that if I write these articles—which it will give me great pleasure to do—they must be printed, and printed exactly as I write them. If Mr. [George] Stevens disagrees with the sentiments expressed in them, he can comment on them to that effect with my complete blessings. But he must neither alter nor cut them without my consent.

Yours very sincerely,

To George Stevens*¹

Dear Mr. Stevens: [May] 17, 1939

All right. Let it go at that. I take it that the remaining articles you want are to be one more of 2,500 words and four of 1,250. I will keep as nearly in limits as possible and if I find I have outrun them, I will indicate the cuts I should prefer.

I am afraid that we shan't be going by the Norwegian freighter on the 25th because my doctor is afraid of the cooking. So we shall go by the Normandie on the 30th. In that case I will make that article one on the literary associations and psychological effects of certain dishes that I will get the chef to cook for us; e.g. *cassoulet de castelnaudary* which prompts thoughts of Provence and Clemence Isaure and the Courts of Love and the Jeux Floraux and the Gaie Saber or *pigeons en geléux* [sic] which automatically suggests Mimi and Shaunard and the *Jolie Colombe qui chantait jour et nuit*—and which they ate at dawn. That will make something gay after the villainies of your friends, the publishers.

Sincerely,

To the Editor of
*The Saturday Review of Literature*¹

Sir: [May, 1939]

I trust you will be good enough to spare space for a protest against the tepidity of the review of James Joyce's "Finnegans

¹ Of *The Saturday Review of Literature*.

¹ See vol. xx (June 3, 1939), 9.

Wake" in your issue of May 6.[2] Mr. Rosenfeld has borne the burden of several frays on several intellectual and agnostic forefronts but, having been reared in an atmosphere of pure reason, he is unfitted to appreciate to the full the peculiar, hieratic qualities of Mr. Joyce's mind. If you are not attuned to the instrument you can hardly do justice to its sound. Hence, Mr. Rosenfeld's lack of sensuous appreciation of the "wit and mysterious poetry" that, intellectually, he perceives in the book. To get a full joy out of Mr. Joyce's polychromatic fugal effects of language, one must have been brought up in either Jesuit or high Anglican neighbourhoods, or in any of the vast territories that lie between those two extremes. Your ears must have been at an early age so impregnated with the verbiage of the mass, the Book of Common Prayer, the Vulgate, and the Authorized Version that the mere vowel sequences of certain passages will be sufficient to call back to you all the associations of your youth. If, say, in the three most impressionable years of your life, you have heard the burden of Collects, Prayers, and Novenas 10,950 times (3 times 10 times 365) in school or seminary chapels, the mere sequence of the vowel coloring of that phrase will give you acute pleasure if you hear it in quite other verbiage. Imagine a paragraph of Mr. Joyce recounting how a Bloom or a Finnegan refuses an invitation to sit at the groaning board of him who had great possessions whilst accepting one to share the unleavened hoe-cake of Lazarus. Imagine the Cranmerian rhythm of the whole paragraph and then the ending: "Rather the bun of the lowly host." To Mr. Rosenfeld that might not be very great fun. But we who recognize the triple fugue implicit in those words, feel the joy that cannot be known to those without the Pale. You have, as first subject, the content paraphrasing the Beatitude, "Blessed are the humble and meek." You have as second

---

[2] Paul Rosenfeld faced the difficult task of appraising *Finnegans Wake* in a brief review. He concluded that Joyce's style "lacks the strong root-feeling of the language. It is cold and cerebral in comparison with that of a veritable 'radical' like Gerard Manley Hopkins. The pressure of passion and driving necessity frequently seems absent. And too often we have the sense of repletion and a work overshot." Ford took up the cudgel for Joyce, signing his letter Faugh an-Ballagh Faugh. It appeared on June 3, but Rosenfeld's reply (June 10) made it clear that he thought Ford's letter did Joyce injustice by its "involuntary minimizations" of Joyce's talent and that Ford was "playing the role of Ham in what I still take to be the illusory nakedness of [Joyce's] Noah."

subject, the vowel coloring. And as third subject, the suggestion of the continual burden of the church's unceasing dedication of herself to the persons of the Trinity. As a free fantasia accompanying the counterpoint, you will have your own emotions in remembrance of shivering winter mornings in the frosty school chapel.

Or again, rightly to get joy out of Mr. Joyce, you must appreciate his chief note, which is a kind of tender picking on God and his Mother, such as the pupils of Jesuits will get a tittering joy at bringing out, whilst chancing that their innocuous blasphemies shall bring down upon their heads the stern voice of their teacher, saying, "Boy, let down your small clothes."

The comprehension of these primary characteristics must be yours if you desire to taste all the joy that can be got out of Bloom or Finnegan; but Mr. Joyce's universality is founded on what Mr. Rosenfeld perspicaciously styles "Mr. Joyce's half tender and half savagely blasphemous picture of human life" . . . and on his unparalleled investigation into the uses to which words and their associations can be put.

English is a language ill-suited to good prose because of the associations that, like burrs, cling undetachable to every English word, and the simplest English sentence is forever blurred because it can always have several meanings. Even "the Cat is on the Mat" can mean so much more than meets the eye. If, for instance, you met the statement on top of a newspaper column you would at once guess that Parliament was discussing the abolition of flogging in the Services. Or Mr. Norman Douglas was right in considering that "They Went" as a title for one of his books would arouse curiosity, since so bold a statement must seem to convey implications such as They Went, flying from fear of disgrace, of threats, of physical violences, of inundations, of earthquakes—with the corollary that you couldn't see their going for dust.

Most of us weaker brothers of the pen try to get round this characteristic of our language by using simpler and always more simple words and constructions. But, wiser and more brave, Mr. Joyce seizes the polysignificance of English as the philosophic basis of his labors, and attracts always more associations to his words until the literal meaning of almost every word is lost in a burr-mantle of local or colloquial colorings. And the world owes gratitude to his huge prodigality, since not only does his prose prove how magnificently hued our language may be but it affords us lesser navigators in the sea of words a chart to show us how far we may go. It maps the verges of the word user's habitable universe.

Thus "Finnegans Wake" stands up across the flat lands of our literatures as does the first Pyramid across the sands of Egypt, and its appearance at this moment is almost the one event of amazing importance sufficient to withdraw our attention from public events. And thus, Mr. Rosenfeld's attempt to turn readers from this masterpiece is one contrary to the interests of the Republic, for, if we are deterred from removing our attention from public circumstances today, there can be no end for us but a blithering lunacy of imbecile phraseologists.

I have the honor to be, Sir,   Your obedient servant,

To Edward Crankshaw*

My dear Crankshaw: May 23, 1939

I owe you a letter about all sorts of things and more particularly one of thanks for the beautiful things you say in your last about the MARCH OF LITERATURE. But I am so hideously [busy] that I can't at the moment take time to say more than one—that we are leaving this place for your side of the world by the Normandie on the 30th inst. and shall bring up in Havre very likely for several months as we want to see something of Normandy. So I hope you and I will meet and be able to exchange news without this weariness of letters for anyhow Havre is quite near you and either you must come to the mountain or the mountain must transport itself into Kent. As things go we are fairly prosperous and but for the daily clamour of the newspaper headings we should be reasonably happy—but the newspapers are even more disturbing here than they are in Europe because they report a great many things that the English and French suppress. So we don't get many let-ups from the almost insupportable tension of public affairs.

Our best regards to Mrs. Crankshaw.

Yours always,

P.S. I have just sent Béhaine to a new publisher—the Harrison Hilton Co. who are energetic and have plenty of money and announce that they are eagerly on the lookout for new French novels. You might try them also with Nizan and [illegible] if you can do so mentioning that I recommended it. Write to Harrison Smith, 420 Madison Avenue. I am also still sending your novel around but I am afraid it is too delicate to find a home here—at any rate, at the moment. The Americans sometime achieve a taste for silver point but that moment is not yet and all the publishers here have the jitters so badly that they won't look at anything new at all.

To Stanley Unwin

Dear Mr. Unwin: May 25, 1939

I forward you herewith the agreement for MR. CROYD duly signed and witnessed. I should have forwarded it before but I was waiting to hear from you in case you should wish to modify the agreement in the direction of including in it the American rights. However, as I have not heard from you on this subject, I think I had better forward the agreement as it is.

I shall be coming to Europe by the Normandie on the 30th and will bring with me the manuscript of the book. As it is the only copy, I do not care to trust it to the mail but I will either bring it myself and give it to you or will give it to my daughter for that purpose.

In the meantime, I have let Messrs. Stokes read the book. They are very pleased with it and would be prepared to publish it at any time. I think myself it will be better to keep it back for some years. It is at present just fifteen years old which makes it have rather the aspect of "dating" whereas if it did not see the light until its majority it will become almost a historical novel. I will leave that matter, however, to you to decide. I think, myself, that the book is in parts rather exaggerated and needs toning down. Messrs. Stokes, however, do not agree with this. I shall be glad of your opinion about this, too.

I am getting on fairly well with the novel I am writing. It is a kind of projection of the way the intelligentsia of practically all the nations have swung latterly towards the left in politics. The scene is laid in New York but the canvas is fairly international. The intellectual and professional classes of this city are extraordinarily mixed in nationalities and there being ever so many characters in the book. I think it is turning out to be fairly lively and what the French call "mouvementé." I expect to finish it about the middle of September and Stokes propose to publish in February under the title of LEFT TURN.

I am signing a contract with them similar to that of ours of the 16th November, 1936. The book to come next after LEFT TURN being the third and completion of the series of which PROVENCE and THE GREAT TRADE ROUTE are the other two.

My health is now definitely or very nearly restored but my doctor here has come to the conclusion that I shall never be ten years younger until I shall have consumed nothing but French cooking for at least four months. So we are going to spend the time from June to October in or in the neighbourhood of Havre with, I hope, an interlude in London or somewhere in Kent. My activities here have become so multifarious and the telephone rings so continuously that, although normally I write better in New York than anywhere else, the practice has become nearly impossible so I hope to find tranquility in Normandy.

All good wishes,

*F*ORD died at Deauville on June 26, 1939. His good friend Edward Crankshaw wrote to Sir Stanley Unwin on July 2: "Ford was buried on Wednesday afternoon in the cemetery behind Deauville, on a hill overlooking the sea. It is rather a dreadful place, but for the time being it must serve. On the other hand, he died in the most pleasant hospital I have ever seen, the Clinique St. Francis, run by the most charming and devoted nuns. They were looking after Mrs. Ford when I arrived and they deserve the infinite gratitude of all who loved or admired him. He was there only two days before he died. He was taken ill on the boat, was fairly ill for the first week in France—at Honfleur—and desperately ill for the next two weeks. Several times he was at the point of death from uraemia, and at last, when he seemed to be recovering from this, his heart gave up."

INDEX

Cecil, Edgar Algernon Robert, 1st Viscount Cecil of Chelwood, 82
Chamberlain, John, letter to, 229
Chamberlain, Neville, 293
Chance, 79
The Chapbook (*A Monthly Miscellany*), 99, 101, 146, 148, 150
Chapman, George, 297
Chapman and Hall, 18, 117, 123
Chatto and Windus, 56
Chaucer, Daniel, 41, 50-51, 131, 132, 212
Chaucer, Geoffrey, 50
Chesterton, Cecil, 309
Chesterton, Gilbert Keith, 21, 44, 59
Chez Swann [*Du Coté de*], 122
Christie, Agatha, 287
The Chronicle, 85
Churchill, Randolph Henry Spencer, 313
Un Coeur Simple, 104
Collins, Wilkie, 245
Commonweal, 300
The Condition of England, 53
Confucius, 285, 286
La Conquête de la Vie, 305
Conrad, Borys, 76, 79
Conrad, Jessie, 72, 76, 78, 267
Conrad, Joseph, 8, 10, 15, 16, 25, 26, 27, 50, 60, 72, 80, 95, 119, 120, 127, 152, 157, 158, 166, 167, 169, 170, 171, 172, 173, 177, 181, 213, 237, 267, 286; letters to, 71, 73, 75, 78, 156
A Conrad Memorial Library: The Collection of George T. Keating, 178
Constable and Company, 43, 57, 286
Coppard, A. E., 142; letters to, 152, 155, 160
The Cornhill Magazine, 16, 17, 266
Covici, Pascal, 177
Crane, Hart, 209
Crane, Stephen, 125, 236, 243, 248, 302
Crankshaw, Edward, 252, 257, 310, 326; letters to, 304, 315, 323
The Creators, 45
The Criterion, 162, 163
Crockett, Davy, 281
Crusoe, Robinson, 53
Cumberlege, E. C., letters to, 262, 263

Cummings, E. E., 152, 319

The Daily Herald, 202
The Daily Mail, 25, 67, 71
The Daily News, 25, 40, 41, 44, 51, 52, 296
Damon, S. Foster, 106
Dane, Clemence, 140
Dante (Durante Alighieri), 287
Dante Gabriel Rossetti: His Family-Letters, with a Memoir, 7
Dark, Sidney, 146
Daudet, Léon, 225
Davis, Jefferson, 274
Death in the Afternoon, 216
de la Mare, Walter, 44, 101
Dent and Sons, J. M., 8, 156, 158, 167, 168
The Dial, 116, 119, 122, 124, 125, 129, 315
The Dial Press, 283, 286, 304
Doolittle, Hilda (H.D.), 107-108, 212
Dos Passos, John, 152
Doubleday, Doran and Company, 178
Doubleday, Page and Company, 167, 170, 172
Douglas, Norman, 137, 140, 322
A Draft of XXX Cantos, 211, 212, 213, 214, 219, 224, 225, 226
Draper, Muriel, 180
Drawn from Life, 177
Dreiser, Theodore, 236, 250, 251; letters to, 201, 216
Duckworth, Gerald, 32, 97, 101, 102, 146, 151, 156, 157, 166, 170, 172, 174, 180, 187, 195; letters to, 168, 175

L'Éducation Sentimentale, 103
Eliot, T. S., 157, 212, 215, 229, 230, 232, 302; letter to, 213
Ellis, Mrs. Williams, 142, 145, 159
Encyclopaedia Britannica, 188
The English Review, 26, 27, 28, 30, 31-33, 34-35, 36, 38, 39-40, 41, 42, 43, 83, 85, 106, 107, 116, 119, 120, 122, 126, 152, 153, 156, 157, 158, 166, 181, 223, 229, 230, 253, 267, 268
Everyman's Library, 194